# On Education

# On Education
## Northrop Frye

The University of Michigan Press
Ann Arbor

Copyright © 1988 Northrop Frye,

All rights reserved

Library of Congress Catalog Card No. 88-50719

ISBN 0-472-10106-4
Published in the United States of America by

The University of Michigan Press

Manufactured in Canada

1991 1990 1989 1988 4 3 2 1

"On Teaching Literature" by Northrop Frye,
©1972 Harcourt, Brace Jovanovich Inc. is
here reprinted by permission of the publisher.

"The emphasis is on the individual . . . " is
here reprinted by permission of The
Harvard Magazine and Justine Kaplan.

The publisher has endeavored to identify and acknowledge the
original occasion for, and where applicable publication of, each
of these essays. Any errors or omissions in this regard will, if
brought to our attention, be corrected in future printings.

# Table of Contents

# *Preface*

This book is a collection of essays and addresses on the general topic of education, written or delivered over a period of about thirty years. I have written similar essays that have been reprinted elsewhere, but I think this collection expresses as clearly as anything else I have written my own convictions on the subject, as transmitted to Canadian audiences (practically all of the essays have a Canadian setting). There is bound to be some repetition in a book of essays that were originally oral addresses: a listening audience, who hears only what is said to it, does not mind if another audience hears something of the same thing, but the situation is different with a book. I hope my editors and I have minimized the repetition, but at the same time I cannot forget the remark of a clergyman on the board of a magazine I once edited: "Don't imagine that you've said anything if you've only said it once". The background for this remark was doubtless his parishioners' resistance to salvation, but the principle holds for a secular (if equally evangelical) context. This preface in fact adds to the repetition by stating, like the overture to an opera, the themes echoed later.

Three of these themes in particular are important. First, there is my own confession of faith as a humanist, and my confidence in the value of what is called liberal education, a confidence that the social and political events contemporary with my seventy-five years of life have left totally unshaken. Here I am speaking as a teacher whose main focus of interest has always been the classroom. Second, there is the record of watching, and sometimes participating in, the Canadian and American educational scenes. As this has covered several decades, there are doubtless contradictory statements in the book, but these should be taken in context: a statement of fact in one decade may well be a statement of fantasy in the next one. Some of the statements in "The Changing Pace in Canadian Education" were true of the fifties and sixties, emphatically not true of the seventies and eighties, but may become true again in the nineties. Third, there is the inter-relation of the subjects of education, the inter-relation implied by the very word "university." The study of science or the performing arts is obviously as humane as the study of literature, and concentrating exclusively on one field makes a scholar sterile even in that field. The audience for "The Bridge of Language" was mainly one of scientists: the audience for "Academy without Walls" mainly one of people interested in the practical arts, including poetry and painting.

Many of the essays are occasional in a fairly restricted sense: for example, one or two convocation addresses are included. A convocation is something I take very seriously, because I try to think of it from the graduating student's point of view, as a major milestone of one's life. Such addresses illustrate the fact that every humanist is likely to become something of a professional rhetorician, employed on public occasions, whether to illuminate the occasion, as he hopes, or at any rate, in difficult situations — and I have had some difficult ones, not recorded here — to save its face. In the humanist tradition one of the central figures — for long *the* central figure — is Cicero, many of whose writings are speeches in law courts or the Senate on very immediate and local issues. A twentieth-century humanist, once past a certain point of seniority, is unlikely to write anything on his own initiative, except when doing what he would call "his own work". Certainly nothing in this book has been written on mine: every essay in the book was a response to an invitation for a specific occasion. Apart from phrases of the "I am deeply grateful to X University" type, the retaining of which would make the book look silly, even though the statement is true, I do not feel that all marks of the occasion should be removed. Nothing written or spoken is timeless or without an immediate social context, and the impulse to "rise above" an occasion is usually a mistaken one. So in a sense the whole book is really occasional, and perhaps I should say how I look at the sequence of these occasions, beginning with the most general and proceeding to the more specific.

My studying and teaching career has spanned the depression, the second world war, the cold war of the fifties, the student unrest of the sixties, and what might be called the expectant stagnation of the seventies and eighties. In my student days it was widely assumed that capitalism would, with or without a revolution, evolve into socialism, socialism being assumed to be both more efficient and morally superior. This led to a good deal of adulation for Stalin's Russia, which all the massacres and famines of that régime failed to disturb. In a world full of the dragons of fascism and the squealing maidens of democracy there simply had to be a rescuing knight somewhere. This evolution did not occur: the two systems settled down into an adversary situation, where both sides improved slightly by stealing techniques from the other. The stealing had to be unconscious, otherwise it would be denounced as open communism on the American side and as bourgeois revisionism on the Soviet one. This situation, though one has hopes of its breaking down, is still essentially with us.

What does a humanist learn from all this? Well, obviously he learns that an adversary situation impoverishes both sides. Also that inconsistency is more of a human virtue than a human failing. In our time we have seen first China and then the Soviet Union discover, to their considerable benefit, that doctrinaire Marxism would not work, simply because no doctrinaire anything will work. I have remained a bourgeois liberal all my life because the serious ideals of democracy — personal liberty, free speech, equality of citizenship and tolerance of variety of opinion — are anti-doctrinaire ideals. The Americans made some effort to be doctrinaire democrats in the McCarthy period, but the fact that that was taking them rapidly in the opposite direction from democracy was luckily recognized in time, even if in far too long a time. It seems to me that what is called academic freedom is the key to all freedom. Once the scientist is allowed to pursue science without reference to political priorities; once the records of the past are thrown open to the historian; once the poet or novelist can write without the restrictions of ideology, I think the worst horrors of the police state will become relaxed and eventually impotent.

The doctrinaire is a characteristic of a mass movement, and mass movements are not genuinely social movements, in the sense of people establishing real human contact with one another. Solidarity (in the general sense: I am not speaking of Poland) seldom breeds love or friendship: it may breed loyalty of a kind, but such loyalty all too quickly turns into suspicion of disloyalty. Everything a humanist most values comes out of some loophole or anomaly in the social order. When one looks at a particularly psychopathic period of history, such as the sixteenth century, when people burned heretics for taking their religion seriously, burned witches for being women, and burned the cottages and crops of peasants for being on the site of a holy war, one wonders how great poets and artists survived in such a world. They survived, I think, because the psychopathic tendencies were not consistent enough or well enough organized to destroy them. The fact that such tendencies always do want to destroy the best and most valuable elements in their culture is confirmed by every period of history, including of course ours.

The greater efficiency of censorship and suppression in our time results from a highly developed technology. Humanists are often ridiculed or denounced for resisting technology, but what they are really resisting are certain social evils that come in its wake. These evils may be, from a historical point of view, short-term by-products, but a short term in history can be a long term in a human life. One of the most obvious immediate results of twentieth-century technology is introversion. Our own time, when, quite suddenly as such things go, the churches, theatres and libraries are largely replaced by television sets, the market-place by the processing supermarket, the floor of the stock exchange by computers in offices, is an intensely introverted time, when most human speech that is a genuine expression of thought tends to freeze up. I note in this book (p. 18) that children, and even more adolescents, exhibit a shyness, even shame, about speaking ordinary language, a tendency that often persists through life.

It matters very little what one knows if one cannot express and communicate what one knows. That is why I think of the study of literature and related disciplines as fighting on the front line of civilization. Free speech can only mean highly disciplined speech: it is normally (there are exceptions, but they remain exceptions) a skill resulting from relentless practice and a relentless search for the exact words that express one's meaning. As is obvious, such practice is a moral as well as a cultural training. Its chief technological instruments are, and I think always will be, books. The book is also often regarded as introverted ("always sitting in a corner reading a book," as many parents say when worried by the fact that their children show symptoms of developing minds), and of course it can be that. But the book is actually a companion in dialogue: it helps to structure and make sense of the flood of automatic gabble that keeps rolling through the mind. This interior monologue, as it is called, never relates to other people, however often it is poured over them. Further, a book stays where it is, and does not vanish into ether or the garbage bin like the mass media. So the book becomes the focus of a community (p. 99), as more and more people read it and are affected by it. It moves in the opposite direction the introversion of what has been well called "the lonely crowd", where no one can communicate with his neighbor because he is too close to him mentally to have anything to say.

Some of the addresses in this book are of particular interest to me because of what they seem to me to symbolize in retrospect. After the "sputnik" was launched in the Soviet Union, the normal anti-intellectual tranquility of America was disturbed, and there was a considerable to-do over improving methods of teaching. In Canada, I became one of the founding members of the Ontario Curriculum Institute, an organization designed to consider elementary and high school education, and my preface to the book called *Design for Learning* was one result. The Institute was obliterated when the provincial government set up OISE: I suppose this was inevitable, but I regretted the passing of a genuinely grass-roots movement that had revealed to me the existence of so many dedicated teachers enthusiastic about making what they were doing still better.

In the United States, I was made a consultant by a publisher interested in issuing a series of readers for grades seven to twelve that would be an improvement on a series they had found very profitable, yet a series that taught no literature but only the mythology of what was then (and doubtless still is) called the American way of life. "On Teaching Literature" was a teachers' guide to a new series produced under my general editorship, and often refers to the volumes in it. Unfortunately, the sputnik affair had not put the fear of God into America, only a fear of Russian technology, and by the time American astronauts had reached the moon, a good deal of the anti-intellectualism was back in charge.

This anti-intellectual current swelled to a flood within the university itself, with the rise of what is usually called student unrest in the late sixties, to which the reader will find many references in what follows. In fact he or she may feel that there are too many references, and that what they add up to is an impression of a bourgeois liberal running scared. I don't think that is true: student unrest was not an obsessive anxiety of mine, but it broke out at a time when I was heavily committed with speeches, partly because society itself was getting obsessive about the subject, and wanted discussions of it from those who had had some experience of it. I had little sympathy with the unrest: it seemed to me to have, unlike feminism or the black movement, no genuine social roots. Those who sympathized with it because they were remembering their own left-wing enthusiasms in the thirties were prisoners of their own metaphors: this movement was anarchist and neo-fascist in its tactics. It enlisted a very small minority of students, most even of them, I suspect, egged on by television cameras, who created "mass demonstrations" with a totalitarian skill. But if I had no use for the protest, I had if possible even less for the kind of opposition organized against it, as the Western convocation address shows.

The lack of any real social base accounted for the fact that student unrest did not so much go out of fashion as simply drop dead. What was much more significant about it was its close relation to the various separatist movements contemporary with it, including the Canadian ones. The two together indicated the importance of the problem of relating cultural to political forces, another theme referred to in this book. I regard this as one of the central social problems of our time, quite important enough at least to be approached with all possible sanity, rather than with violence and paradox. The decentralizing movements of culture, the centralizing movements of politics and economics, the need for distinguishing the two and yet recognizing their constant inter-involvement, is a situation at the heart of present-day society, and Canada is, I think, further along than most countries of its population in getting some sense of direction about it.

The age of hysteria, in Canada, peaked with the murder of Laporte, the news of which came the day after the Windsor convocation address. By that time it was clear to everyone that such terrorism was both futile and obsolete. My own activities, however minor, had brought me into touch with more genuinely long-term issues. In the spring of 1957 I went to Ottawa from Harvard, where I was teaching that term, to deliver the inaugural speech, "The Study of English in Canada", at the founding of what is now called ACUTE, the organization of professors of English. In thirty years this has become a large and flourishing group, with its own periodical. There was, if the reader is interested, a certain personal wistfulness in the references to "supporting a common cause," because the publication of my book *Anatomy of Criticism* about two weeks previously had started me on what seemed at the time a lonely and rather frightening path. A few years later I spoke at a conference of the arts meeting in the O'Keefe Centre ("Academy without Walls"). One almost has to read the speech in the context of the issue of *Canadian Art* that reprinted it to recall the extraordinary excitement aroused by this conference, an excitement that seemed inexplicable at the time, even to its organizers. In retrospect, I see it as a realization, however unconscious, that Canadian culture had finally begun to awake from its sleeping-beauty isolation.

Fifty years ago it would have been true to say that Canadian literature was totally unknown outside Canada and that there was every probability that it would remain so. Today there are about a dozen Canadian writers who are world figures, and at least another two dozen who should be. Institutes of Canadian studies have been set up in what once seemed very unlikely parts of the non-Canadian world, and Canadian poetry and fiction has been translated or otherwise made available in most of the major languages. This maturing of Canadian literature (mainly English Canadian, despite so many wonderfully impressive French figures) is the greatest event of my life, so far as my own direct experience is concerned. The paper on the Ontario bicentenary, apart from being by accident confined to Ontario, perhaps does not really convey the intensity of this feeling. I have been very fortunate: it does not fall to everyone's lot to see everything one believes in so triumphantly reinforced by a social and cultural movement on such a scale. Over a long period, say two centuries or more, no society is respected for anything whatever except the evidences of cultural vitality that it has produced in that time. The vagaries of the book business and related enterprises, and their constant preoccupation with what I think of as the Agatha Christie syndrome, the bungling of bureaucracies, and the pressure on schools to squeeze out all serious reading from their curricula, may yet destroy the continuance of what has been achieved; but Canadian writers have been struggling with such things for years, including the years of the greatest productive energy.

I have called the last two decades a period of expectant stagnation, because it is clear to most of us that our world is in the midst of a gigantic revolution, mainly technological in form, and that such problems as chronic unemployment and inflation have to wait on the unfolding of whatever that revolution may contain. I do not mean a revoltion of the traditional type: such things seem very antiquated now, along with wars and strikes and government emergency regulations. Later on in the book (p.93) I recall that in my younger days George VI was Emperor of India, and that Hitler ruled an empire stretching from Norway to Greece. The conflict of empires, their growth and decay, produces only phantasmagoria and illusion. This has been said for many centuries, but we have come to a point in history when we cannot afford illusion any more, and must either be destroyed by it or turn to reality. I do not know of anything except the arts and the sciences that can tell us anything about reality.

At seventy-five the sense of perspective becomes more important than the sense of discovery. And yet the perspective includes a recapturing of discovery: the sun has been told often enough that it shines on nothing new, but it knows better, and keeps rising as placidly as ever. Any temptation I might have to say "this is my last word on the subject" is checked by the realization that it is probably also my first word. For I find myself constantly returning to the assumptions and intuitions of my earliest critical approaches, but the return is not simple repetition, rather continuity into a different life. I suspect that every critical or creative effort in words is a beginning, a reconstructed creation myth. Its model, for those in my field, is Wordsworth's last work, published after his death at eighty, and bearing the title of "Prelude".

# The Beginning of the Word

If I speak of myself to begin with, it is to make clear, so far as I can, the personal origin of my attitudes to the study and teaching of literature. They are attitudes that some of you may consider only the prejudices of my generation, as they may well be. I started teaching in Victoria when it was a small college, and recruits to the teaching staff were selected on what would be now the heretical basis of personal knowledge. My own chairman, Pelham Edgar, had previously appointed to the English staff a demonstrator in psychology in his late thirties who had published virtually nothing, on the ground that he would not only make a good professor or English, but quite probably a poet as well. It sounds like an utterly idiotic thing to do, except that the unknown psychologist was Ned Pratt. I never had the anxiety of lacking tenure: as long as my superiors knew me I was unlikely to lose my job, so I could pick the very difficult subject of Blake's prophecies for my first book, and take the time to do it within the scope I wanted. At Victoria, and at Toronto generally, there was still a strong enough Anglophile feeling for the Ph.D. not yet to be compulsory. So, being very impatient to start both teaching and collecting a salary, I avoided it, and have never been systematically trained as a scholar. I should have been better off with such a training, and this statement is far from being a boast. But it explains why my main interest was teaching from the beginning, and a teacher I have remained.

For most of my career at Toronto the University possessed the Honour Course in English, which many of you will remember, and a new teacher was simply assigned a course to teach if nobody more senior wanted it. That was how I acquired what knowledge I have of many fields, such as nineteenth-century prose, that I should otherwise have left uncultivated, probably for a long time. Texts were prescribed and examinations were anonymous, because students from four colleges, all taught by different people but all proceeding to the same degree, were involved. What this meant in practice was that everywhere a teacher of English turned in Toronto in those days, he was confronted by the impersonal authority of the subject he taught. He could not teach courses he had invented himself, except, within very strict limits, in the graduate school; and the student could not avoid his courses if that student had chosen Honour English — perhaps a more dubious advantage. Once you chose Honour English, that was your last choice: from then on you got English, in various courses covering the whole field from Anglo-Saxon to what had so far emerged of the twentieth century.

I have been accused, if that is the word, of defending the Honour Course whenever I get a chance, and this is one more chance. I remain obstinately of the opinion that the Honour Course, with all its rigidity and built-in administrative absurdities, gave the best undergraduate training available on the North American continent, and the best teacher training for the instructor as well. At the same time it required a much greater maturity from students than many students were able to bring to it, even with the extra year in high school. It takes a good deal of maturity to see that every field of knowledge is the centre of all knowledge, and that it doesn't matter so much what you learn when you learn it in a structure that can expand into other structures. The containing overall structure at Toronto was mainly historical, and options in philosophy and history that covered the same historical period as the English provided an exhilarating clarity of vision into culture. I do not think I am reconstructing when I say that there was a high morale then among both students and teachers of English, and what held us together was encapsulated in a remark I heard Professor Woodhouse make at one of the spasmodic efforts to organize societies of teachers of English that preceded the one I am addressing now. "After all," he said, "we do have the best subject-matter in the world".

I am not mourning the loss of something that has gone and can never come back in anything remotely like the same form. I am saying only that I was lucky to have what I have had, and whatever deficiencies I may feel as a scholar or teacher of English cannot be blamed on anything outside myself. I am also trying to explain how I acquired my sense of cultural priorities, such as it is. Clearly, no one who believes that he teaches the best subject-matter in the world is going to worry very much about the goals of teaching. I can seldom understand the statements about goals that departments of education set for the end of public school, for the end of high school, for the end of anything that seems to have a discernable end. They all sound like much the same set of goals, and the entire operation reminds me of the *New Yorker* cartoon of a man lying in bed and reading a book called "How to Get Up and Get Dressed". There can really be no goal where taking the journey itself is the best thing to be done.

Although Toronto has always put a strong emphasis on undergraduate teaching, I soon got to learn about the common university attitude to teaching. The common attitude is that the university's primary function is to produce scholarship, and the scholar is the man on the frontiers of knowledge who keeps pushing them back. The teacher imparts the knowledge that has already been established to less advanced students, hence the more seniority a teacher has, the more likely he is to confine himself to supervising a few graduates and withdraw from undergraduate teaching. This is, I say, a common attitude, and should be, because much of it is true. It *is* the university's primary function to produce scholarship, and a great many scholars do want to be relieved of undergraduate teaching as they grow older, and rightly. What is wrong about the attitude, I think, is its conception of the teaching process, which seems to me a quite different one from the retailing of information.

I have never felt that I was necessarily an uncreative writer merely because I have confined myself to works of criticism, and I have often attacked the fallacy which says that writers who produce poems and stories are creative, and critics and scholars non-creative. The fallacy, once more, consists in ascribing creativity to the genres used instead of to the people working in them. Some poems and stories and works of critcism are creative; other poems and stories and works of criticism are simply variant verbal patterns. No system of valuation, beyond the tentative hunches of practical experience, will tell us in advance which ones are "alive" and which are not. As with the question of which seeds of a plant will grow, the only practicable answer is "wait and see". I am often assumed to know the answers to such questions as which contemporary Canadian writers are the best, or will be judged "truly great" in the future. There is no answer I know except to ask the question again in two hundred years, and even then the answer would reflect all the limitations of posterity, which has no infallibility in such matters. It seems to be difficult for some to understand that a contemporary writer cannot be "great", whatever his merits or his future reputation, because greatness includes the dimension of having been dead for a long time.

My view of my own work revolves around my growing realization that in my writing I am also a teacher, rather than a typical scholar. My books seem to me now to be addressed essentially to teachers, concerned with new perspectives rather than new data. Such books would be of little use unless more typical works of scholarship were still the main staple of university production, but fortunately they are. I may be said to have blundered into this form of criticism by accident, and it took me a long time to understand what I was really doing, although I might have learned something from the remarks of others. A very old and dear friend, now deceased, remarked over thirty years ago, when my book on Blake had been out for some months: "When I think of that book of yours masquerading as a work of scholarship, I nearly split myself laughing". Perhaps it is high time to look at some of the theoretical implications of my own practice.

Let me begin with an illustrative parable. The older one gets, the more clearly one's childhood comes back into the memory, and I recently recalled a story I had forgotten for over half a century about my mother's experience as a teacher in the late eighteen-eighties. One of her pupils was a girl named Susan, who had been nicknamed "Confusion" by the previous teacher and ridiculed as a dunce. My mother discovered that she was blocked by the theorem in Euclid that the angles at the base of an isosceles triangle are equal, a theorem that for many centuries has been a famous *pons asinorum* or crucial obstacle. My mother spent most of a day going over this theorem with her: she was a desperately honest girl who would never say she understood something if she didn't, and my mother said that the expression on her face when she finally said "I see it, Miss Howard" was worth not only the day but her whole career as a teacher.

Those were very different times, and such a situation could hardly occur now, but even so I can see some contemporary morals in the story. First, the initial change would have to be psychological: she would have to realize, on a deep level of consciousness, that this time she was being required to react as a student and not as a dunce. It has been proved any number of times that the main problem with a learner's so-called stupidity lies in his belief that he is or is considered stupid. Second, what she said was "I see," not "I understand"—perhaps an accident, but still every breakthrough in education is a breakthrough in vision. Third, it made no practical difference to her life whether she understood the theorem or not—in the eighteen-eighties not much was open to a young woman except marriage, and no matrimonial advantages were bound up with isosceles triangles. But it had everything to do with her sense of identity. As long as Susan remembered that she had once known why the angles at the base of an isosceles triangle were equal, some part of her identity would remain inviolate.

All of which indicates how inadequate it is to think of the teacher as primarily someone giving out information to someone else who doesn't have it. The teacher's function is to help create the structure of the subject in the student's mind. That is why it is the teacher who asks most of the questions and not the student. The student already knows a great deal more than he realizes he knows. But this greater knowledge is concealed from him, partly by the fact that it is unstructured, lying around in bits and pieces, and partly by certain repressions operating in his mind. All around him is a world of advertising, propaganda, brainwashing, casual conversation with all its prejudices, news with all its slants, everything conspiring to say to him: "it's all you can do just to take things in; if you try to put things together you'll probably go nuts even if you succeed; let it go. If you go on you'll become different from other people, and you're not smart enough to get away with that". This is not a natural state of mind, which is why so many students are at their keenest when still children, before the full force of social conditioning makes itself felt. I have long been aware that students are more sensitive to poetry, on an average, in grade four than they are in second year university. I thought at first that this problem was peculiar to the humanities, but those concerned with the teaching of science and mathematics don't think so.

How does this situation arise? I think it lies deep in the nature of mass education and the social motives for maintaining it. In a civilization as complex as ours it is crippling and dangerous to be without the rudiments of reading and writing and arithmetic. If we are stopped on the street and asked directions by someone who cannot read, we become as consciously aware of his handicap as if he were blind. At the same time, the main motive in keeping a system of mass education going is, and must be, a regulating one. The primary motive in teaching reading and writing and arithmetic is to produce the disciplined, that is, the docile and obedient, citizen. Of course we must learn to read: how else are we to respond to traffic signs? Of course we must learn to count: how else can we make out our income tax forms? There is nothing sinister about this: it is a simple law of social cohesion. But it means that society aims at a level of literacy that is primarily passive, a training in the ability to make conforming acts. There is no real motive for a society to aim at anything more than this in education, and no obvious tangible benefit for it if it does. It produces the adjusted citizen, and in relation to originality it is anti-intellectual. It is only the born and dedicated teacher who can realize that this motive of adjustment to society, however benevolent, is an enemy to be fought.

The students he can win over to his way of thinking are his allies, but in the nature of things they will seldom be a majority. The situation is further confused by its historical context. In the educational process there always a tendency to hand down a cultural tradition with as little change as possible, which derives from a very primitive conception of wisdom as the voice of antiquity. The myth of ancestral wisdom goes with the authority of seniors, the anxiety of continuity, the sense of the need for preserving the tried and tested way, the supreme virtues of prudence and precedent. As a matter of fact this does characterize a good deal of what is most valuable in education, especially in the humanities. It is only when it becomes inorganic, not recreated for each generation and each student in that generation, and above all when it becomes exclusive, ignoring its connections with the contemporary world, that we get an impression of a fossilized cultural heritage being passed on merely for the sake of passing it on. Such a lifeless continuity can survive only when the traditional heritage, like the Classics in the public schools and universities of England in the eighteenth and early nineteenth centuries, becomes a symbol of upper-class prestige. This can be a very powerful social support, and as long as the symbolism is accepted, such education may survive the dullest reading over of crumbling lecture notes, or even, for younger students, physical brutality.

This symbolic and class-structured approach to education, however, hardly survives anywhere now, and in America at least it collapsed long ago. For well over a century American education has been increasingly geared to society's demand for regulated conformity within a more open class context. It is not called conformity, of course: it is called independence of judgment, learning to think for oneself, fostering the original and the creative, sending the whole student to school, and so forth; but conformity is what it is. Some years ago I was asked to investigate a series of readers that represented literature as taught in grades seven to ten in a large number of American schools. They showed no interest in literature, but a great deal of interest in the stereotypes of middle-class Americanism. They presented some of these with legendary names attached, like Washington and Lincoln and Franklin, others as types, like the pioneer and the inventor; but their greatest object of reverence was Helen Keller, to whom all the volumes recurred, because she represented so triumphant an adjustment to the normal. They were called the "Adventures" series, and the frontispiece of the first one was a picture of a little girl staring into a mirror. That is, what they pretended to suggest was mental adventure; what they actually suggested was narcissism.

There are other reasons why America has had a particularly pervasive kind of anti-intellectualism built into its educational system, at least on the younger levels. The United States is a revolutionary country, starting with a written Constitution and proceeding deductively from it. Any society which has gone through a consolidating experience like a revolution feels itself drawn together and mutually involved in its own coherence. De Tocqueville carefully studied the sense of engagement, the sense of actively participating in the immediate social data, as the characteristic feature of American life. Dickens ridiculed the same kind of thing in *Martin Chuzzlewit*, where the British hero visiting America is nauseated by someone's table manners, and another American remarks on the hatred of outsiders for American "institutions". In a post-revolutionary society everything one does had immediate political relevance, but the conforming act is the typical symbol of this relevance. The last thing a post-revolutionary society is likely to produce is revolutionaries. Canada has had very difficult historical and cultural traditions from those of the United States, but of course it has been thoroughly (and in education increasingly) permeated by American social attitudes.    For most young people, male or female, the code of the gang, the attitudes held by one's contemporaries, is the strongest and most attractive form of conformity. Nineteenth-century American fiction is full of stories about schools where the new teacher could survive only if he could lick the biggest boy in the class, who because he was that was the representative of the local gang spirit. The same condition of entrenched violence is still present, in a much more sinister form, in the jungle schools of some of the big cities. Elsewhere conditions may be more overtly peaceful, but there are still many tensions around the generation gap. There is a wide difference between being aware of the world and being "with it": the teacher ought to be more aware of the world, as older and more experienced, but when it comes to being with it he usually finds his students a jump or two ahead. The deliberate debasing of the literary curriculum that goes on in so many schools is often less an attempt to attract the students than to educate the teacher. If the teacher replaces a Shakespeare play with a contemporary thriller of passing interest, it is not because his students find Shakespeare stale and outmoded but because he does; not because they need to know about the world of thriller but because he feels left out of it. But these efforts to bridge over the generation gap soon fall into the separating abyss.

I feel a profound sympathy with the clergyman who looks over his congregation, sees nobody under sixty in it, and imports a number of gimmicks to make his church more relevant to young people. But, as he is practically sure to alienate his sixty-year-olds without gaining any additional following among the young, one should look for the fallacies involved as well. The main fallacy is that the church, if it is worth maintaining at all, is an educational institution like the school, and can never be sustained on the basis of relevance. Relevance is a disease for which education is a possible, though by no means a certain, cure. It is a disease of nervous degeneration, like St. Vitus's dance, and it ends by destroying the sense of individual identity. We begin by trying to relate social phenomena to ourselves, but end by partitioning ourselves among the phenomena.

The so-called "student unrest" of the late sixties was caught in this double bind of conformity and generation resistance. Students felt obscurely that they were being pushed into conforming modes of action and resented it, but they were too conditioned themselves by the same process to know where or who their enemies were. They spoke darkly of "establishments", and caricatured the university as an agent of reaction and repression, encouraging learning by rote and forcing students to "regurgitate" their lecture notes. I read at least enough student editorials using this word to produce the effect it referred to. There was actually not much of this kind of teaching in the major universities where the unrest centered; but it was essential for them to pretend that there was, as they could not conceive of undesirable conformity except as a fossil from the past. Nor had they any vision of a better order except an intensified conformity, enforced in many places, especially in Europe, by terrorism. I noted earlier that a post-revolutionary society tends to conformity, and in the sixties the SDS (Students for a Democratic Society) hoped to mastermind a total revolution modelled on the "gang of four" regime in China that would introduce a total conformity. Fortunately the next generation of students took a saner view of democratic society.

I have called this talk "The Beginning of the Word", and I suggest that the literary teacher's role is to stand out in the current drifting towards conformity and work his way upstream, like the fisherman in Yeats' *Tower*, towards the headwaters of his cultural tradition. I shall not recapitulate arguments I have made elsewhere about putting poetry in the centre of literary education, but merely repeat that poetry is at the centre, because it is the most primitive and powerful way of stylizing utterance, that prose surrounds it, and that the specialized forms of jargon known as communication skills are on the periphery, where a proper literary education would never get around to reaching them. Trying to reverse the procedure by starting with the kind of gabble fostered by textbooks in "effective writing" and working one's way in a vaguely literary direction does nothing for anybody. I do not trust any way of teaching writing except composition from models, feeling one's way into the idiom of cultivated prose. Again, I need not repeat my contention that the Jourdain fallacy, as I have called it, that prose is the language of ordinary speech, is totally wrong. How wrong it is nobody fully realizes except a teacher of literature. Students may believe that prose is the language of ordinary speech, at least to the extent of distrusting and disliking poetry, but they seem not to be disturbed by the paradox that the language of ordinary speech is something that most of them cannot speak themselves, much less write.

Yet the ability to speak in a relaxed, colloquial, associative rhythm, recognizably close to prose, that is, a lucid but articulate speaking style, is the foundation of all good writing: in fact it is the foundation of any cultivated life. The biggest problem a teacher has to meet in this area is the sense of shame or embarrassment about speaking articulately that so many young people have. It makes their speech stand out from the uniform bleating of the herd, and hence threatens exposure, like a nightmare about appearing naked in public. In times of social unrest, as we saw in the hippie movement of the last generation, there arise cults that make a fetish of inarticulateness. Prose is a difficult and complex form of expression, and I do not see how it is possible to master it without entering into the technicalities now associated with linguistics.

I am aware of the objections brought against the old-fashioned Latinate grammar I learned myself at school, and against them can set only my own experience. My training in grammar, such as it was, was of immense practical benefit to me, and I feel I could have accomplished very little as a writer without it. It may have analyzed the language in the wrong way, but at least it conveyed the fact that there was a structure in language, of a most exciting kind. It was also a curious and oblique introduction to philosophy. There is no reason why such rudiments of philosophy as the distinction of concrete and abstract, the conceptions of universals, of predication, of the relation of subject and object, cannot be absorbed early in public school. I learned them from Latinate grammar, and am still learning from them. So I read with no sympathy an allegedly "contoversial" newspaper article of some years ago called "Grammar is Snobbish Nonsense". The title sums up many of the anti-intellectual fallacies I have been dealing with, and the word "snobbish" expresses the feeling that education is to be distrusted because it might create "elitism", which, whatever it is, is bound to be something simply awful. It can hardly be said too often that "elitist" is a bogey word without content, with the same resemblance to reality that a child's Halloween mask has to the child. Like "heretical" or "atheistic" in a previous age, and like "communist" in many quarters still, it expresses certain social anxieties but defines nothing, and raises only pseudo-issues.

The social goals of the teacher of literature are not reactionary, but he should not feel upset if they are often called that by people who do not think beyond reflex. Man cannot attain his true dignity until he exists in time, in a historical dimension as well as in his spatial surroundings, until some of the gates of the past have been opened, and he can see something of the relativeness of his own standards and values. The centre of literature in time, the historical beginning of the word, is, as it always has been, the great classical tradition, which in English normally runs from Chaucer down to the great symbolic age that ended around 1950. This is what young people, to whom it is new, have a primary right to learn about, and it is our duty to see that they are not cheated. Canadian literature is an offshoot of the central classical tradition: that does not mean that it should be neglected, only that the teacher should have the same sense of proportion about its place in literary tradition as a whole that all the Canadian writers he is likely to choose for study have already acquired. In a sense one may say that the social ideal of the teacher of literature is a pre-revolutionary society, which his teaching helps to recreate. By that I mean a society in which new ideas, new structures of intelligence and imagination, can still have a revolutionary impact. The foundations of such a society are in the classroom, where old ideas and old structures are striking new minds. In this kind of society the educated person discovers a social function for himself that transcends the immediate function of his job or career.

There is, then, a positive and a negative pole, to be respectively sought and avoided. The two poles have been clearly identified ever since the writings of Plato. What has caught everyone's imagination primarily in Plato is the figure of Socrates, especially the Socrates of the *Apology*, facing his mob of accusers and telling them that if they are going to condemn him to death they had better get on with it, as he has no intention of stopping what he is doing. But Plato was a revolutionary thinker, and in one of his last works, the *Laws*, he gives us a blueprint of his post-revolutionary society. There everything turns on the rigid control of the teachers, who are to have no freedom to choose what they teach, but must teach under the strictest instruction and supervision. In such a society no Socrates could exist. We should understand the full dimension of Plato's betrayal of the spirit of Socrates here: he is really assuming that those who condemned Socrates were right in principle, and wrong only, if wrong at all, in their application of it. Similarly, Christianity was founded on the teachings of a prophet who was put to death as a blasphemer and social menace, hence any Christian ready to put someone else

to death as a blasphemer and social menace is assuming that Pilate
and Caiaphas were right in principle, and should merely have selected
a different victim. The teacher's function, I suggest, is to turn his
back on all such post-revolutionary terrorism and face the unpredictable world of Socrates and Jesus, where anything can still happen,
in the mind or in society.

Socrates remains the archetypal teacher, and the modern teacher
finds that Socrates' irony is equally essential to him. He has to answer
all questions with a deep reserve and elusiveness, suggesting the ten-
tativeness of all answers, because progress in understanding is a progress through a sequence of questions, and a definitive answer blocks
this progress. This is particularly true when the student himself gives
the answer, which demands a very active use of irony in counteract-
ing it. Irony has also a peculiar importance in the teaching of literature
because the emotional response to literature is quite as important
as the intellectual one, and is much harder to awaken to maturity
and flexibility.

It is very easy for a teacher to turn himself into an opaque substitute
for literary experience, presenting himself and his personal influence
as the substitute. This is a subtle and insidious temptation he must
fight against every moment in the classroom. His ultimate goal is the
abolition of himself, or the turning of himself into a transparent
medium for his subject, so that the authority of his subject may be
supreme over both teacher and students. In four or five of the great
Socratic dialogues everyone is united at the end in a vision of one
of the Platonic forms, love or justice or eternal life, a union that draws
them into a single body and then releases them. Even with Socrates
this kind of vision did not appear very often, though often enough
for education to be haunted ever since by the ghost of the symposium
and its fleeting glimpses of the forms of the good. Whitehead speaks
of education as the habitual vision of greatness, but I question if such
a vision can ever be habitual, and the greatness in any case is not
that of a person but of the spirits from the deep that the great writers
may summon.

At his trial Socrates compared himself to a midwife, using what
for that male-oriented society was a deliberately vulgar metaphor.
Perhaps the teacher of literature today might be called a kind of drug
pusher. He hovers furtively on the outskirts of social organization,
dodging possessive parents, evading drill-sergeant educators and

snoopy politicians, passing over the squares, disguising himself from anyone who might get at the source of his income. If society really understood what he was doing, there would be many who would make things as uncomfortable as they could for him, though luckily malice and stupidity usually go together. When no one is looking, he distributes products that are guaranteed to expand the mind, and are quite capable of blowing it as well. But if Canada ever becomes as famous in cultural history as the Athens of Socrates, it will be largely because, in spite of indifference or philistinism or even contempt, he has persisted in the immortal task granted only to teachers, the task of corrupting its youth.

Ontario Council of Teachers of English Keynote Address, October 30, 1980. *Indirections* 6 (Winter 1981)

# The Study of English in Canada

I suppose the most obvious reason for forming a society of Canadian English teachers is the need of keeping up with new techniques in literary criticism. The variety of these, and the speed with which they develop, make it extremely likely that a scholar, no matter how central his situation, may be for a long time unaware of new advances in fields relevant to his own, without the help of the kind of association that it is here proposed to establish. I think, as a useful analogy, of the English Institute, founded at the beginning of the war and still meeting annually in September at Columbia University. This is a group of about a hundred and fifty scholars, most of them primarily concerned with English, who meet to discuss, not research in progress, but techniques of criticism as applied to research. Nobody gets or gives a job as a result of going to the Institute: its members meet for the sole purpose of acquainting themselves with what is going on in such fields as editing, linguistics, the history of ideas, analytical bibliography, *explication de texte*, the study of myths and archetypes, and so on. My own experience of the Institute, the amount I have learned from it and the friends I have made at it, convince me of the value of a parallel organization in Canada.

We step into a different world when we pick up, say, a volume of the Eleventh Edition of the *Encyclopedia Britannica*, published in 1910. Here we find Edmund Gosse writing on the seventeenth century, Austin Dobson on the eighteenth, while for such Romantics as, say, Landor or Victor Hugo, after some dull hack has looked up the mere brute facts, Algernon Charles Swinburne can cut loose with a panegyric on the style. The eleventh *Britannica* is an extraordinarily useful reference work, and I am far from belittling it: I say only that no science that was in existence at all in 1910 has developed further, or changed its techniques more drastically, than literary criticism has done. Such developments are, of course, common to the whole critical field, but English studies are clearly now what Classical studies used to be, the clearing house of the humanities, and scholars concerned with other languages have much the same need to keep up with advances in English criticism that English scholars have themselves.

These new developments are rapidly covering the field of literature itself, and I imagine that the next few decades will see an increasing interest in the relations of criticism to other verbal disciplines, such as history, philosophy, ane the social sciences. It is becoming more obvious that we do not teach or learn literature, in universities or elsewhere, and that only the criticism of literature can be directly taught and learned. This fact is more important than it sounds, for literature, like the other arts, does not improve or progress: it produces the classic or model, and the masterpieces that literature has now will always hold their present rank, however splendid those still to be written may be. But while the arts do not evolve or improve, the sciences do, and there is a scientific element in criticism that will keep it expanding its range and consolidating its findings. The extent to which philosophical problems are rhetorical ones, and hence the concern of criticism; the role of metaphor in conceptual thought; the social and political uses of poetic myth; the relation of symbolism and imagery to faith and conduct, are a few of the questions that are likely to engross us in the near future.

The old notion of criticism as a secondary literary activity, following the creative writer at a respectful distance and distributing his largesse to the crowd, is no longer with us. Critics are beginning to understand that literature, like everything else, has a theory and a practice, of equal importance, and that their own place in modern culture is no longer a subordinate one, but ranks with those of the philosopher, the scientist, the historian, and the poet. And as criticism is being faced, as it has never been faced before, with the challenge to take a major place in contemporary thought, literary scholars may be seen dividing into two groups. One group's motto is "Why should it?", that of the other, "Why shouldn't it?" It would clearly be the second group that would be interested in the kind of association now proposed.

What English does the humanities do, and the humanities are the index to the university. Apart from new developments in the criticism of English, the university as a whole is rapidly changing its relation to society, and our role as teachers and scholars is affected by the change. I think it is arguable that the day of the *great* scholar is over, and that he is being replaced by a type of organization man that would better be described as an intellectual, whose social reference is closer to Newman's gentleman, or even to Castiglione's courtier, than to the erudite prodigies of sixty years ago. The intellectual admires and respects scholarship, and he wishes he had more time for his own; but what he actually has is an administrative desk job, often a nine-to-six desk job, the intervals of which he must fill up with such scholarly work as he can. He is not protected, as the great scholar was protected, from the exhausting versatility that continuous contact with modern life demands. His intellectual role has an immediate social importance, sometimes a political importance. An American intellectual, for instance, may be summoned at any time to get into a plane and go off to explain American culture to the Japanese. The public is at present in a somewhat repentant mood over their underestimating of intellectuals in the past: this shows their awareness of the changes taking place, and foreshadows the much greater social demands that will be made on our eggheads in the future.

Of late years the development of professional and graduate schools has overshadowed the undergraduate core of the university, but it is possible that even now social influences are setting in which will counter-act this tendency. Already centres of pure scholarship, like the great research libraries and the Institute of Advanced Studies in Princeton, are beginning to separate from the university proper. We may be moving back again to the Newman conception of the undergraduate university as less intellectual than, in the highest sense, social, less concerned with research as an end in itself than with a definite social aim, an aim that might be described as realizing the idea of a free society. Similar tendencies are at work in the university itself, not least in English studies. At present the advance of critical techniques seems to be increasing the professionalizing of literary study, and thereby widening the gap between the critic and the plain reader. I think that this is a temporary result of rapid growth, and that we shall soon see the gap beginning to close again, as criticism becomes more coherent and more aware of its own unity.

Liberal knowledge of course was never quite its own end: it was always to some extent the vocational training of responsible citizens. And as the university becomes less of a fortress and more of a market place, it might be well to recast our conception of it along the wider lines indicated by Arnold's conception of culture or Mill's conception of an area of free discussion. No one concerned with the Church would confine the conception of the Church to the aggregate of buildings called churches, and it is equally a fallacy to identify the true University in the modern world with the aggregate of degree-granting institutions. Wherever two or three are discussing a subject in complete freedom, with regard only to the truth of the argument; wherever a group is united by a common interest in music or drama or the study of rocks or plants; wherever conversation moves from news and gossip to serious issues and principles, there the University, in the wider sense, is at work in society. The candor and liberality of a society's cultural life indicates the social effectiveness of its universities.

Undergraduates in arts and sciences are being trained to form an educated public, an amateur rather than professional goal. Such university training thus comes in between the specialized research or professional training centre, and the teaching institution or school. Undergraduates usually speak of the university as "school," and expect to be taught, but it is part of the function of a university to disappoint them, to insist on treating them as adults. It is an axiom of university life that teaching takes care of itself, that lectures (to use an admirable distinction of Mill's) should be overheard rather than heard. A scholar who cannot teach by virtue of being a scholar must have either a cleft palate or a split personality; it is hard to see how one can master the world's most difficult technique of communication and still be unable to communicate. There have been such scholars, but their frequency and importance in the modern world is easy to overestimate.

As education is not itself an academic subject, its introduction into university life makes for confusion, exaggerating the difficulty of teaching at that level, and compromising with, or deliberately prolonging, the immaturity of students. In universities, as in schools, instructors will knock themselves out trying to become conscious of everything their students are unconscious of; professors will revise their courses and wonder whether putting B before A instead of after it might not revolutionize their students' comprehension of the whole subject. But "teaching methods," however important in dealing with children, achieve in university classrooms only a dreary and phony magic.

Students of science who are any good are proud of the impersonality of their subject: their self-respect is increased by its demand for evidence that cannot be faked or manipulated, for facts that have nothing to do with individual preferences. The humanities are of course more directly concerned with values and with emotional and even subjective factors. Nevertheless it may be a mistake to try to popularize the humanities unduly, to neglect the very large degree of impersonal authority that the humanities, no less than the sciences, carry with them. University teachers of English are certainly not being false to their subject if they suggest to the student that he does not judge great works of literature, but is judged by them; that while he should be encouraged to make statements about Shakespeare and Milton, the statements will be about himself and not about them. Whatever changes of fashion in literature may come or go, the difference between an informed and responsible tast and a whimsical or erratic one remains constant. The English teacher's ideal is the exact opposite of "effective communication," or learning to become audible in the market place. What he has to teach is the verbal expression of truth, beauty and wisdom: in short, the disinterested use of words.

A student cannot call himself a student without acknowledging the prior authority of the university and of its courses of study. Joe Doakes at college is not necessarily a student, nor is a degree-granting institution necessarily a university. It is a university if it trains its students to think freely, but thinking, as distinct from musing or speculating, is a power of decision based on habit. Reason is but choosing, Milton says, but to choose is to eliminate the other choices: the greater the freedom of thought, the less the freedom of choice. The process of education is a patient cultivating of habit: its principle is continuity and its agent memory, not rote memory but practice memory. The university is doing its proper job when it presents the student with a coherent area of knowledge and enables him to progress within it. Universities with department-store curricula that allow him to leave an instructor in the middle of a sentence in order to pick up a credit somewhere else are not enfranchising him; they are merely cheating him. Such pseudo-educational procedures are an assault on the memory; they undermine the habits of continuity and repetition which are the basis of learning. All the distinctions which are fundamental to education: the distinction between concentration and attention, between knowledge and information, between education itself and instruction, depend on such habits. Thinking itself is not a natural process like eating, but an acquired skill like playing the piano: how well one will think at any given time will depend primarily on how much of it one has already done.

It is because education is rooted in habit that its technological basis is the book. The book is a model of patience, for it always presents the same words no matter how often one opens it; it is continuous and progressive, for one book leads to another, and it demands the physical habits of concentration. Popular and mass media are discontinuous: their essential function is to bring news, and to reflect a constantly changing and dissolving present. It is often urged that these media have a revolutionary role to play in education, but I have never seen any evidence for this that I felt was worth a second glance. The arts of phantasmagoria can only stimulate a passive mind: they cannot, so far as I can see, build up habits of learning. The university informs the world, and is not informed by it.

One of the superstitions that beset the teaching of English is the notion that the student should not be directly confronted with the heritage of the past, but should sidle into it cautiously from the present, spending his first year on the *Atlantic Monthly* or some collection of topical essays, but gradually learning about the history of literature from what is quoted in Eliot. It is hard to see how any university that is apologetic about the literary tradition can do much to develop writers. For not only is tradition itself a creative force in writing, but the structural principles of literature do not exist outside literature. As far as form and technique are concerned, poems can only be made out of other poems, novels out of other novels. Hence however much a new writer may have to say, his ability to say it can only be developed out of his reading: in other words it will depend on his scholarship.    In fiction this fact is partly concealed by the importance of content, which is normally contemporary and derived from experiences outside literature. But we notice that in contemporary painting there seems to be less interest in realism and documentation, and more emphasis on the formal or structural principles which are brought out in abstract or non-objective painting. The formal principles of painting are quasi-geometrical; in literature they are myth and metaphor. And in literature too, at least in Canada among the younger writers, one notes a decline of interest in fiction and an increase of it in poetry, especially mythopoeic and symbolic poetry. Whether this is a good or a bad thing, it is a trend toward forms of expression that are inextricably involved with the academic study of literature, and hence is something on which our help might reasonably be called for.

I think it probable that writing in Canada in the near future will become more academic, in the sense of being preoccupied with the formal principles of writing, with myth, metaphor, symbol and arche-type. This does not mean that it will become less popular, for these have always been the popular and primitive elements of literature. It is much easier for me to imagine Dylan Thomas popular than to imagine some documentary and naturalistic novelist like Dreiser popular. We have always had a crucial responsibility for the quality of writing in Canada, and we have always had a good deal of imper-sonal and professional influence on it, but that fact seems to me likely to become increasingly obvious, to ourselves, to the writers, and to the public, as time goes on.

At the same time we cannot forget that there are different types of originality, and that while we may encourage some toward fame and applause or even fortune, others may have to travel a lonelier road of indifference, hostility, even of persecution. This is also a cen-tury in which great novels have been seized and burned in custom houses, in which a frighteningly long list of writers have been driven to madness or exile or suicide. Not all Muses are soft cuddly nudes: some are obscene harpies that swoop and snatch and carry off, and faced with a writer like this we can do little but understand what is happening and sympathize with his plight. For our function, like his, may not be always a socially approved one: it may make the greatest demands on our integrity, may force us to withstand hysteria and the pressure to conform, may call not simply for intelligence but for a rare courage. If so, it will surely be some advantage to feel that there is a community of us, engaged in the same work and concern-ed to maintain the same kind of standards, not merely filling similar positions in different places but supporting a common cause.

Lecture to a group of Canadian Teachers of English in Ottawa, 19 June 1957. *Dalhousie Review*, 38 (Spring 1958)

# The Critical Discipline

The present paper deals with the relation of the liberal arts to education as a whole and to the conditions of life in Canadian society. This sounds like very familiar territory, and it is; but I am still not sure that the objectives of undergraduate teaching in this country are generally understood. I do not believe in conflicts between science and the humanities, or between religion and science; but we do have conflict when different theories attempt to explain the same set of facts. The theory of education, like other theories, should be based on the whole of its practice. We have suffered much from the theories that generalize from the practice of the kindergarten; but we should examine these theories, horrifying as they are, to understand why they arose. The liberal arts have suffered also from theories based on the practice of professional faculties, including the graduate school, perhaps the least liberal of them all. Then, just as some of the confusions surrounding undergraduate teaching were beginning to clear up, along came the wealthy foundations, as obsessed with "projects" as any teachers' college, and showing a marked preference for projects as disruptive of normal university routine as possible.

In this situation all the millions of words that have been written about the humanities and the liberal arts fail to do much to improve either the morale of the staff or the motivation of the students. And that both need improvement is clear to such an audience as this at such a time of year as this. Many of us are university teachers who have just finished marking undergraduate papers, and are all too familiar with the baffled stare with which the Canadian youth confronts his cultural heritage. As Coleridge is prominently featured in this session of the Royal Society, we may adopt Coleridge's method of studying existing practice in an effort to see what theoretical principles may underlie it. I use the term "critical" because it seem to me that criticism, in Matthew Arnold's sense, is the only conception that will cover the whole area that we are interested in.

It has become an axiom in educational theory today that the skills developed from the study of specific subjects are not transferable to other subjects. The study of Latin, for instance, is not "good for the mind" in the sense that it can directly contribute to mental efficiency in a business or professional career. This particular discovery became very popular among the "progressive" educators of the last generation, because it seemed to fit so neatly into their programme of replacing intellectual with social training. A little Latin, so the argument ran, is a dangerous thing, for all it can lead to is more Latin, which is practically a fatal thing. Such educators often assert that all emphasis on content in education derives from the old fallacy about transferring mental skills. I have no desire to defend the fallacy, but as the fallacies that replaced it were much more disastrous superstitions, the inferences drawn from its refutation may have been the wrong ones.

To speak of a general mental ability developed from specific mental skills is merely a mistaken way of stating an obvious fact. The specific things a student learns or experiences do contribute, directly or indirectly, to the formation of his opinions and behaviour. All experience educates, and our social personality forms underneath our vanishing experiences like layers of chalk under a rain of dying protozoans. Primary education, in the broad sense, is concerned with acquiring the minimum of specific skills and information that one must have in order to live in modern society. As experience, it is being assimilated to a developing social attitude, but this is a process which is steadied by the nature of the child's society. The child's society is a primitive society, and like other primitive societies it is an extremely stable one. Its folklore, codes of behaviour, humour and modes of speech have probably changed very little since Neolithic times. Hence primary education is, or should be, almost entirely specific and useful, and the basis of its theory is, or should be, research into the learning process.

In secondary education the student is old enough to notice that his social opinions and attitudes are taking shape underneath his studies. He is still immersed in a primitive society, rigid in its etiquette and in its demands for conformity; but he is now swept by moods of oppositions, ranging from rebelliousness to idealism, that seem to have a more consistent pattern in them. All his experience continues to educate him, as it did before, but he is becoming aware of an underlying conflict in his situation. On one side of him is his ordinary social environment, the world of his television set, his movies, the family car, advertising, entertainment, news, and gossip. On the other side is the school, and perhaps the church, trying to dislodge him from this lotus land and prod him into further voyages of discovery. On one side of him is a difficult theoretical world or art and science, the principles of which he has not begun to understand; on the other side is a fascinating world of technology and rhetoric, which he can already handle with some competence, and in which he must live in any case. The school has only five hours a day in which to fight the influences which keep soaking into the student from the rest of his experience, and which usually command an authority that the school cannot command. As a rule, therefore, the world of technology and rhetoric wins out, whether the student goes on to university or not. In moments of depression one feels that the majority of university students have already been conditioned beyond the point at which the university can affect them at all.

The educational theories generally called progressive tried to abolish this conflict by making the school the agent of society. Education thus became a matter of social adjustment to the world one must live in. But this world, in itself, provides no real standards or values. It stands for immaturity and a cult of youth, for social values rooted in entertainment and advertising, and for emotions rooted in the erotic. Besides, the world, unlike nature, always betrays the heart that loves her. It changes very rapidly, driven on by forces that the socially adjusted cannot comprehend, and can only cope with by the fixations of prejudice and stock response. Thus understanding the world, if it is made the goal of education, is forced to become an acceptance of the world, and that in turn becomes increasingly an acceptance of illusion. The forms of illusions are familiar: there are the illusions of advertising and its status symbols; the illusions of slanted news, and the illusions of entertainment, where the "fixing" of a television programme or ball game is so much more emotionally disturbing than major corruption or crime. What started out as a fearless grappling with the conditions of present-day life finishes in a neurotic prison of credulity, bewilderment, and cynicism. I am speaking of the logical consequences of a theory, not of what invariably happens in practice, but it happens often enough to be a grave social danger.

The university demands, first of all, that the student recognize and accept a dialectic between his social environment and a cultural environment which crosses it, so to speak, at right angles. He should understand what he must do to live in his society; but he must understand too that that society has no criteria for judging itself or one's actions within it. The criteria (or at least the secular criteria) can come only from the arts and sciences, the co-ordinated vision of the greatness and accuracy of human imagination and thought. The university then demands that the student devote his main energies for several years to a study of his cultural environment. This entails a voluntary commitment which includes both a physical and a mental withdrawal from ordinary society. It entails too the atmosphere of academic freedom, which means among other things that ideas and works of the imagination must be studied as far as possible without reference to ordinary society's notions of their moral or political dangers. In practice this freedom may be limited in various ways, but it is sufficiently present to make it forever impossible that any open-circuit television programme can ever reproduce the actual conditions of university teaching. For that, one must always have a closed door.

In primary education only the surface of learning, the acquiring of information and skills, is ordinarily visible; in secondary education social opinions and attitudes begin to come into view. In the university the basis of the whole structure appears, in the form of a vision of what the world is in comparison with the higher society of art and science which shows us what humanity can do, the society that Arnold called culture. The university is thus a kind of social laboratory in which the most revolutionary conceptions may be valuable, not necessarily as programmes for action, but as insights into the structure of society, nature, or the human mind. This conception of a social laboratory was, I suppose, the basis of the old Classical training, where a completed civilization could be studied as a laboratory specimen of a social organism. The student often reacts to academic freedom by developing a naive radicalism or a naive conservatism. Which it is will depend on whether he is more impressed by culture's power to transform society or by its power to hold it together.

One familiar feature of university practice is particularly puzzling to the student, and not only to him. The authors of a recent book, *The Academic Marketplace,* were equally puzzled by it, though they devoted the entire book to a study of it. The young man who starts out on a university staff is earning his living by teaching. Yet he is given no instruction in teaching, and is not appointed for his teaching abilities at all, but for his scholarship. Questions are unofficially asked about his classroom effectiveness, but there is something conspiratorial about such questions, like the questions about the political views of government employees. Promotion, too, is based on scholarship, and any appointment made primarily on teaching ability is generally regarded as a second-class appointment, just as appointments that involve no teaching are generally regarded as the juiciest plums on the academic tree.

However much snobbery and confused thinking may be involved with this practice, it seems to be the assumption that in the university teaching should be left to take care of itself, that every scholar can teach, and that if he cannot teach there is merely something the matter with his scholarship. In practice, this assumption works fairly well. The majority of competent scholars are also effective teachers, and become so without benefit of any instruction in teaching. Those interested solely in teaching, on the other hand, often find that their lack of interest in scholarship increasingly isolates them from the classroom as well as from every other aspect of university life. Exceptions are less important than they seem because the really keen student, faced with an inarticulate scholar, can cut the lectures and work on his own. I am not suggesting that the university instructor is fulfilling his social function by cheating his mediocre students out of their tuition fees. I am merely saying that the university's practice of regarding teaching as a by-product of scholarship is apparently a sound one.

It is clear that in many respects the university is not primarily a teaching institution at all. The more mature the student, the less the teacher becomes the dispenser of learning, and the more he becomes a transparent medium of it. In the primary grades the teacher is an apparition from a strange and mysterious adult world; by the end of secondary school he should have become a fellow-student. The significance of the priority of scholarship to teaching in the university thus becomes clear: it means that in the university the relation of teacher and student is strictly subordinated to the authority of the subject being taught. In the university there is no longer any such thing as "education": there are only literature, chemistry, history, and similar subjects to be studied. The university does not ask if a man is educated: it asks only "What does he know?" But this "what" is not, as the progressivists say, mere content, to be used as material for personal development. What he knows is literature or chemistry or history or whatever it is, and these are the organized forms of knowledge: no genuine scholarly knowledge exists outside them.

The emergence of the teacher, as a professional person on a social and cultural level with members of other professions, is a result of the series of social revolutions which have produced modern democracy. In Plato and Aristotle we hear much of education, but much less of teachers as such, and in fact Plato says explicitly in the Laws that a well-run society cannot afford to leave anything to the teacher, but must prescribe everything he does. Such an attitude today would be called totalitarian. But in our society, too, we discover that a child-centred theory of education soon becomes an administration-centred theory, where the individual teacher is absorbed into the teacher's conference. The independence and autonomy of the teacher is only possible if he owes his main allegiance to his cultural and not to his social environment. To subordinate teaching to scholarship is the only way of guaranteeing the independence of the teacher within the university, and of encouraging his independence outside of it.

Thus the university, so far from assuming the transferability of mental skills, assumes the exact opposite. The discipline of the subject studied becomes an end in itself in proportion as the student matures. He advances from "taking" a subject to being taken up in it. The general course in arts assumes that an integrated curriculum, even in so specialized a world as ours, is, up to a point, possible at the university level. The honour course, on the other hand, is based on the assumption than any genuine discipline can be used as a centre of knowledge, the radius of expansion from the centre being the student's responsibility. Either assumption is justifiable, but that of the honour course is perhaps closer to this age of intellectual pluralism.

But whatever may be true within the university, it is of course concerned with returning students to their social environment after graduation. Its product is the social product that we think of as the educated citizen, or what Newman called the gentleman. The word gentleman does not now mean, however, what Newman meant by it, and we badly need a word to describe the man who tries to live in his social environment by the standards and values of his cultural environment. The difference between the ordinary citizen living by purely social standards and the educated citizen aware of a cultural environment as well is, or should be, a difference in personality. It follows that the conception of personal development, so dear to the hearts of educational theorizers, is not a simple conception.

The ordinary social personality is an adjusted ego, and its energies are the energies of self-expression. The shrewdness and accuracy with which this self-expression adapts itself to a social situation makes up one's ordinary practical intelligence. In all areas of the cultural environment we meet with something additional that may be called renunciation: the surrender of the ego to the laws and conditions of the discipline being studied. The student of science is proud of the impersonality of his subject, of its serene preoccupation with evidence and its independence of whim and fancy. The professional man is not qualified until he had gone through some ritual acknowledging the priority of the standards of his profession over his own needs and desires. Poets, from Homer to Eliot and Joyce, have consistently spoken in the same terms about poetry. It is impossible to teach the humanities properly if we think of them as ornaments or graces of ordinary social life. They have their laws and disciplines like the sciences, and must be taught as impersonally as the sciences, despite their emotional and aesthetic connections. Normally it is only after prolonged contact with a specific discipline of thought or imagination that one can face the kind of reality that detachment reveals, a reality unaffected by socially acquired prejudices or the passions of the ego.

It follows that such a cliché as "teaching the student to think for himself" is not a simple conception either. In ordinary social experience, thinking for oneself is a matter of putting one's expressive energies into socially acceptable forms. In real thinking we first study a given subject long enough to enable its laws and categories to take possession of our minds, after which we may move around inside the subject with some freedom. There is no real thought outside such disciplines. Those of us who are in universities have heard the protest of the delinquent undergraduate in some such terms as this: "You tell us we should think for ourselves, and when we do you throw the book at us." It is a complicated matter to explain to such a lad that what he means by "himself" is a being entirely incapable of thought. Of course a thinker should be able to return to society with an enormously heightened power of practical decision, but by that time he has lost interest in thinking for himself.

Whatever one studies at a university, whether humanities or science, one is studying a subject in a state of continual intellectual ferment, which has gone through many revolutions of perspective in the last century and is certain to go through many more in the next one. Such a mental training is becoming almost indispensable for living in a society of which great revolutions in perspective will also be demanded. Communism has the tactical advantage of a revolutionary point of view; its overthrow of previous governments is recent and it asserts to its people that it is progressing in revolution and that they are participating in history. By contrast, the democracies seem to be forgetting their revolutionary traditions, and their will to face the future seems to be sapped by a morbid fear of losing what they now have. But both religion and democracy teach us that ordinary society is highly expendable. Christianity insists that man's ordinary actions are worth very little in the sight of God. Democracy was not founded on a maudlin enthusiasm for the common man, but on an inference from original sin: that men are not fit to be trusted with too much power. Our students have been conditioned to regard such doctrines as depressing, although they were part of the vision of life that inspired Milton and Lincoln. Without the sense of expanding possibilities that such a vision brings, it is hard to see how the democracies can mentally adapt even to the social changes that will be forced on them, much less develop the creative energy to make their own.

We hear much about the increased numbers of students coming to universities; and surely this great mass of potential public opinion is more important than merely a vaguely alarming statistic. Most of these students will, inevitably, be processed rather than educated, and for the really keen student in the future the great difficulty will be, not to get to university, but to get his proper education instead of processing. I say difficulty for the student, because the initiative will be up to him. The university, by virtue of its emphasis on the cultural environment, the supremacy of mental discipline over personality, and academic freedom, has the resources for forming a bridgehead of flexible and detached minds in a strategic place in society. It should not think of doing this as an additional task, or even as a manipulating or directing of its present task. The university can best fulfil its revolutionary function by digging in its heels and doing its traditional job in its traditionally retrograde, obscurantist, and reactionary way. It must continue to confront society with the imaginations of great poets, the visions of great thinkers, the discipline of scientific method, and the wisdom of the ages, until enough people in the democracies realize that a way of life, like life itself, must be lost before it can be gained.

Address to the Fellows of Sections I and II of The Royal Society of Canada, June 1960. *Canadian Universities of Today: Symposium Presented to the Royal Society of Canada in 1960*, ed. George Stanley and Guy Sylvestre. Toronto: University of Toronto Press, 1961.

# Academy Without Walls

I suppose everyone here has been asked by someone, at some time or other, to explain contemporary art to him. I cannot explain contemporary art, but I can point out two of its characteristics without moving very far away. In the first place, this is a *conference* of contemporary arts. Artists have always formed cliques, schools, groups, and isms; they have formed societies and guilds; they have organized manifestoes, little magazines, co-operative housing and insurance schemes. But the conferring artist, the artist who goes to a conference of artists, is a product of this age alone. In the second place, I am the third university man in a row to address you this afternoon, which means, whatever else it may mean, that we are well into the twentieth century. At no other period of history would academics be so willing to talk to artists or artists be so willing to listen to academics. At no other period of history has the university's devotion to the liberal arts been so closely associated with the actual arts.

One obvious fact about the culture of our time is the enormously increased awareness of its past, and the variety and range of tolerance in its sense of tradition. The greenest student in a conservatory may learn more about pre-Mozartian music than Mozart himself ever knew; and even if, say, Watteau or Goya had known anything about Bushmen painting or Haida masks, they could hardly have seen much connexion between them and the traditions of art that they accepted. But the artist of today cannot think of himself as being pushed along at the end of a thin line of historical development through Greece, Rome and Western Europe. He is now a citizen of all time and space: Javanese puppet-plays, Chinese calligraphy, Benin bronzes, Peruvian

textiles — anything that has ever been produced as art or is now realized to be art may take its place in his tradition. Immense erudition
is needed to understand the variety of influences on contemporary
artists, and the work of Picasso, of Stravinsky, of T.S. Eliot, might
from one point of view be studied as a mass of quotations and allusions.

An artist may serve his apprenticeship in many ways: he may start
at the age of eleven in a master's studio grinding colors and laying
in backgrounds; or he may attend slide lectures in a university scrib-
bling indecipherable notes in the dark about Carolingian manuscripts
in the Ottonian Renaissance. What he is doing in either case is learning about the conventions of his art. For no artist ever faces his world
directly: he enters into the conventions provided by the art of his time.
One does not learn to paint landscapes by studying landscapes, any
more than one learns to compose fugues by listening to street noises.
After a little study of Italian painting, one may learn to distinguish
at a glance across a room what century a particular picture was
painted in. This would be impossible if any artist really had the power
to face nature directly, outside the prism of convention. The novelist
may gather his material from the life around him, but his ability to
make anything of it will depend on his knowledge of novel-writing,
which begins in his knowledge of how other people have written novels.
An artist's technical ability, in short, comes out of his craftsmanship,
and his craftsmanship comes out of his scholarship.

Consequently, an increase in the sense of the variety of tradition,
of the number of legitimate influences it is possible to have, becomes
part of an increase in the technical resources of the arts. Art is, Aristotle tells us, an imitative activity, and what it imitates, according
to the critics, is nature. Other authorities have assured us that art
is also a creative activity, and that what it creates is an aspect of human
society. But in the twentieth century "nature" is no longer so firmly
rooted a world of familiar physical objects, nor is "society" a group
of familiar personalities growing out of it. You heard that a conference
was being held in Toronto and came here by plane or train or car:
in other words your "society" or environment is a co-ordinated series
of points in space. Twentieth-century life does not radiate from a
centre but rotates in an orbit, moving from point to point at will.
Nature has become similarly abstract and conceptualized. The ease
of moving around has become central in our imaginations, and our
sense of objectivity is no longer identified with fixed objects. The ob-

jective world appears as a swirling mass of electrons even to those who do not know what an electron is; the view of the world from an airplane window, as an abstract pattern of crop and fallow fields or a geometrical network of city lights, is the world-view even of those who have never been in a plane. Vision is relative to the choice of a point of view: this has always been true, of course, but never before so obviously true. Consciousness itself is a chosen point of view; there is no reason why the world of dream and fantasy should not be an equally valid choice.

This vast expansion in the possibilities of form has given the artist unprecedented resources in technique. Representationalism in painting, diatonic harmony in music, strict metre and rhyme in poetry, are as legitimate techniques as they ever were, but each is now regarded as one among a great many possibilities. Like man in existentialist philosophy, art is in a state of unqualified freedom. To begin with, anything goes: difficulties may come later, but they come as consequences of a free choice. At times one feels that the artist is rather in the position of Adam in Paradise, who had so much freedom that all he could do was sin. And yet much of this sense of unlimited freedom is an illusion, or rather, it exists for the art as a whole, but not for the individual artist. The artist is in theory free to commit himself to any one of a dozen conventions, but all that he can choose is a convention. Tachism, abstraction, twelve-tone harmony, free verse: these are loose terms for groups of conventions each of which is as rigid as the conventions of plain chant, Russian ikons, or a beatnik's vocabulary.

Contemporary art is neither popular nor esoteric. It is academic and scholarly, newly possessed of tremendous technical resources and still experimenting with their use. It is therefore an integral part of the educational system of our time, which is why the artist and the scholar can be so naturally associated as they are in this conference. It has always been said that the artist's function was to delight and instruct, and in an age like ours his importance as an instructor cannot be ignored. There will always be artists for every variety of creative expression, but a large part of the creative energy of our time is bound to be directed toward the exploring of technique. It is natural that poetry should turn to myth and metaphor, painting to the abstract of pattern and color, music to a neo-classical absorption in form. How long this academic phase of art will last I do not know, not having a clouded crystal ball handy, but other things being equal it should outlast the century. There will be reactions against it every year or so, eddies churning in the stream, and each will be hailed in turn as the beginning of something totally new. But, as Samuel Butler remarked in *Erewhon* a century ago: "There is no way of making an aged art young again; it must work out its salvation anew, and in all fear and trembling." I am not making a value-judgement on contemporary art: I am merely trying to characterize it. Being an academic myself, I feel that if art is academic there is nothing better for it to be, and that there is no reason why our age should be cultural-ly inferior to any other.

When the ideals of modern democracy were formed, there was some hope that patronage in the arts would be replaced by popularity; that art would cease to be a status symbol for connoisseurs and would take a central functional place in society. It has done this to some extent, but in a way that has disappointed many. Some of you may recall a tedious and foolish harangue that covered an inordinate amount of a Toronto newspaper a few weeks ago under the title of "Cult or Culture." There is, of course, no "or" about it: culture has always been a cult, in the sense of being a group of specialized and exacting disciplines. It is natural that some people should resent this, just as it is natural that some people should resent the fact that years of hard work in education are necessary for the best life. It is natural that some people should feel a strong urge to tell artists that whatever they are doing they are doing it all wrong, and ought to "return" to something they regard as more satisfactory. The trouble is that the artist does not have all that freedom of choice, once his initial choice (and even that may not be a choice) has been made. He can paint or write or compose only what takes shape in his mind: he can-not will to become a different kind of artist. It is possible in a totalitarian society, and it might be possible in this one, to lay down certain approved norms that all artists must conform to, and to ensure that no one who does not have the specific talents required will ever get to be an artist. But that would not make realists out of artists; it would merely mean that a very different and much less genuinely creative group of people were taking over the arts.

The contemporary artist is dependent neither on patronage nor on popularity, but on something in between. Because his work is in-creasingly regarded as an academic and scholarly activity, he depends on recognition by critics, reviewers, directors of museums and art galleries, members of the advisory boards of councils and wealthy foundations, university administrators who employ him as a summer teacher or resident artist — almost entirely a community of scholars. The artist may dislike this situation, or pretend to do so. He may dream of appealing to the general public over the heads of such scholars: he may attack them as unimaginative, culturally sterile, parasitic, prissy and hidebound: he may fall into cliches of nineteenth century romanticism about the creator's virility and the critic's lack of it. We find this in the work of the writer who produces, for middle-brow magazines, the kind of highly conventionalized essay about his view of the modern world that is designed to give the impression of a writer writing like a writer. Or the artist may have been brought up to think of the academic as the opposite of the creative, and be genuinely bewildered by a world in which they have become the same thing. Nevertheless, scholars are the public on whom the artist must make his first impression, and from his point of view he could hardly do better. Advisory committees and the like are as a rule liberal to a fault: they know how many mistakes have been made in the past, and are not anxious to repeat them; they do not require conventional morality or subservient behaviour; they expect the artist to take the odd nervous bite out of the hand that feeds him. There are exceptions, but they are far fewer than when Samuel Johnson could list the hazards of the mental life as: "Toil, envy, want, the patron and the jail." For many a modern artist, supported by benevolent foundations until he can be handed over to the women's committees of symphonies and art galleries, the course would be better described as: "Prize, study, grant, the matron and the kale."

The patronage of the arts by various semi-official bodies, and the employment of artists by universities, do not mean that the country is trying to buy itself a culture, or that foundations are seeking for more virtuous and better publicized ways of paying income tax. Such things mean that in the twentieth century the creative arts have become absorbed into the educational process. The artist is recognized as a teacher and educator, and society is exposed, however reluctantly, to the contemporary arts because they are a necessary part of education. The "difficulty" of contemporary art is precisely the same as that of any other subject of education, which means that most of the difficulty, like beauty, is in the eye of the beholder. Algebra is neither difficult nor easy to the keen student, but to, say, the girl who has already decided on a life of bridge and Saturday shopping it is impenetrably obscure. She "can't do" algebra because it has no place in her vision of life. Nevertheless the educational system mildly compels her at least to try a little algebra, because this is a democracy, and it is her right to be exposed to quadratic equations however little she wants them. The arts are much less like alegebra than, for example, a well-planned football game, but still they do demand some concentrating of attention. It is the right of people to be kept in contact with the contemporary arts because the public is partly paying for them, and the public ought to get what it ought to get. It is entirely impossible to know nothing of art and yet to know what one likes: what one likes is always a measure of what one knows. Those who deny that society is responsible for guiding and developing its own taste are people who cannot distinguish a democratic society from a mob.

The result is that there is now an unprecedented tolerance for experiment and originality of all kinds in the arts. It is difficult even to imagine what sort of pictures would go today into a *Salon des Refusés*. Gone are the days when radicalism in the arts could be regarded as a sign of atheism, communism, and moral turpitude. I remember passing behind two gentle old ladies in the Art Gallery of Toronto as they were contemplating some rather strident pictures by a young painter, and hearing one of them say: "And when I knew him he was a nice clean boy." But such comments are now rare. T.S. Eliot, with his Order of Merit and his odour of sanctity, must look back with some nostalgia to the days when *The Waste Land* was a new poem and he could be described as a "drunken helot" and a "cultural Bolshevist". On the contrary, even the Museum of Modern Art in New York is old hat now, and crowds line up before the elevators in the Guggenheim Museum waiting to be sucked down into the vortex of that preposterous building. As art becomes increasingly fashionable, anything new in art becomes a new fashion. To encourage it is ever so revolutionary, and yet completely safe. The Canada Council has no qualms about supporting the magazine *Canadian Art*, however radical the art may be that it illustrates. *The Canadian Forum* is a magazine that the Canada Council, according to its own statement, will not support, on the ground that it expresses opinions. Some things, apparently, can still be disturbing; but the arts, like the religions, seem to have become immunized.

Pseudo-tolerance has an insecure basis, and carries its own disadvantages. Hazlitt, a tough Romantic radical who was both painter and critic, once spoke of music as a thing without an opinion, and though I do not share the view of music implied, I can understand his attitude. In their younger days artists may form in groups issuing manifestoes and endeavoring to impress the public with the importance of their work by making defiant gestures at it. But as the artist grows more successful he becomes less fond of other artists and more fond of the people who buy his work and advance his reputation, and so tends to fall into the social attitudes prescribed for him by them. And academic art, like any other kind, has the defects of its virtues. For the arts reflect the world that produces them, and everything the detractors of modern art say about it is true, except that what they are objecting to is not so much something in our art as something in our lives. Painting, music, and architecture, no less than literature, reflect an anonymous and cold-blooded society, a society without much respect for personality and without much tolerance for difference in opinion, a society full of slickness, smugness and spiritual inanity. But as long as the arts are thought of as educational they can teach as well as reflect. It would be an appalling disaster if the arts became merely decorative, identified with the qualities they do, to some extent, illustrate.

It is a great mistake to imagine that the end of education in the arts is simply to admire the works of art themselves. Education in the arts makes one more critical and detached, not more impressionable. Of course one does appreciate what one has learned to understand; but the arts have something to teach beyond themselves, a way of seeing and hearing that nothing else can give, a way of living in society in which the imagination takes its proper central place. Just as the sciences show us the physical world of nature, so the arts show us the human world that man is trying to build out of nature. And, without moralizing, the arts gradually lead us to separate the vision of the world we want to live in from the world that we hate and reject, the ideals of beauty from the horrors portrayed by art when it is in the mood that we call ironic. All genuine art leads up to this separation, and that is why it is an educating force.

Our present society is not predestined to go onward and upward, whether with the arts or without them. We are trying to marshal all the resources of culture and intellect we have in order to struggle with the problems that our civilization has created. We have outside us nations with different political philosophies, and we think of them as dangers, or even as enemies. But our more dangerous enemies, so far, are within. I spoke a moment ago of the difference between a mob and a democratic society. Our effective enemies are not foreign propagandists, but the hucksters and hidden persuaders and segregators and censors and hysterical witch-hunters and all the rest of the black guard who can only live as parasites on a gullible and misinformed mob. Yet the only real permanent way to turn society into a mob is to debase the arts: to turn literature into slanted news, painting into billboard advertising, music into caterwauling transistor sets, architecture into mean streets. As an educator, the artist today has a revolutionary role to play of an importance of which no nineteenth-century Bohemian in a Paris garret ever dreamed. He has powerful friends as well as enemies, for in his commitment to his art he has the fundamental good will of society on his side.

Presented at Canadian Conference of the Arts, May 1961. *Canadian Art* 18 (Sept.-Oct. 1961)

# Design for Learning: Introduction

Near the beginning of 1960, some trustees and officials of the Toronto Board of Education approached a number of professors and administrators in the University of Toronto, including the present writer, to discuss problems of common interest. A loosely organized *ad hoc* committee began to meet during the summer, talking somewhat at random in the hope of defining a central question. There were several things that caused us some concern: the number of students not finishing high school, the number of able students not reaching university; the number of secondary school graduates unable to adjust to university methods of work; the role of Grade 13 in the transitional process; and so on. But for the most part we were merely following the mysterious law which says that no society can flourish, or in the modern world even survive, until it learns never to let well enough alone. Even so, we were a little surprised to discover what our central question was. It turned out to be an academic question: does teaching in the schools, or at least the secondary schools, reflect contemporary conceptions of the subjects being taught? The answer was no. Changes of perspective have taken place in all fields of knowledge which teachers outside the university find great difficulty in keeping up with, and even greater difficulty in applying to their present curricula. Before we began to meet, refresher courses had been started for teachers in history and science, but these could go only so far. There was no question of the school curriculum being false in its philosophy or dangerous in its social effects; but a synoptic survey of it, in contemporary terms, did seem to be called for.

The non-university members of the committee pointed out that in front of the theoretical question lay a practical one. Does not the university have a heavy responsibility in the larger educational process? The university, unlike the schools, has the resources for keeping up with advances in scholarship, and hence has some obligation to make its knowledge socially effective. The University of Toronto has always assumed (correctly in this writer's opinion) that "education" as an academic subject has no place in a liberal-arts undergraduate programme, and belongs to postgraduate professional training. But there is some danger that the university may withdraw too far from other educational operations. A professor is not doing all he can do to maintain educational standards merely by cursing the secondary schools for not sending him better prepared students. Perhaps he knows nothing about secondary school curricula, much less anything about the difficulties or the positive achievements of the secondary schools. Perhaps he can't teach, and so has no sense of proportion about what a good preparation would be. Perhaps he is not making a first-rate job himself of training those of his students who are going to be secondary-school teachers. As all the latter have to pass through the university, the university ought to be fully aware of its own educational context.

The university members of the committee of course admitted all this, and we felt that we were beginning to get somewhere. This was, so far as I know, the first time in Toronto's history that the University and the Board of Education had really talked to each other about education. (We have since gathered that such meetings are extremely rare in North American cities generally.) Clearly there was some value in breaking down barriers. But of course the real barriers to break down were those between the three major divisions of education, the elementary, secondary, and university levels, each of which tends to become a self-enclosed system, congratulating itself on its virtues and blaming whatever deficiencies the educational process as a whole may have on the other systems. How could we get these together? We discussed the possibility of a conference. But obviously any conference would have to have a great deal of preparatory work done for it if it were to reach any conclusions likely to impress the public. Eventually we began to see that it was this preparatory work which it was our business to organize.

So our *ad hoc* committee sought and obtained the blessing of the Board and the University, was formally constituted a Joint Committee and, after some changes in personnel, settled down to become a steering committee for a group of study committees of teachers. Five of these were set up, in English, foreign languages, mathematics, science and social science, each with representatives from the Toronto elementary and secondary schools, and the Unversity of Toronto. After four or five meetings they brought in preliminary reports which while brief indicated that full-time work might produce unusually interesting results. A grant from the Atkinson Charitable Foundation made it possible to finance a full month's work for three of them, the committees in English, Science and Social Studies. Once the steering committee had decided on its proper strategy, its tactics became very simple. What we had to do was to get the best teachers we could find and then leave them alone. The three committees worked hard and long during the summer of 1961, and their reports are the substance of this book.

Obviously we need corresponding surveys in mathematics and in non-English languages, perhaps, too, in art, music and other subjects. But even without them we now have the outlines of a survey telling us a good deal about the gap, which exists in teaching as in all areas of human effort, between stated objective and actual achievement. It is easy enough to formulate the most admirable statements of aims in education ("All the ones we have seen are very nice," the Social Science report remarks dryly), and such statements enable us to see what is being done in our classrooms in some kind of perspective. There remains the question of whether the statement of aims is realistic or not, and this is connected with the state of scholarship contemporary with the subjects being taught. In reading through the English report, the only one of the three that I can comment on with any technical assurance, I was struck by the fact that when the authors ran into a difficulty, the difficulty was usually caused by a defect in contemporary critical theory. It looked as though there should be some regular means by which the teaching programme could be re-examined continuously in the light of advances in scholarship.

So on the horizon of our immediate problem there loomed a much larger task, the outlines of which only gradually took shape. This we are now able to describe as a kind of institute of curricular research, a permanent centre where scholars and teachers are engaged in working out the implications for teaching, at all levels, of improvements in scholarship in the subjects being taught. The axiom underlying its activity would be that the ability to explain the elementary principles of a subject to children is the only real guarantee that the subject itself is theoretically coherent. The physical sciences are theoretically coherent by this test at present; literature and the social sciences much less so.

## II

These reports are academic in the sense in which academics themselves use that term. They do not represent any educational pressure group or interest. They are not aimed at the Provincial Department with a view to influencing its policy; they are addressed to the informed public, and discuss the kind of thing that might be done. The Department has two observers on the steering committee, and is interested in and sympathetic towards the work presented here, but obviously the relationship cannot be more official than that at this stage. The reports have been approved in principle by the steering committee, but not without sharp expressions of specific disagreement from some members of that committee. They do not in fact wholly agree with one another, though there is an underlying unity to them which it is the purpose of the present introduction to elucidate. If the reader also finds himself disagreeing with them, he will learn something from his disagreement that he would not learn by compulsory agreement with a mass of platitudes. They have not been written in committee jargon, but in lucid, often brilliant, prose; they are designed to be read, and read with an active and critical response. They are, in short, a candid, independent, disinterested fresh look at what we are trying to do in our education.

The authors are teachers, unfamiliar with the typical stalling devices of educational bureaucrats. One of the commonest of these is the plea that no theory of education will be of any use until we have a statistically, psychologically and neurologically irrefutable theory of the child's learning processes. This subject in itself is certainly important enough: the steering committee has two advisers who are experts in this field, one attached to the University and the other to the Board. But, as all the reports clearly indicate, one of the essential data for research into the child's learning processes is an intelligible programme for teaching him, and every improvement in the latter changes the situation of the former. Further, the authors are good teachers, and consequently have none of the maudlin enthusiasm for the "inspired" teacher which assumes that an inspired teacher of, say, mathematics can get inspired by something which is not mathematics. What inspires a good teacher is a clarified view of his own subject. There will always be average teachers as well as average students, and what inspires a good teacher will at least help an average one. The Social Science report observes that the criteria of adequacy are the same for students going on and not going on to university: "What is good for one group is good for the other." The English report asks: "Is not what these young people have in common as human beings more important and more relevant than their differences?" But these things can only be true when excellence sets the standard for mediocrity, for in education, as in religion, we may be inspired by a vision of something that we cannot reach. If mediocrity becomes a kind of censor principle setting the standard for excellence, all teachers and students at all levels suffer alike.

Because the authors are writing as teachers and not as educators, their approach is pragmatic. Nevertheless one can see the reflection in them of a considerable change of emphasis in recent educational theory. This change of emphasis is something very different from what is discussed in newspapers and in popular rumour. The learned have their demonologies no less than the unlearned, and the bogey of the "progressive" educator, with his incessant straw-threshing of "teaching methods," his fanatical hatred of the intellect, and his serene conviction that everyone who is contemptuous of his maunderings must be devoted to the dunce cap and the birch rod, still haunts university classrooms. He does in fact still exist, though educators today pay him little attention and no respect. Never, perhaps, a major threat to Ontario schools, his incompetence elsewhere helped to create the power vacuum which has done much to make education more subject to political interference than the other professions. The Canadian aspect of this problem has been discussed by Frank MacKinnon in *The Politics of Education* (University of Toronto Press, 1960). The kind of vague panic which urges the study of science and foreign languages in order to get to the moon or to uncommitted nations ahead of the Communists is equally remote from the educational issues that these reports face. Human nature being what it is, serious educators would probably not have got as much public support for their efforts without headlines about sputniks, but they could see the facts of the situation without benefit of such headlines. I recently talked to a supervisor of curriculum in an American public school who told me that he had been sent a science text-book for elementary grades, from a usually reliable publisher, which he had rejected out of hand, on the ground that it contained no science. I was gratified to hear this, but ventured to suggest that he might not have thought it a real objection to the book a few years ago. He said: "No, but we're teaching stuff in third grade now that we didn't use to touch until junior high." Hence books containing only advice on what to do if one's playmate turns anti-social, and the like, can no longer be used for "science" text-books. This was not Ontario, but Ontario is bound to be affected by the eroding or shoring up of educational standards elsewhere.

The assumption in all these reports is that the school and the teacher, *qua* school and teacher, have no other function than an educational one. Hence the aim of whatever is introduced into the school curriculum, at any level, should be educational in the strict and specific sense of that word. It was the confusion of educational and social functions, implicit in the motto, "The whole child goes to school," that made "progressive" theories so fatuous. The axiom that the entire school programme should be specifically educational leads naturally to questions of proportion and distribution, or of what may be called the economy of education. How much science, social science, and English is appropriate at each year of training? What is the point at which repetition ceases to be a means of sound learning and becomes discouraging and sterile? Another problem, outside the scope of these reports, is that of priorities. Which are the basic disciplines at each level, and we how can decide between the claims of two subjects competing for the same place in the timetable? We need additional reports for these questions, as it is particularly the tendency to push foreign languages further back into elementary schools that is likely to cause traffic jams in the near future. Many of the problems of the rhythm of education, which should be that of leisurely progress, a golden mean between dawdling and cramming, cannot be solved by theory but only by the tactics of the classroom. Yet there are questions of theory which strike their roots deeply into the structure of the subjects taught and into the nature of democratic society.

From the beginning, the study committees were interested in the remarkable success of the Woods Hole Conference of 1959 in the United States, and in the book by Jerome Bruner, *The Process of*

*Education* (Harvard University Press, 1960), which consolidated the results of its findings. Dr. Bruner was invited from Harvard to visit and address the committees in February of 1961, and it was he who suggested the idea of an institute of curricular research (already alluded to). The Woods Hole conceptions of a "spiral curriculum" and the prime importance of structure in elementary teaching have entered deeply into all the reports. These conceptions are, as we should expect, new only in context; inherently they are very old conceptions, but they have to be revived in a new form with every generation.

It is doubtless true, as Bruner says, that the original thinker pushing back the frontier of knowledge and the child confronting a major conception for the first time are psychologically in very similar positions. But they are not in the same context of the subject itself. The original thinker is probably (almost certainly if he is a scientist) proceeding inductively, making new experiments in a new conceptual area and drawing new conclusions from them. Once his conclusions become established, the procedure for everyone who follows him and repeats his experiments becomes deductive. The theory comes first and the experiments test it, and at last, when the theory is fully established, simply illustrate it. It follows that elementary teaching is naturally of a strongly deductive cast. Once this is realized, a great deal of time can be saved, and a great many random observations and experiences may become examples of central principles. The conception of the subject to be taught should therefore be, not a conception of content, or of so much information to be "covered," but a conception of structure.

The Science report is particularly careful and successful in explaining how genuinely scientific principles can be introduced to the youngest children when made sufficiently simple and concrete, and in showing that they are no more difficult to comprehend than nonscientific or pseudo-scientific activities like washing woollens or feeding pets. We are thus led to the startling but quite logical conclusion that children six years old can, and should, be studying physics, chemistry and biology, presentations of which can be made intelligible to the six-year-old mind. Such principles as energy can be illustrated by almost everything a child does, and the fact that he gets warmer when he runs may introduce him to laws of thermodynamics and the principle of entropy. As the child's mind develops from the sensational to the conceptual, the things he understands unconsciously, such as how to calculate the speed and trajectory of a ball thrown at him, become translated into the language of consciousness. Thus we arrive at the principle of a "spiral curriculum" of the same structural elements of a subject being repeated at progressively more complex levels. This principle takes care of the point raised in the Social Science report about the need for fresh starts and unlearning as essential in the continuity of the educational process. The English report also urges that the study of English must be literary from the beginning, and that reading texts "too low in vocabulary count, too dully repetitive, too vacuous" belong to the outmoded and pernicious scheme of postponing all real education as long as possible.

Increase in complexity of understanding is largely an increase in the capacity of verbalization. This fact gives the English report a more difficult situation to consider than the other two. In the first place, "English" means a literature which is one of the major arts, addressed to the imagination, and in a group with painting and music. In the second place, "English" is the mother tongue, the means of understanding and expression in all subjects. The first "English" is chiefly a language of metaphor and analogy; the second is a language of description. These two aspects of English cannot be separated. Mathematics is often said to be the language of science, but it is a seondary language: all elementary understanding of science is verbal, and most of the understanding of it at any level continues to be so. The verbal understanding of science, at least on the elementary level, is quite as much imaginative, quite as dependent on metaphor and analogy, as it is descriptive. Here is a passage from *The Intelligent Man's Guide to Science,* by Isaac Asimov (Basic Books; University of Toronto Press, 1961), which illustrates how metaphorical a writer must become when he has to explain science to scientific illiterates: "Cosmic rays bombarding atoms in the earth's upper atmosphere knock out neutrons when they shatter the atoms; some of these neutrons bounce out of the atmosphere into space; they then decay into protons, and the charged protons are trapped by magnetic lines of force of the earth." This functional use of metaphor is one of the many reasons why no programme of study in English, however utilitarian in its aims, can ever lose contact with English as literature.

In "English" conceived as the language of understanding and description, there is an inductive study of the phenomena of language called linguistics, which is descriptive in its approach, and there is a traditional "grammar," which starts out from the normative position, laying down accepted standards of conventional communication as its premises. One is inductive, the other deductive, in its general direction. The English report shows how completely elementary education in English has to be based on the deductive approach of grammar, at whatever stage its nomenclature needs to be learned. Hence the so-called quarrel of linguists and grammarians, as far as school-teaching is concerned, is a pseudo-problem.

The structural or deductive pattern in literature is less easy to see, largely because so few contemporary literary critics have reached the point of being able to see it. The authors of the English report get little help from Bruner's book here, beyond a somewhat vague suggestion that tragedy is a central structural principle. As a matter of fact tragedy is one of four modes of literary fiction, the other three being comedy, romance, and irony. Of these, comedy and romance are the primary ones, and can be introduced to the youngest children. Those whose literary tastes do not advance beyond the childish stage never learn to appreciate any form of fiction outside these two modes. Tragedy and irony are more difficult, and belong chiefly to the secondary level. The main line of the argument of the English report on this point is based on the fact that literature is highly conventionalized. The young child can be introduced to the myths, fairy-tales, legends, Bible stories, which are central to our imaginative heritage, because all he needs to do to comprehend them is to listen to the story. This is not a passive response, but a kind of imaginative basic training, which those who are continually clutching for meanings and messages in the arts have not learned. As he grows older and his literary experience increases, he begins to realize that there are a limited number of possible ways of telling a story, and that he is already in possession of all of them. Hence he has, not only a sense of the structure of story-telling implanted in his mind, but a potential critical standard as well, which he badly needs in a world of sub-literary entertainment.

In all learning there is a radical pioneering force and a conservative supporting force, a learning that explores and a learning that consolidates. It seems to me that there are three main phases in the relationship of these two forces, three main turns of the spiral: a primary phase, a secondary phase, and a tertiary phase, which correspond roughly, if not exactly, to the elementary, secondary, and university levels of education.

In the primary phase the consolidating or conservative force is memory. Children seem to have good memories, and many children enjoy the power of using them: like the poets of primitive societies, they have an affinity for catalogues of names, accentual verses, and lists of all kinds that can be delivered in the chanting rhythm of a child's speech. Behind whatever I know of the social and cultural effects of the Norman Conquest is a primitive mnemonic chant of "William the First, William the Second, Henry the First, and *Steephen* !" I remember encountering a small girl in California who had just "taken Canada" in school, and who saw in a Canadian visitor an approaching captive audience. She backed me into a corner and recited the names of the provinces of Canada, complete with capitals, quite correctly. A question or two revealed that she had no notion where any of these provinces were. It was unlikely that she had been so badly taught; much more likely that she had simply remembered what interested her, the roll-call of strange names, and tuned out what did not, such as their location in space. Perhaps much the same thing was true of the lad in the Social Science report, with whom I have a good deal of sympathy, who remembered the three voyages of Captain Cook but not the fact that he was an emissary of eighteenth-century British imperialism.

Perhaps in our justified distrust of "mere" memorization we underestimate the power in it that can be harnessed to education. What we are apt to underestimate, in a civilization which is almost compelled to identify education with book-learning, is the role still played in memory by oral and visual experience. Many a boy who cannot remember what countries are in South America can tell the year and make of an automobile a hundred yards away, a feat mainly achieved within what literary critics call the oral tradition. A comic strip recently made an extremely shrewd comment on such extra-curricular learning. Two children in Kindergarten are out for recess; a plane flies overhead; one calls it a jet, the other disagrees, and a quite technical discussion follows on the difference between jet and piston planes. The recess bell rings, and one of them says, "Come on, Mike: we gotta go back and string them beads." What is true of sensational learning is even more obviously true of practical learning, especially in practical skills and sports, where memory develops into motor habit. Elementary science has to be deductively taught, but it does not follow that children should be discouraged from experiment at first hand;

and learning to write and to speak intelligible English are practical skills also. There is a core of truth in the principle of learning by doing, as long as "doing" is not assumed to exclude reading and thinking, and as long as motor activity is not thrust into studies where it has no business to be.

The difference between a good and a mediocre teacher lies mainly in the emphasis the former puts on the exploring part of the mind, the aspects of learning that reveal meanings and lead to further understanding. In English, this means ensuring that a child knows the meaning of what he reads as well as the mechanics of reading; in social and historical studies it means understanding why things happened instead of merely that they happened; in science it means; understanding central principles illustrated by what without them would be a bewildering variety of unrelated phenomena. Unless there is reason and system to give direction to the memory, education burdens the memory; and however resilient a child's memory may be, nobody is going to keep a burden in his mind an instant longer than he is compelled to do. What is merely learned is merely forgotten, as every adult knows. Those who never get psychologically beyond the primary phase of learning are apt to retain a conviction all their lives that total recall is the same thing as intelligence. Until some scandals, which however regrettable were extremely useful to educators, changed the fashion, there was a widespread belief that the "smartest" people were those who proved on television programmes to have the largest stock of information on non-controversial subjects. But it was the sense of how much they themselves had forgotten which gave their audiences a superstitious reverence for those who had been unable to forget.

It is important to realize that the pioneering element in the primary learning process has to do with the reasonable and the systematic, with what makes learning continuous and progressive. It is not a matter of arousing interest or stimulating a student, even to the pitch of enthusiasm. Civilized people respond readily to intellectual stimulation all their lives. Those who speak at business men's luncheons and women's clubs, from pulpits on Sunday morning or through the microphones of the CBC, find intelligent and receptive hearers. But these activities, however valuable in other ways, are not strictly educational. The sense of continuity, of one step leading to another, of details fitting gradually into a larger design, is essential to education, and no sequence of individually isolated experiences can possess this. The fact that all three reports stress the genuinely educational aspect of teaching, rather than the psychologically attractive aspect of it, is one of their most distinctive features. They do not, like so much writing in this field, fail to distinguish between interest and concentration.

Because memory is the more passive element in the learning process, mediocre students tend to rely on their memories, and even good students do so for the subjects in which they are less interested. Mediocre teachers, similarly, and examinations where the marking-schemes have been ossified by a desire to make them mechanically accurate, are also apt to stress memory at the expense of intelligence. Sometimes attempts are made, especially in science, to simplify the grasp of structure into a methodology, but we note that the authors of the Science report, like most scientists, have very little to say about "the scientific method." A scientist enters into the structure of his science, and then uses the same mixture of hunch and common sense than any other mental worker would use. Literature, like mathematics, is practically all structure, and the attempt to master it by memory forces the student to grapple with a pseudo-content, something not really there at all. A teacher who boasted of his ability to get his students through Grade 13 English, would, when teaching Browning's *Epistle of Karshish,* ask his students how many letters Karshish had written (the poem contains the line "And writeth now the twenty-second time"). He admitted that remembering this number was not very central to understanding the poem, but, he argued, unless students had something definite to learn they just gave you a lot of boloney on their examinations. This is the kind of thing I mean by pseudo-content, and its victims are strewn all over the first-year university results in English.

In the secondary phase of learning the pioneering and consolidating forces become more conceptual. The former is now the power of understanding that asks the radical questions: What good is this? How true is it? Could we get along without it? The latter asks the conservative questions: What does this mean? Why is it there? Why has it been accepted? It is particularly in the social sciences that these questions seem relevant, and the Social Science report devotes much attention to them, especially the radical ones. Even with things admitted to be bad, such as slavery or persecution, it is worth asking conservative questions about why the human race has practised them so widely and with such enthusiasm; and even with things admitted to be good, such as religion and democracy, it is worth asking radical questions about what would happen if we did not possess these things, or possessed them in different form. In literature the student is now advanced enough, not simply to listen to stories, but to inquire within them for real motivation and imaginative causality. Hence his questions here also fall into similar patterns: Why does the author say this? Would this kind of thing really happen? and the like.

Thus the secondary phase of learning revolves around the problem of symbolism. There are realities, and there are appearances related to them. Some appearances represent the reality, as a thermometer represents the temperature or, in a different way, as a drama represents a certain kind of human conflict. Some appearances partly conceal or disguise a reality, like the appearance of the sun "rising" in the east. And some appearances masquerade as reality, like the appearance of lofty intentions in a government about to grab someone else's territory. Learning to sort out these various relationships, or in other words developing what is in the broadest sense a critical intelligence, is the main preoccupation of students on the verge of becoming adult citizens.

In education properly so called, radical and conservative questions are asked within the subjects themselves. If a student asks, "What use is the conception of gravitation or relativity to physics?" or "What was the point of fighting the Crusades?" or "Why did Shakespeare put a ghost into *Hamlet?*" it is possible to give him a scientific, a historical, and a literary answer respectively. Asking questions about the relation of the subjects themselves to ordinary life is another matter. With young children the educational process competes on fairly even terms with the social one: the young child is interested in everything, and he might as well be interested in his education. But as he gets into his teens the growing power of his social adjustment, where he feels the immediate response of possession, and does not have to be in the humbler position of questioner and seeker, begins to fight against the learning process. This is at the stage at which we may see some highly intelligent fourteen-year-old firmly closing his mind to further education, while parents and teachers stand helplessly by, knowing how much he will regret it later on, unable to make the slightest impression on him now. This is the stage too at which many questions are likely to take the form of: "What good is this subject to me when it has no place in the kind of life I now think I want to live?" or "Why should I study science (or history, or literature) when I don't particularly want to study anything?" It is impossible to give a student real answers to such questions, and the weary and helpless answers he does get (e.g., without science we couldn't kill our enemies with bombs or our friends with automobiles) have nothing to do with the actual "good" of these subjects.

We can now see, perhaps, how serious the confusion between social and educational standards, on which the old "progressive" theories foundered, really was. It is because so many intellectually stunted lives result from it that all three reports speak out sharply about every aspect of the confusion that comes to their attention. The Social Science report attacks the "rosy cosy" view of society, of giving a child his own situation (if it *is* his own situation) in the ideal form of a Blakean song of innocence before he has any song of experience to compare it with. The point is that presenting the child's society to him in the form of a superego symbol is deliberately weighting social standards at the expense of educational ones. The English report says much the same thing about primary readers, and the Science report insists on the difference between science and technology, on the impropriety of calling by the name of science the various devices for providing the North American middle class with the comforts of home. I remember a word recognition test given to children in a school which drew from a middle-class group, a lower-middle-class group, and an "under-privileged" group. One of the words was "gown." Children of the first group said a "gown" was what mummy wore when she went to a party; children of the second group said it was what mummy wore when she went to bed; children of the third group had never heard of the word. Such intrusions of class distinctions into tests of learning and intelligence are not always easy to spot, and may in themselves seem very trifling. But the more fundamental problem of weeding social standards out of educational ones is something that requires constant vigilance and astute criticism. The principle involved is the most important in the whole process of education.

Secondary learning, we suggested, revolves around the relation of appearance and reality. What education as a whole deals with is the reality of human society, the organized forms of intelligence, knowledge and imagination that make man civilized. The middle-class twentieth-century Canadian world the student is living in is the appearance of that society. Education, freedom, and nearly all happiness depend on his not mistaking it for the real form of society. The young student needs to be protected from society, protected by literature against the flood of imaginative trash that pours into him from the mass media, protected by science against a fascination with gadgets and gimmicks, protected by social science against snobbery and complacency. The crisis of his education comes when he is ready to attach himself to the standards represented by his education, detach himself from his society, and live in the latter as a responsible and critical citizen. If he fails to do this, he will remain a prisoner of his society, unable to break its chains of cliché and prejudice, unable to see through its illusions of advertising and slanted news, unable to distinguish its temporary conventions from the laws of God and man, a spiritual totalitarian. Whether he has voluntarily imprisoned himself or whether he has been betrayed by educators under the pretext of adjusting or "orienting" him, he cannot live freely or think freely, but is pinioned like Prometheus on his rock, oriented, occidented, septentrionated, and australized.

The reports do not cover university teaching. But the presence of the university, or at least of its liberal-arts undergraduate programme, in the educational process is implied throughout. Each report attempts to outline the programme of study that will be of the greatest value to a student whenever he drops out of it; and they at least imply that the more drive and energy the planning of studies has, the longer the average duration of its appeal to a student is likely to be. The university is concerned specifically with the third phase of learning, where the conservative aspect is the consciousness of the presence of one's own society, with all its assumptions and values, measured against the radical criticism of that society by the standards of accuracy, profundity, and imaginative power to be found in the arts and sciences. The detachment required for this is symbolized in a four-year physical withdrawal from full participation in society. The very small number of university graduates who really achieve such detachment, along with those who achieve it outside the university, are enough to keep our society's head above water. One hardly dares to speculate about what might happen if the number were suddenly to increase.

The reports that follow are witty and pointed, sharply critical, and fearless in their expression of criticism. This does not mean that the educational system they discuss is ridiculous or that the authors consider it to be so. They are criticizing something to which they themselves are completely committed. One's vision of life, like the units of one's elementary understanding of science, is a metaphor, and the natural metaphor for any responsible man's job is that of a complex machine, likely to be smashed up in incompetent hands. Contempt for the amateur critic is built into all professions: it is a part of what the late Professor Innis calls the bias of communication. And those who have places of trust in education must often feel, when reading books intended to stir up public resentment, like a farmer seeing his crops trampled and his fences broken by a hunting pack in clamorous pursuit of an enemy that he could have disposed of quickly and quietly with his own shotgun. But these reports have not been written by amateurs, and they are not indictments but specific and sympathetic suggestions. The real power that drives the educational machine, or, in our other image, the final twist on the "spiral curriculum," is the power of self-criticism in teachers, which means the renewing of the vision of the subject they teach. It is such a renewing of vision that is here presented to the public.

from *Reports Submitted to the Joint Committee of the Toronto Board of Education and the University of Toronto,* ed. Northrop Frye. Toronto: University of Toronto Press, 1962.

# The Changing Pace in Canadian Education

The reward of surviving in universities is to become an educator, and the more technical and administrative problems of education have been forcing themselves on me in the last four years or so involuntarily. One thus finds oneself in the constant position of having to make pronouncements on liberal education and related topics. These are easy enough to make, being like sermons except that they have no text and no context. But it is curious that there are so many pronouncements of this kind, and yet that there should be relatively little attempt to define the function of the university in contemporary society, particularly at a time when it is obviously changing its relation to that society. Many areas of thought today are left undeveloped through a kind of wait-and-see policy: what, for example, is the use of trying to work out a coherent political theory for a world that may blow to pieces at any moment? The attitude of the chief fireman at a burning rubber factory: "We'd best let it burn up a bit, so we can see what we're doing", is one that we find everywhere today, not least in the intellectual attitudes of students. And as a major revolution in the function of the modern university is clearly only beginning, it is natural that speeches about that function should be ritual rather than prophetic, concerned more with the habitual than with the impending.

The university is becoming so powerful and influential in society that legislatures, churches, sport-conscious alumni and opinionated philanthropists are no longer able to bully it with the same old zest. In this very increase of freedom, however, there is a subtle threat of a new kind. The public has become much more interested in education at all levels, including the university level; and when the public becomes interested in something, it demands as payment for its interest the right of breathing down necks. What academic freedom the university has so far been able to preserve has been preserved partly by a general lack of such public interest: it may have to be preserved by more positive means in the future. If so, it will be well to be clear in our minds what academic freedom consists of, and why its defence is important, under the new social conditions.

At the same time, we have steadily increasing swarms of young people, earnest in their aims and wondering, justifiably wondering, what is expected of them by the university in particular and by society in general. Not unreasonably, they want to know what the university can guarantee to do for them, if anything, and they often find themselves baffled by the situations that they encounter. They have been, through elementary and secondary schools, taught with varying degrees of efficiency. At university they sometimes encounter, especially in the bigger universities, instructors who can't teach and are proud of it. They discover that their university instructors are given no training in teaching; they learn to teach in much the same way that a dog learns to swim, and are not promoted for their ability in teaching but for other qualities altogether. I have not myself any sympathy whatever with the instructor who regards it as a status symbol to be a bad teacher, and certainly in my field of literary criticism it is hardly possible to achieve genuine excellence as a critic without being a teacher as well. At the same time, once the student crosses the boundary line between high school and university, he leaves a place which is primarily a teaching institution and enters one which is not; and some of his natural expectation of being taught in the same way as before is bound to be disappointed. Still less, of course, does the university have anything to do with any such aims as the improving of one's mind. Yet here again the university needs a clear sense of its own function in order to explain to the student what the limits of its teaching powers are.

The traditional view of the university is that it is a function of the church, the classical exposition of that view being Cardinal Newman's in the nineteenth century. I happen not to believe in this account of the university's origin and function: I do not think the university is especially a medieval idea, or that it is, at least now, in any respect a function of the church. Yet the university does resemble the church in one respect, that it stands for some kind of detachment from the moral standards of its community. It needs the sense of such a detachment in proportion as it becomes involved with its community. The older type of scholar, commemorated in the comic strip figure of the absent-minded professor, did exist in nineteenth-century universities, discovered by his scout in the evening with a pile of books over his table and the lunch which he had forgotten to eat buried beneath the books. But the professor becomes managerial like other professional men in contemporary society, and there is danger of his acquiring the kind of moral insensitivity which goes with his new place in society. I am thinking of a social scientist I was talking to recently who had just been to a conference — I think in Bermuda — in a luxurious hotel where the theme of the discussion was assistance to under-developed nations. He remarked that the amount of money spent there on liquor alone would appreciably raise the standard of living in South Indian village for some years. This is the kind of thing I mean by moral insensitivity. If the university, like so much of the rest of our society, falls into the habit of rationalizing its own prosperity as a kind of virtue, it will have been kidnapped by that society and will have betrayed its specific function. There is a well known phrase popularized by Chaucer, "to make a virtue of necessity," but it is equally pretentious to make a virtue of freedom, if one interprets freedom as the possession of middle-class comforts.

Whenever I think about the approaching change in the social context of universities, I begin by contrasting the university today with its position when I was an undergraduate about thirty years ago. At that time it was the depression, and the younger university instructor had approximately the social status of a door-to-door pencil salesman. There was even competition for students. I remember talking with a sardonic young woman at a reception desk in New York who told me that after she had been graduated she got a letter inviting her to enter the graduate school. This had flattered her considerably because she was by no means a model student, but she soon realized that there was an economic motivation involved. This had given her a view of society which convinced her that, in her own words, "Education's the biggest damn racket there is except maybe religion." The young instructor, if hired, was paid rather less than the driver of a delivery truck, and was also told that even to earn that he would have to go through the long, laborious and expensive business of acquiring a Ph.D. — or else. Having acquired the Ph.D., he would then have to produce a regular series of publications under the general motto of "publish or perish," until, somewhere around middle age, he would finally be given "tenure," which to an American academic was not unlike an appointment to the Senate for a Canadian politician. The situation of the instructor today is a very different one. Instead of having a status of a door-to-door pencil salesman, he now has — or soon will have — approximately the social status of a free taxi in a pouring rain. It is becoming obvious that the cumbersome routine of the Ph.D., followed by the series of articles in learned journals, is no longer necessary to support his wife and children. If he shows competence in teaching in a university classroom, no university in its senses is going to let him go, whatever degrees he has. His economic motivation for becoming a scholar and producing articles in learned journals will be, not to avoid getting fired, but to become known in other universities so that he may leave his job for a better one.

Then again, universities do a great deal of worrying, and rightly, about the coming population explosion of students. For some reason we hear less about another problem which is even further advanced: a population explosion in scholarship. There will be a vast increase in the number of bright young men, all busily writing and producing articles; and as a result, the general field of, say, English, which I know best, is bound to become specialized to an unprecedented degree. I can visualize within my own time departments of English in which the professor of English will be the professor of Dryden; and underneath him will be lecturers in *Lycidas,* fellows in *Othello,* and readers of Blake Prophecies. There is already one learned journal in Canada devoted entirely to the scholarly organization of Canadian literature, and within a short time we may look forward to definitive scholarly editions of *Beautiful Joe* and *Anne of Green Gables,* together with definitive biographies of their authors. When I was an undergraduate at the Unversity of Toronto, the University of Toronto Press produced relatively little in the way of books; tended in fact to disgorge the President's report early in March and call it a year. Today, of course, it is a first-rate press with a first-rate publishing list, and similar presses are now being established in universities in Montreal. We take this development of the university press to be normal as a university grows, but we have to multiply that by about two hundred to realize what is happening; because there are probably about that many ambitious universities all developing presses, all with distinguished lists and with people to write books for them. I have had a good many students who are now engaged in scholarship, and a constant shower of off-prints keeps pouring on my desk. A few of them were people who had little vocation for university work, and whenever I get an off-print from one of them I discover the existence of a new learned journal which I had not previously heard of. But of course that will in its turn become one of the recognized journals.

What all this means, among other things, is that the sense which has always been endemic in the university, a sense of a universal mutual unintelligibility among departments, is clearly going to increase as well. As a member of Section Two of the Royal Society, which covers the humanities and social sciences, I find myself unable to read even the abstracts of the papers contributed to Section Three, which is mathematics and physics. For a time, I thought that exclamation marks in the equations of the mathematicians represented some enthusiasm for the beauty of their subject, and that there was at least that much communication possible; but I was undeceived on this point. I question whether there is anything at all to be done about this situation. I do not warm up to the notion of integrating or co-ordinating subjects. I can understand the statement that literature and mathematics are both attempts to communicate, but I feel that any such subject as "communications," designed to communicate between them, tends to become enclosed in its own special language, and merely to add one more unintelligible voice.

I have similar reservations about attempts to base an entire educational curriculum on a synoptic view of the heritage of western culture. There are colleges devoted to the study of great books which attempt to give the student a co-ordinated training in humanities, mathematics and at least the history of science. These projects strike me as, to some extent, efforts of remedial education, which are significant partly as indicating a breakdown of the organized curriculum between kindergarten teaching, which is relatively efficient, and university education, which, if often inefficient as teaching, is relatively well informed. In a properly organized educational system, in which the sequence made consistent sense from kindergarten through to the end of high school, the student would have acquired, in however immature a way, some sense of the synoptic view of culture which the curriculum of great books designs to give. When he entered university he would have earned the right to specialize, and it is my experience that the majority of exceptionally keen and brilliant students at university want to specialize. University courses need not be afraid of dealing in separate disciplines intelligible only to those who have studied them. The subjects in the university have to be revolutionized from within: there is no other way of adjusting them to changes and advances in knowledge, and it is far more important for each subject to be intelligible to itself than for the different subjects to be intelligible to one another. Nobody can work out a master plan to make the student understand the relations of geology to physics, but the subject of geophysics will take its own form from those relations.

The attempt to give the university student a kind of perspective on what the whole of the learned human race has done and is doing is often bound up with the desire to formulate the beliefs or the aims or the purposes of a democratic society. We are often told that we suffer from a disadvantage, as compared with communism, in not having a set of clearly defined statements which say what we believe about society and constitute our vision of it. There is still some danger, though less than there was a few years ago, to put social pressure on universities to force them to work out and teach some kind of democratic philosophy — what kind does not matter too much as long as it is sufficiently anti-communist. It seems to me the essence of democracy that such things should be left undefined, and that individual subjects, however difficult and esoteric, should be left to themselves. Every science is the queen of sciences, or, if it is a new science, a pawn that may become a queen. Whether the universe is pluralistic or not, there is no doubt that the world of the intellect is. In approaching the problem of the relation of the university to a democratic society, I think we need a radically different point of view.

I start with the fact that there are two levels on which the reason may be employed. There is a speculative level, and there is a practical level. The speculative level is that of the knowledge of the objective world. On this level the great virtues are detachment, impartiality and suspension of judgment. The university teaches on this level, and to the extent that the university is a moral as well as an intellectual influence, these are the moral qualities it appeals to. This kind of thinking consists in identifying oneself with a body of thought, so that one then becomes capable of adding something to it. There is no thinking on this level apart from such identification with a specific discipline. Thinking is not a natural process like eating or sleeping, nor a process centered in the personality, like social behaviour. It is an impersonal skill, developed by habit and practice, like playing the piano. On the level of practical intelligence, on the other hand, man is a citizen of a society, and here the relevant categories are not so much truth and falsehood as freedom and necessity. On this level the human being, as a member of a society, is first of all engaged or committed, and his intelligence on this level expresses itself primarily in the making of a choice. This is a kind of intelligence that Milton was thinking of when he said in *Areopagitica* that reason is but choosing.

Moral as well as intellectual qualities are also different on this level. Here the personality is involved, and conflict may become personal: in a crisis, the bad argument may turn into the bad man. If a person is maintaining views about white supremacy and the inherent inferiority of the colored races, we do not say that he is using syllogisms illogically: we say that he is sick. We do not feel impelled to argue: we merely feel impelled to say: "What is the matter with a man who feels compelled to argue in this way?" Suppose, for example, that some ambitious Canadian McCarthy were to try to build a career out of spreading slander and hysteria. Undoubtedly many Canadians have already conditioned themselves to climb on the bandwagon of such a person as soon as he opens his mouth. On the level of practical intelligence what is demanded of the educated person is not the ability to see facts as they are, but the courage to fight. Whoever pretends that on this level there is still room for detachment and impartiality is merely rationalizing his own cowardice.

It is not difficult in practice to see how the same problems reshape themselves on these different levels of intelligence. I remember attending a meeting of social scientists a while ago and listening, as I always do in such discussions, to the metaphors. I realized that the mood was fairly cool because the metaphors were mechanical. They were talking about co-operating and adjusting and dealing with breakdowns. I realized that if they were more concerned about their subject they would start using organic or medical metaphors, and talk in terms of health and sickness. If they were still more deeply concerned, moral conceptions of good and bad would creep in, and if they were discussing something like the Nazi persecution of Jews, they would be compelled to go one step further into religious metaphors. They might have no explicit religious views of their own, but they could not avoid speaking and thinking of such things as being under the judgment of God.

What I have been revolving around in the last few minutes is the problem described in the famous Rede lecture — C.P. Snow's "The Problem of the Two Cultures" — the humanist's ignorance of science and the scientist's ignorance of the humanities. I have tried to suggest why I do not think this a major problem in our society. It is not the humanist's ignorance of science or the scientist's ignorance of the humanities which is important, but their common ignorance of the society that they are living in, and of their responsibilities as citizens. It is not the humanist's inability to read a textbook in physics or the physicist's inability to read a textbook in literary criticism, but the inability of both of them to read the morning paper with a kind of insight which is demanded of educated citizens. You are doubtless familiar with the book of Robert Jungk, "Brighter than a Thousand Suns," the story behind the lives of the scientists who made the atom bomb. The book begins in a kind of academic paradise at the University of Gottingen in Germany where they were living in a state of intellectual ferment and high excitement, yet oblivious to the fact that the greatest concentration of evil and malice that the world had ever seen was slowly gathering in the society around them. They were utterly bewildered when they found themselves refugees in Denmark, and in reading the remainder of the book one hardly knows which to wonder at more, their brilliance as scientists or their chuckle-headedness as citizens.

The practical sense is obviously central in the process of education but as it cannot be directly taught, it is at best a by-product of university training and not something that the university specifically aims at — apart from the fact that it can be held quite as firmly by people outside the university. The question next arises of where the practical sense is derived from: that is, where one gets the power to make choices in the interests of one's freedom. The easiest answer is in adjustment to society itself, but that clearly is a wrong answer, because society changes very rapidly; rapid change breeds hysteria, and adjustment to rapid change merely breeds more of it. In a book which many of you may have seen, "The Gutenberg Galaxy," Professor Marshall McLuhan speaks of contemporary society as a post-literate society; that is, a society which has gone through a phase of identifying knowledge with the written word and is now gaining its knowledge from all kinds of other media which affect the ear as well as the eye. The ability to twitch ears is the mark of the animal which is constantly exposed to danger, and Mr. McLuhan is well aware of the extent to which the increase in such media brings with it an increase in panic. He quotes one or two examples of panic in contemporary writers, including some very intellectually respectable ones, and remarks: "Terror is a normal state of an oral society, because everything is happening to everyone all the time." The sense of panic is occasionally rationalized on the level of practical intelligence itself, by people who speak of commitment as though it were a virtue in itself: don't just stand there, get yourself committed. This is the attitude which was described many years ago by H. G. Wells as the attitude of the "Gawdsakers" — the people who continually say: "For Gawd's sake, let's do something."

No, we need a better answer to the question of what the source of the authority of the practical intelligence is. One possible answer is that it is derived from some kind of overall vision of society. Every person with any function in society at all will have some kind of ideal vision of that society in the light of which he operates. One can hardly imagine a social worker going out to do case work without thinking of her as having, somewhere in her mind, a vision of a better, cleaner, healthier, more emotionally balanced city, as a kind of mental model inspiring the work she does. One can hardly imagine in fact any professional person not having such a social model — a world of health for the doctor or of justice for the judge — nor would such a social vision be confined to the professions.

It seems to me in fact that a Utopia should be conceived, not as an impossible dream of an impossible ideal, but as the kind of working model of society that exists somewhere in the mind of every sane person who has any social function at all. At the end of Plato's *Republic*, Socrates, after having described his ideal state, asks his disciples if they think that any such state could ever be established. Those who had not, by the ninth book, either gone to sleep or fallen under the table, say that they suppose not. Socrates then says that he doesn't either, but that the wise man will always live as though he were a citizen of such a community, no matter what the society around him actually is. Very frequently, however, such social visions become the basis of revolutionary activity. This is why, as I said earlier, I distrust the tendency to define social ideals too explicitly, because to define a social vision is to make that curious identifying of religious and secular feelings that is characteristic of the revolutionary mind, especially, today, in the attitude of communism. Communism has no God, but that does not prevent it from being a religion with prophets, revealed scriptures, a body of infallible doctrine, heresies, saints, martyrs and shrines. Such a religious attitude results from its defined conception of social change. It is obvious that our own time is a revolutionary one, and the communist countries spend a good deal of their time and energy arguing about which is the correct form of revolution. That is the issue which divides them whenever Russia expresses its disagreement with China by abusing Albania. There are two possible attitudes to social change: one is to think of the revolution which has happened, once and for all, in some countries and is going to happen in others; the other is to think of our society as in a constant state of change, and try to deal with it accordingly with the flexibility which that fact demands. The latter seems to me the view of social change that we are committed to in the democracies.

I have a slightly different answer to the question of where the origin of the practical intelligence is. The fact that we are living in a revolutionary age means that the society around us is not real society at all, but the transient appearance of that society. The students going to college now were born into a world in which the King was Emperor of India, in which China was a friend and Japan an enemy, and in which Nazi Germany ruled the most powerful empire that the world had ever seen. It is obvious that the twentieth-century middle-class Canadian society we belong to is too transient and to fitful in its manifestations to be regarded as real society at all. I think the real society that man lives in is the society which is revealed to him by the arts and the sciences with which his education brings him into contact. The goal of education is social, an initiation into the form of human society that won't go away, and will not have disappeared within the next generation. It is this vision of society which operates as a kind of informing vision in human activities, as the vision of Plato's *Republic* is supposed to do for the disciples of Socrates. I suggest that the simplest way to characterize that informing vision of society is to identify it with the university itself, with that total body of arts and sciences which, in their totality, are the real form of society and into which the student is initiated.

And yet, I have also said, the university as an institution of teaching and research cannot go beyond the speculative level of knowledge, where thought consists in identifying one's mind with a specific and highly specialized discipline. This is why it is so important to understand how much, in university education, must be left to student initiative. In the universities of the immediate future, the student's problem, despite all the limitations that universities will be forced to put up, will be not so much the difficulty of getting to college as making sure that when he gets there he will be educated and not merely processed. In the nature of things no instructor, however deeply interested in students, can take the initiative in this. The student must cultivate all the virtues of education, and the virtues of education are mainly social vices. He must become anti-social; he must make an unmitigated pest of himself in sitting on his professor's doorstep armed with questions; he should have the kind of maladjusted unpleasantness that goes with the genuine student's mentality. When a good student displays arrogance, it often means that he is pulling away from the kind of well adjusted social behavior that leads to security, popularity, and the death of the free mind.

Such anti-social qualities may be forced out of a keen student by the sense that unless he develops some form of intellectual resistance, he will be, in university as elsewhere, merely sliding by smoothly on a kind of assembly line. I should hope too that the university of the future, however much it had to offer intellectually, would not be reserved for professional students only. Restricting the university to students of a certain academic standing may often be necessary, but is too simple to be a total solution to the problem of admission. I should prefer to see the university continue to be what it is now, something of a cross-section of the more intelligent and well-meaning part of the community at large. It is also, or should be, a more heterogeneous community than the student has been accustomed to. In Canada, to give one obvious example, it is a place where students from Africa and Asia can mingle in Canadian life more easily than they can anywhere else.

At present the university is a centre of scholarship and research also concerned with the liberal and professional training of young people in their later adolescence, much of the most bewildered and bemused period of their lives. Perhaps the next century, as society develops more leisure with automation, will see the university expanding its relation to society and less monopolized, as a teaching institution, by the routine of granting degrees. I can envisage an ideal university which would be a community which a person could enter at any time in his life, as, say, an adult with grown-up children, as both a retreat and as a place of study in which an accumulation of practical experience could be brought to bear on academic training. A university in this expanded sense would be the institution of the theory of society as opposed to practical society: it would be the clearing house of cultural and intellectual pursuits, in fact the embodiment of Matthew Arnold's "culture," which for Arnold was not merely the ornamenting of life, but the source of all genuine order and stability in our civilization.

Second Annual Kenneth E. Norris Memorial Lecture, Sir George Williams University, 24 January, 1963. Montreal: Association of Alumni, Sir George Williams University, 1963.

# The Social Importance of Literature

I will be talking about the University because the university is what I know, and I shall leave it to your many years of professional experience to translate what I say into the context of your immediate professional concern. I think that the difference in contexts gets less all the time and that in particular at the present moment we are turning a corner in the rapprochement between the different groups of people concerned with the educational process.

I should like to start with a fairly concrete situation, and one which is being exploited *ad nauseam* in the news: that is the question of what is euphemistically called student unrest in the universities, and which impresses some people as being rather a kind of cult of bumptiousness. The student unrest is of course partly kept alive by the mass media, in pursuit of their general policy of making up the news and of going into a trance whenever they hear the word controversial. Students are instinctively docile, but this time they appear to be docile in relation to other things than the university itself. In this situation the staff attitude is very confused. Every university teacher worth his salt has a great affection for his students, and although he has, if he has a social conscience, always been very vigilant against threats to academic freedom, it has, in my experience, never occurred to any university teacher that the threat to academic freedom might conceivably come from the student body itself. Those who take the side of the student include a great many earnest and dedicated liberals, who are trying hard to emphasize the genuinely liberal elements in the student protest. Others are less scrupulous people who feel that they can, by fishing in these troubled waters, get a shorter cut to public attention than is afforded by scholarship. The author of a recent article on *The Student as Nigger* is clearly one of those, and I think that the students have been making a mistake to regard such writers as being on their side.

One does have to realize that there is a core, along with much that one has to sympathize with, of something anti-intellectual in student unrest. The kind of student who used to say: "Are we responsible for this on the examination?" can now rationalize his question by saying: "I feel that what I have been exposed to lacks contemporary relevance." There are many complaints about the process of taking down notes from a lecture, and then, in the stock phrase, "regurgitating" these lecture notes on the examination. But this process, whatever its limitations, still does not prevent the student from thinking for himself, even about his lecture notes. On the other hand, the regurgitation of the clichés and the slogans and the half-truths of social activism does tend to cut off free and flexible thought, and the process of re-examining one's own assumptions.

At the same time the movement is an important one, and we have to try to look into its causes with some care. Naturally one thinks first of all of the general frustration with a society in which the world's greatest democracy, the country which is bound to lead the democracies of the world, can only offer us Nixon, Humphrey and Wallace as choices for their chief executive. At the same time, there was a time, back in the nineteen-fifties — it seems an eternity ago now — when everybody was complaining about the apathy of students, and I can remember a girl saying to me then, with exasperation in her voice: "But what do they want us to get excited about?"

Well, of course, students are now being told on all sides what they ought to get excited about, but the real cause, I think, is of a rather different kind. We come closer to it when we realize what a loss of commitment there has been to the economic goals of society, and how the whole process of developing a professional or business career has been questioned in its moral basis, in a way it was not questioned, even in my own student days, when there was a very lively and highly organized Marxist group on the campus.

This means that the so-called "New Left" is by no means the same as the old Marxist Left, as is clear from all the newspaper reports of student protest movements in Columbia, Paris and elsewhere. The old Marxist Left accepted the work ethic quite as completely as Henry

Ford, and it is the work ethic itself that is now being attacked and ridiculed. Again, the modern leftist student, if he is protesting against Negro segregation or the Vietnam war, does not think of those things as a Marxist would do, as merely by-products of a class struggle. He sees rather the emotions and prejudices involved in these issues as primary and as the real target to be fought. Consequently, the new protest movement is anarchist, rather than communist; it is much more deeply concerned with the imaginative and the emotional and it raises even more directly the question of the vision of society which one should have here and now. One difficulty with the Communist movement, as you remember, is that it conceived of the revolution as the means to an end, the means being a proletarian dictatorship, the end a classless society; and there is always a tendency in all such movements for the means to take the place of the end, and for the end to disappear. The new movement of social protest is much more concerned, as the nineteenth century anarchists were concerned, with goals of direct action, and their attitudes are much harder to argue with. It is no good even calling them absurd, because absurd is also an in-group word now.

But I think that the real cause is to be sought rather in the history of education as it has developed in this country and our western civilization, over the last century. As universal education came to be regarded as more and more the necessary condition of a civilized and democratic society, naturally a great many more people of professional competence came to be involved with education, and it was soon realized that, in order to teach, one needed rather more equipment than merely a Latin grammar and a taste for sadism. In this process, of course, while the basis of elementary education remained, in theory, accessible to everyone, the pyramid tended to become more selective as it went up, and in, say, the twenties of this century, the universities were still regarded, very largely, as middle-class playgrounds. This meant of course that the institution of the university could hardly be questioned by students. The psychological effect of the new university, the sense of universities as something in process, was almost unknown to students of my generation during the depression. Then came various crises, of which perhaps the most obvious one, from the newspapers' point of view, was the reaction to the Sputnik in 1957, when a sense of the importance of education in society suddenly became strongly and emphatically dramatized.

What we did not notice, all through this period, was that by treating students with so much affection and creating the kind of community that we had been making out of the universities, we had also been making, unconsciously, a proletariat out of the student body. A proletariat, in the Marxist sense, is a group of people excluded from the benefits of society to which their efforts entitle them. We were showering students with privileges, and yet, at the same time, carefully excluding them from the general process of adult society.

Students, not being fools, drew an obvious inference from the reaction to the Sputnik and other such developments. They said: "Well, if we are students, then we must be fully participating in society, simply by being students. And, if so, why are we being excluded from society and from its responsibilities?" This meant of course the decline, to the point of collapse, of the conception of education as a preparing for life. The present day undergraduate no longer believes that he is spending four years of college sitting around waiting for something more important to happen to him. He realizes that he is in just as real a world at college as he is ever going to be, and, if he is an intelligent student, he also realizes that the educational process is never finished and that his teachers are, of course, students too, assuming that a student is a person who does not know enough about a subject and wants to know more. Along with this decline of the notion of preparatory education goes the decline of what I might call initiatory education, that is the aspect of education that has to do with learning the rituals of society. This is a matter of great importance when you have an élite and in, for example, the universities of Oxford and Cambridge during the eighteenth and nineteenth centuries, the process of learning certain social rituals, although it was not featured on the curriculum, nevertheless was a very important part of the whole educational process. In our own society, where the conception of a governing élite, recruited from a certain class of society, is being so sharply and radically questioned, it is obvious that this conception of education as, in part, an initiation into social rituals has also collapsed, and other conceptions of education have to take its place.

I have perhaps already indicated that I feel that the movement of student protest has rather shallow social roots, and does not have a very long-time career ahead of it. The analogy to student protest is not anything like the Negro movement or anything genuinely rooted in long-standing social injustices. The analogy is rather to the feminist revolution of about fifty years ago. When women were agitating for the vote, it was widely predicted that when the women got the vote, the democratic machinery would be cleaned up, and when all the votes of that pure and noble sex were dumped on the electoral market, corrupt political machines and ward-heelers and things of that kind would disappear. Nothing of the sort happened, and yet, if I had been active then, I think I should have supported votes for women on grounds of general human fairness and on the fact that it is silly to create unnecessary proletariats in society. Whenever you have a proletariat in society, you always have, sooner or later, a revolutionary situation. Student representation on university bodies is not difficult to arrange, but I think that, as with the women's vote, it will make very little difference in practice.

And yet I think that I should support the movement, again on general grounds of fairness. I think too that the situation between teacher and student will be re-established (so far as it has really been disturbed), perhaps with a greater frankness on both sides. There is at present a great deal of prejudice against the teaching lecture as a form of education, on the ground that it suggests an active teacher and a passive student. There is correspondingly a great development of the mystique of the seminar, in which the myth of a fully participating and articulate student occupies a prominent place. But I think that in a short time the teaching lecture will re-establish itself, in the seminar and outside it, as the normal method of instruction in a university. Again, when relations are re-established on the basis of greater frankness, it will not be necessary for the teaching or the administrative staff to pretend, out of politeness, that students are more mature than they ought to be. I have known a good many mature students, who were as undergraduates exactly what they were going to be forty years later, and a most depressing lot they were.

If we examine the curve of student protest from Berkeley to Columbia, we can see how it has worked itself out. The demonstration at Berkeley was carried through by Grade A students almost entirely and the staff support behind it was overwhelming. But by the time we reach Columbia we have professional organizers brought in from outside, a very sharp division in the student body itself, an equally sharp division in the staff, and a number of social issues raised which are peripheral to university affairs. I see a good deal of danger in this, of hardening the cleavage between the protesting students and the kind of student who has social goals which may be conventional, but which are still legitimate. It seems to me that the university is rapidly ceasing to become the real target of social protest, and the protest is actually moving out of the university in other social areas. The university is, of course, a good place in which to carry out social protest, because it is a flexible and tolerant place, and occupationally disposed to argument. And as the private said when he saluted the sergeant-major: "You'll do to practise on." But in all activist situations there is likely to develop what we know familiarly as the "we-and-they" mentality, where "they" become, from the students' point of view, something authoritarian and established and to be described in solid metaphors. That is, the establishment is a structure, and however much corroded with dry rot and the death watch beetle, however near to collapse it may be, it is still to be thought of as something solidified and frozen. On the other hand the freedom of the individual is associated with liquid metaphors, of getting things stirred up and the like. Neither of these metaphors really covers, of course, the situation they are describing.

Recently there was an interview printed in the Varsity between the editor of the Varsity and President Claude Bissell. The editor was the author of the article and although he was clearly trying to give himself the best lines his success was not unequivocal. After a more than usually incoherent remark about authority President Bissell finally said: "What do you mean by authority?" and the student said: "Authority is other people telling me what I have to do". Now I can understand that this should be the conception of authority held by someone whose habitual reactions are still clearly those of an adolescent. But neither President Bissell or any other responsible officer of the University is fool enough to think in terms of an Institution, with a capital I, which has to be kept running in working order without regard to the human lives concerned with it. The answer to the student's question about authority — what he wanted, of course, was simply unrestricted electives to study whatever interested him — is that interest is not enough for an educational process. That is, there are many things that are interesting, many things which are profitable, but which are nevertheless not educational. Teach-ins, for example, are entertainment of a very high quality but they are not a form of education. We cannot have education without incessant repetition and practice, drill, and going over the same things over and over until they become automatic responses.

The kind of authority that the University is interested in is the authority which is inherent in the subject being studied. The authority of the fruitful hypothesis as opposed to the crack-pot notion; the authority of the great imaginative classic as contrasted with the mediocre or the merely sensational. Authority of this kind is not a limitation of freedom; it is merely the completion of freedom. Every subject studied in the University or elsewhere is a structure to be entered into, and if the University insists on certain compulsory prerequisite courses, the compulsion is not the compulsion of a truant officer; it is simply the compulsion inherent in the subject itself. In the present climate of opinion it may sound insufferably smug to say that a student's first duty is to study, but if I do say so I am simply applying to students the same principles that I would apply to any other member of the University, the other members also being students. Whenever a person is considered for a senior administrative appointment at a University, the question is always asked: "How good a scholar is he?" because if he has no idea what scholarship is he has no idea what a University is either, and consequently the administrative staff, the teaching staff and the undergraduate body are all involved in the same process.

What seems to me to be an even deeper fallacy in this kind of argument is the notion that freedom is subjective, in the sense of being related to an individual. The genuinely individual protester is a rather rare bird: he is usually a crank, though once in a hundred years he may be a genuine prophet. But, on the whole, protest is the expression of a social attitude, and is not subjective, in the sense that it is geared to some kind of social feeling. One of the most important things in a democracy is to keep such a social attitude from embodying itself in a power structure so that it cuts off all further freedom of investigation. I feel that our attitudes towards education have been very largely dominated by a conception of reality which is confirmed by reason and by experience. That in itself, of course, is reasonable enough. There is such a thing as a right answer and a wrong answer, and the right answer is usually the one in the book, though by no means invariably. This conception of reality as embodied in reason and experience is, of course, particularly congenial to the sciences. And the sciences, however essential and central in the educational process, can also be congenial to an authoritarian society simply because science tries to escape from controversy — it appeals to evidence in which there is no room for argument. That is, I take it, the goal of the scientist's investigation: to have his hypothesis confirmed by experience. But we should remember that there are two kind of reality. There is an objective reality confirmed by reason and experience, and there is another kind of reality, which does not exist to begin with but is brought into being through a certain kind of construction or creative activity. Let us take as an example a work of art, the reality of a picture, of a book, of a musical composition. The fact that the painter's or the composer's or the writer's vision is a genuine vision is confirmed by the existence of the work of art, but this work of art cannot be said to be either right or wrong. In other words, the arts belong to the conception of reality in which reality is something that man makes, something that man constructs himself, so that when the issue is raised about the rights and wrongs of such reality, we have to raise the question of what our vision of society is in the largest sense.

The humanities and the arts and many other areas of knowledge cannot escape from controversy because in them there are fewer right and wrong answers. There can only be discussion over conflicting visions of what society's goals should be, and of what kind of world man should make for himself. For man is in two worlds: there is the world that he sees around him, and which science interprets, and there is a world that he makes for himself and wants to live in. That world is governed by a vision of which the arts and the religions and similar areas of knowledge are the instruments. When there are no rights and wrongs and no end to controversy, there can only be a kind of continuous discussion in which gradually, if the conditions are right, the liberal, the flexible, and the tolerant begin to make headway against the bigoted, the anxious and the superstitious. The humanities in general, the arts and I would say religion too, are the subjects which deal not with external realities studied by the reason, but with something which should be called, rather, concern with man's fundamental questions about his whence and his whither, his nature and his destiny, and above all, the kind of society that he wants to live in. It seems to me that the arts, and more particularly literature, are the obvious vehicles of education in concern and in social vision. Religion is also involved in concern, And Paul Tillich speaks of ultimate concern, that is concern about man's relation to eternity, as being the special area of religion. But while in theory it is an excellent idea to teach religion, in practice religion is attached to a number of social groups, and consequently the teaching of religion bogs down into insoluble problems of teaching Christianity to Jews and the like. The study of literature is a training in a constructive and imaginative vision of man's own sense of his social goal. In that sense, literature belongs with the sciences in the centre of the educational process.

The teaching of literature is, I think, subject for its effectiveness to two conditions. One of those is very difficult to meet; the other is widely regarded as impossible. The first condition is that literature should be taught as a subject like other subjects: it has its own systematic progression within it, just as mathematics has, and the study of literature should never be corrupted or adulterated or weakened by the study of what is not literature and has simply been thrown into the English curriculum because there seems no other place to put it. The second condition is that literature at all levels needs to contain a large contemporary element, because historical imagination is a difficult thing to develop in students, and when so it should be fully contemporary and taught without censorship and without moral anxiety. Nothing infuriates young people so much as the feeling that they are being excluded from adult conversation on grounds which they regard as frivolous. I feel that *Pride and Prejudice* and *Great Expectations* are admirable novels, very well worthy of sustained study, but the mere absence of bad words or explicit descriptions of the sexual act do not seem to me valid reasons for studying books even on that level.

The study of literature, as I define it, is not a panacea; it is not a cure; it does not solve social problems. What it does is to base education on the sense of a participating community which is constantly in process and constantly engaged in criticizing its own assumptions and clarifying the vision of what it might and could be. The teaching of literature in that sense, and in that context, seems to me to be one of the central activities of all teachers and educators in their continuous fight for the sanity of mankind.

Canadian Association of School Superintendents and Inspectors, 17 September, 1968. In *Educational Courier*, 39 (Nov.-Dec. 1968).

# The Day of Intellectual Battle:
## Reflections on Student Unrest

May I say first how greatly honored I feel at being made a graduate of Western; it is a university where I have so many close personal ties, and the memory of so many pleasant visits, that the university itself has become an old and familiar friend. I am also honored by the degree in particular, because in conferring it the University is recognizing that a life devoted to scholarship and teaching represents its own commitment to society. Neither Western nor myself would want to have anything to do with a degree that was simply an established symbol, a reward for being relatively senior and conservative.

And may I congratulate, most sincerely, all of you who have reached your first degree today. For four years you have been secluded in the ivory tower of the world, reading papers, making love, attending meetings, expressing opinions, playing or watching games, enjoying all the delights of suburbia. Now you are going out into the great wide university, and whatever your profession, for the rest of your lives you will have to assume the responsibilities of university teachers. Other people, including your children, will get their notions of the university through you; and whatever you do or think, the university will be doing or thinking too, in the place where you are. You have been at Western: now you are going to be in *the* University, along with St. Thomas and Milton and Einstein, and most of you will feel grateful to Western as long as you live because it has given you your passkey to your own real society.

Man is first of all a social being: what is true and real for him is what his society declares to be true and real. This is his primitive state, the state of social concern and anxiety, where he clings to his community for all mental support. As society matures, this anxiety relaxes a little, and man becomes aware of another kind of truth and reality, the kind that depends on logic, evidence, verification, and the recognizing of imaginative power in the arts. All education is built on this second kind of truth and reality, and the university is the keystone of education. And because the university is a community as well, it shares to the full man's sense of social concern, though it adds a new dimension to it. But the primitive social anxiety, the fear of the intellect, the desire to accept as true and real only what society accepts as true and real, keeps nagging at the student with some kind of trumped-up moral challenge. Isn't there some primary social obligation that we are dodging by being at college, like fighting a war or a revolution ending poverty, or simply earning a living? Shouldn't we be "out there", doing something, anything, so long as it is busy enough to drown out the intolerable inner quiet of the soul?

I have been facing groups of students for thirty years, and have never ceased to be impressed by the amount of sheer courage it takes to keep on studying and ignore the infinite resources of anti-intellectual suggestion. I have watched students resisting the temptations that came through all the disguises of the second world war, the cold war, the atom bomb, the McCarthyist witch-hunts, and have finally seen the enemy enter the university itself. It is students, to-day, who repeat the formulas of the ignorant and stupid of a generation ago, that the university is a parasitic growth on society, that academic freedom is old-hat liberal rhetoric, that because complete objectivity is impossible degrees of objectivity do not matter, that the university seeks for a detachment that ducks out of social issues, that scholarship and research are all very well but of course aren't real life. It is not an accident that the more extreme this attitude becomes, the more closely its social effects come to resemble those of the youth movements set up by Hitler and Stalin. For the totalitarian impulse is the primitive impulse, the longing to return to the narcotic peace of society's version of truth and reality, where we no longer have to cope with the conflicts of intellectual freedom and social concern.

I have just come from the Berkeley campus, where I have been teaching during the spring quarter. In the previous quarter there had been a students' strike called over the issue of a "third world college", mainly for black and Mexican students. The university was willing to start such a college, though less willing to have it become simply a training school for professional revolutionaries, which was what many of its advocates wanted and still want. The university was deeply divided and troubled over this issue, and the majority of staff and students resented the open contempt that so many of the militants showed for the university and its values.

The first six weeks of this term were very peaceful, and then, on Thursday, May 15, a state of war began. Like other wars, it was not started but simply blundered into. The issue was a vacant lot owned by the university that was being illegally made into a community park by the "street people", a phrase very difficult to translate into Canadian. The black revolutionary leader, Eldridge Cleaver, had advised his fellow militants to "establish a territorial imperative", in other words, attach a symbolic value to a piece of land. And so we had the "people's park,", symbolizing the rights of people against those of property, on land which, we were solemnly told, was also covered with blood because it had been stolen from the Indians. So the "people's park"came to fill the empty space in the militant noddle that a genuine education would have filled with the Garden of Eden and the murder of Abel. The quarrel was not a students' affair to begin with, but student sympathies were soon enlisted. The next few days were days of violence and terror, as the police got out of hand.

I am not speaking of agitators assaulting or reviling the police and getting what they asked for: I am speaking of ordinary students, including some of mine, who were clubbed and beaten and gassed and prodded with bayonets while trying to get to lectures or enter their own residences. After such events it was impossible to think in terms of a riot being controlled by law and order. It was the police who were rioting, and wherever the social order was, it was not in this hysterical rabble, for all their bayonets and tear gas. And while argument and dispute went on, at every level, I got a strong impression of the whole university, staff and students alike, closing its ranks. The immense cohesive force of the university as a community was making itself felt through all the rumors and half-truths and accusations, through all the clichés of militants and the blustering of officials.

Both Governor Reagan and the local SDS issued statements. and there is a curious similarity in their statements. They both say that the people's park was a phony issue, and that the real cause was a conspiracy—the Governor says of hard-core student agitators, the SDS says of right-wing interests operating "probably at the national level."

Both are undoubtedly right, up to a point. There *is* a hard core of student agitators: one of them was grumbling in the student paper, a day or two before the lid blew off, that "not a goddam thing was happening at Berkeley", and that something would have to start soon because Chairman Mao himself had said, in one of his great thoughts, that revolution is no child's play. On the other side, Governor Reagan is clearly staking a very ambitious career on the support of voters who want to have these noisy young pups put in their place once and for all. Both are very pleased with the result: the Governor is visibly admiring his own image as a firm and sane administrator, and the SDS are delighted that the police have "over-reacted" so predictably and helped to "radicalize the moderates". But the more one thinks about these two attitudes, the clearer it becomes that the militant left and the militant right are not going in opposite directions, even when they fight each other, but in the same direction. For both the Governor and the SDS, the university is ultimately an obstacle, which will have to be destroyed or transformed into something unrecognizable if their ambitions are to be fulfilled.

And this is precisely what I do not think is going to happen. We notice that the progression of sit-ins and demonstrations and confrontations and the rest of it never gets anywhere: one university goes through such a seizure, then collapses in exhaustion, and then another university goes through it. It never gets anywhere because the tactics of trying to revolutionize society by harassing the university are not serious tactics. The university is relatively easy to harass, but student unrest, as it is called, has had no real effect on the social and political life of the country, for all its headlines. I think students are getting a little weary of vague and vaporous revolutionary clichés, and of having their idealism exploited by leaders who do not share it. I think we may be turning a corner in student unrest, that a stage of serious and effective social action is about to begin and that the children's crusade is on the way out.

I keep thinking of the analogy of war. Wars ought not to start and accomplish nothing when they stop. Their professed aims are lies and the sacrifices they demand are useless. And yet, out of the midst of a war, there comes, occasionally, a sense of interdependence, of the vast increase in the intensity of awareness when we realize how our own life is bound up with other lives. It is ordinary citizens, whether in the army or on the home front, who are most likely to have such a feeling: career soldiers and professional patriots know little of it. We think that if we could only hold on to such a feeling after the war there is nothing that society could not do. But, of course, we are so relieved to have the war over with that we soon go back to our normal attitudes.

During the past week I caught a glimpse of the profound concern that teachers feel for their students and that students feel for their teachers and their studies, as they struggled to read and think and write and discuss issues with police helicopters buzzing overhead and tear gas seeping through the windows. I realized, in direct experience, something that I had always known: that the university is the centre of all genuine social order, and that all serious and effective social action has to begin by strengthening and unifying the university community. The university is changing and will change more, but change is simply adaptation to new social conditions: it is not itself a good thing or a bad thing.

A convocation is not a dismissal: it is not an occasion for saying that you have been welcome at your university but that now you may depart in peace. A convocation is rather a calling together, a summoning of a tocsin to those who care about the university, to tell them that society must renew itself if it is to survive, that the university is at the centre of society, that those of us who are professionally concerned with the university are doing what we can, but that for what we have to do every one of you must help.

Convocation Address, University of Western Ontario. 27 May 1969

# A Revolution Betrayed:
## Freedom and Necessity in Education

The role of a convocation speaker in these days is hard to define. A university convocation is a ritual, and a ritual is among other things an expression of concern, concern for the community, for one's soul, or for certain emphases and values in society. The church, politics, business, all have rituals that we are well accustomed to, so accustomed that we hardly give much thought to their meaning, or even notice their presence. But radical concern also has its rituals, and the rituals of demonstration, protest, terrorism, confrontation, sit-in, love-in and folk festival are still new. In another two or three years they will become as conventionalized as an Empire Club lunch, but right now they attract more attention. With the newspapers full of rituals of burning brassieres and bombing libraries, a convocation seems as genteel and uninvolved as an actress with her clothes on.

But a university is not, like a church, a political party, or a pressure group, primarily a concerned organization. The people in the university are citizens: they have the same concerns and commitments as anyone else. But the university itself stands for something different: it is not trying directly to create a certain kind of society. It is not conservative, not radical, not reactionary, nor is it a facade for any of those attitudes. Its goal is liberal, in the sense that we speak of a liberal education, but that is not a liberalism in any concerned or political sense, with however small an l. Even if everybody connected with a university voted unanimously to denounce the FLQ or the Vietnam war or racial segregation, that would still not commit the university as such. Still, as citizens, we are all concerned: any notion of being neutral, of standing above the conflict, of seeing all sides and joining none, is only an illusion, and a very dangerous one. So the university cannot be standing for this kind of Olympian detachment either, at least not as an ideal for the people in it.

What it does stand for is the challenge of full consciousness. Concern is close to anxiety, and anxiety is close to hysteria. In a world as hysterical as ours, we are all, like bad swimmers, continually getting submerged, gasping and spluttering out the clichés of a partisanship that we do not ourselves wholly understand. The university tries to show us that the intellect and the imagination provide the air which it is more natural for us to breathe. For example, there is such a thing as reason, and philosophy and the sciences show us how it operates. In ordinary life we do not reason, we rationalize. There is nothing that cannot be rationalized: terrorists can rationalize blowing up a plane as political idealism; homicidal maniacs can rationalize murder as an indictment of an evil society; indecisive leaders can rationalize doing nothing as prudence or wisdom. The university does not claim that anybody ever has, ever could, or ever ought to order his life entirely by reason. It merely says that there is a reason beyond rationalization, that if we pursue it we develop philosophy and the sciences, and that if we develop philosophy and the sciences we get something more useful than the rationalizings of thugs and ditherers. Again, there is such a thing as imagination, which operates in literature and the arts. The university does not say that we should learn how to live from poetry or fiction, or how to see from painting. It merely says that there is in the arts an imagination better than the melodrama and poster-painting of our ordinary social imaginations, of our constant efforts to create a knight in shining armour out of Tweedledum and a foul belching dragon out of Tweedledee.

This is where the freedom that the university offers comes in, the freedom that the phrase liberal education refers to. Most of us never outgrow the childish notion of freedom as freedom of will, as something opposed to the external constraints that other people, starting with our parents, put on us. Freedom, we think, must still be for us what it was at the age of four, freedom to do as we like, without realizing that what we like to do may be as compulsive as anything that the most obsessed parent could think up to prevent it. There is a strong popular sentiment in favour of this kind of freedom: everybody is for it, like motherhood. We have a revolution when one organized group is able to exploit this sentiment as a means toward gaining power for itself. All dedicated revolutionaries are traitors, not because they are trying to upset an established authority, but because they can only succeed by promising a freedom that they have no intention of granting, and could not grant if they wanted to. Every revolution, in short, is a revolution betrayed. The unrest in the United States today is partly the result of a growing feeling that this was true even of the American Revolution, which looked for so long as though it were an exception to the rule. What was exploited in the American Revolution, and again in the Civil War, was a desire for domocratic freedom, but what came to power was an oligarchy, and for many Americans the desire for freedom is as frustrated as ever.

Meanwhile the university keeps talking about a different kind of freedom. We notice that as soon as we enter the world of intellect and imagination, the whole notion of an opposition between freedom and authority disappears. One is free to reason only when one follows the inner laws of reason; if an artist is painting a picture, what he wants to do and what he must do are the same thing. The authority of the logical argument, the repeatable experiment, the compelling imagination, is the final authority in society, and it is an authority that demands no submission, no subordinating, no lessening of dignity. As this authority is the same thing as freedom, the university is also the only place in society where freedom is defined. We may think of freedom, first of all, as something to be gained or increased by attacking the symbols of external compulsion in society. A good many of these, in every society, deserve to be attacked. But if we destroyed the external compulsions, we should still have the internal compulsions that made us attack them, and they would instantly produce a whole new set of external ones.

The university helps us to get out of this rat-race of trying to resist one compulsion by obeying another, and never getting any closer to freedom. We cannot struggle to achieve a better society without a vision of what such a society might be, and it is only the arts and sciences, the forms that the human intellect and imagination have achieved, that can provide such a vision. But freedom exists in the vision itself, not in the means of reaching it, because the goal to be attained in the future is, in the intellect and imagination, already there. In this neofascist age there are many people who hate the very thought of freedom, and it is a sound if vicious instinct in them to attack the university. Naturally they encourage us to think of academic freedom, which is really the freedom to live in the world of the intelligence, as an outmoded concept. But apart from the purely negative freedom of being out of jail, human society is not capable of any freedom except academic freedom and what is derived from it. Nothing short of that is really human life at all.

It is usual for a convocation speaker to congratulate the people in front of him on having got their degrees. I am doing this now, but I wanted to explain first why my congratulations are sincere and not merely perfunctory: why, in short, I consider it a genuine achievement for you to have your degrees. When we hear so much nonsense about how a degree is a mere piece of paper, a mere this or a mere that, it is perhaps as well to say that you have a degree not only because you have done the work required of you, but because you have had the moral courage to concentrate on it. The Indian teachers of yoga say that when a novice sits down to meditate, all the demons for miles around come to distract him, because they are terrified of the power of a concentrated intelligence. I often think of Bunyan's Christian, plodding through the Valley of the Shadow of Death and having to listen to all the silly gabble of the voices in the valley, which, says Bunyan, "he verily thought had proceeded from his own mind". You may have had your demons too, some telling you to go in for relevance, which means trying to educate yourselves by echo, by listening to the sound of your own prejudices; some telling you that there are no goals in society worthy of your efforts; some telling you to become radicalized, or to transcend your ego-consciousness, or whatever other synonym of goofing off is currently fashionable. There is always something more exciting and picturesque to do than to cultivate the intellect and imagination. But whatever issues demand commitment without critical intelligence today will be stone dead tomorrow, and it is always disconcerting to discover that one has been embracing a corpse.

I began by saying that a convocation was a ritual, but it is a ritual of an unusual kind. Most rituals are devoted to adherence, to solidarity, to professions of faith, to consolidating a group or community. We have very few rituals of separation, and the ones that do exist, like political purges, are mostly very sinister ones. You will, of course, be approached by alumni organizations, and I hope you will respond to them: it seems to me a natural and healthy instinct for you to think of the university from which you were graduated as your lifelong intellectual home. But still a convocation is a separation, as each one of you leaves the University of Windsor to become the University of Windsor in yourself. It is a kind of benediction indicating that the essential ritual act has already taken place. As at a church service, you have been shown something that is both mysterious and substantial, infinitely beyond us and yet inside us, something we can never reach and yet something that is essentially what we are. It is quite possible to go through university without realizing this, but, even if you have, that does not mean that you have for ever lost the university's vision. It makes a good deal of difference, to you, whether you respond to that vision, but it makes much less difference when or how you do. It is still here; it won't and can't go away: it is independent of time and place, but it is only because it is here that time and place have meaning.

Convocation Address, University of Windsor. 17 October 1970

# Education and the Rejection of Reality

Most of us are perhaps old enough to remember the world of 1943, in the middle of the war. Japan was a totalitarian enemy and China a bourgeois friend, the King of England was Emperor of India, Nazi Germany ruled the most powerful empire the world has ever seen. When we look back on that world we realize that what we are living in, the world of current events and of news, is actually a kind of phantasmagoria. It is an illusion of what is really happening. What really happened between 1943 and 1971 is something that we cannot get from news media. They are not set up to give us that kind of information. Not only is the world we live in a phantasmagoria, it is also a world which seems to be dominated by an almost continuous hysteria.

This has its equivalent in education. In education, and particularly in the universities, there is an obsessive over-production of graduates. The economy of waste and of deterioration works here too. We have to keep on producing more and more and more graduates; we educate them less and less and less, just as the more automobiles are produced the cheaper and more trashy is the vehicle turned out. But there is another kind of continuity, and educational theory does not always distinguish the obsessive or neurotic continuity from the kind that actually does preserve our identity throughout the day. It is true that we change roles very frequently during the course of a day, and yet we know that there is a continuity of our own individual life underlying that. We know that we are, for all the variety of appearances we make, the same person. We know that beyond all the conflict and whim and caprice of our lives there is an underlying con-

93

sistency of purpose. This consistency is the basis of all virtue: it is the basis of all human dignity. The only person who is honest is the person who is consistently honest, and what is true of the moral life is true of the intellectual life as well.

The basis of education is repetition in the form of habit and practice, and freedom emerges from and flowers out of discipline. One is only free to play the piano after one has disciplined oneself to practise the piano hour after hour. In the Middle Ages the word *habitus* or habit was used to describe the process of education. A man who could read Latin was said to have the habit of Latin, and the art of education consists in administering the discipline of habit and holding the goal before the student of what emerges at the end of it. It is this that enables a person to maintain his identity throughout his life and to meet the threat to the identity which is posed by the variety of situations that he is in.

The end of knowledge is, of course, wisdom, and if we think of what is meant by the word wisdom, of what a wise man is, we can see that it has something to do with a sense of the potential. The wise person is the person who we feel could meet any number of potential situations in a roughly consistent and yet flexible way. Our lives are founded on a kind of invisible continuity and it is this invisible continuity which enters into both education and ordinary social life. At certain times there are cumulative points where we have a kind of break-through, a feeling of an emergence into a new and a greater kind of freedom. A scientist may go through five or six hundred experiments which get him nowhere and in the 631st (I think that was a famous number in science), suddenly the experiment comes through. He has done what he has been trying to do and his whole sense of what he is doing crystallizes.

The most impressive example of this kind of repetition in literature, I suppose, is the final volume of Proust's *Remembrance of Things Past*. In that volume Proust describes how the repetitions of certain experiences which held his life together kept his attention focussed throughout a long, futile, dilettantish existence drifting from one party to another in the upper crust of Parisian society. Suddenly at one of these parties the pattern of repetition cleared up and expanded, and this futile, dilettantish life suddenly took a new shape and new form, the form of one of the great works of imagination of our time.

For the most part real life cannot be discovered except through the continuous and the structured forms of the arts and the sciences. That leads me to make a very different definition of education from the usual one. I should say that life in the world is life in a continuous illusion, and that education is the encounter with life on the level of reality. That is the opposite of the usual notion which we accept in practice if not in theory. That notion is that education is a preparing for real life and that real life is what I have just called a dissolving and hysterical phantasmagoria. It is this notion which has led us to concentrate all education on one end of existence and make it a monopoly of the young.

It follows that all discussions of education which use that silly phrase "ivory tower" have got the whole subject the wrong way round. The question of relevance is an example: it is not the relation of education to the world that matters, it is the relation of the world to education that matters. There is no such thing as inherent relevance. No subject is more relevant that another: it is only the student who can establish the relevance of what he studies, and the student who does not accept this responsibility does not deserve the name of student. A much more serious result of our regarding education as a preparation for real life instead of being real life itself is that we have created in modern society that curious being that we call the adolescent. I say creation because I think the adolescent is a deliberate creation of an adult society, and that we have done with young people what Victorian society did with women: on the pretext of coddling and protecting them, we have subordinated them and kept them out of any real social role or influence, and we have done this because they represent a kind of projection of our own anxiety. Young people very much resent being used as a projection of adult anxieties, but the more they protest against it the more apt they are to fall into the role that society has prescribed for them. The more they talk about the necessity for being treated like grown people, the more adolescent and shrill-voiced their protests are apt to sound. In many of the demands of student protestors in the university, one senses not so much an immaturity as a kind of infantilism, and one feels that to many of their pronouncements and proposals what they unconsciously expect is not the response "How cogent!" but rather the response "How cute!"

As I said earlier, there is a law of diminishing returns in the educational process. Clearly there is something in this notion of concentrating all education at one end of life which does not succeed in making people more mature or wiser, nor does it really enable them to think for themselves. If one looks at student newspapers, for example, one does not see any real individuality of opinion: one sees the same outpourings of cliché and slanted news that one sees in any other bad newspaper. This situation is one that carries with it an increasing expense and a heavier burden on the taxpayer and a consequent growth of panic about a process which still appears to be something of a middle class playground.

My own view of an ideal system of education is a Utopian one which could not be achieved without a very extensive restructuring of society. The moral of that is, of course, that the cure for whatever is wrong with education does not lie within education itself. It lies within a much broader conception of society and what society could do. But the value of Utopianism is that it gives one a kind of model to consider and to keep in mind.

The basis of my view is my own experience of teaching in the university. When the war was finally over, the returned people came back and there was a tremendous leap forward for all university teachers. Their students were not only older and more mature but they also realized that they had been wasting many years and they wanted to return to real life, which was life in the classroom. The challenge which their liveliness and their independence presented to the teacher is something that nobody can ever forget who went through that period of teaching in a university between 1945 and about 1948 or 1949 — after which, as a colleague remarked to me one day, "we're back again to teaching children."

That made me realize how important it would be if there were some means of alternating schooling and some other kind of experience as early in life as possible. Socialist countries have experimented a good deal with this, though not on a basis that many of us would find acceptable. It seems to me that the bogy of child labour is not so much of a threat as it was, and we notice how serious students pick up for themselves various interests which involve them with the community around them. We have many students at university concerning themselves with Pollution Probe, with Zero Population Growth, and with other things of that kind. That is a rather significant trend and one which I would hope would grow rapidly in the future.

I should like to see all educational institutions open for people to return to as frequently as possible in adult life. I wish that the university had students of different age levels, who were not simply in adult education programs but who were making a full-time return to university life. This would be essential for many groups of people: teachers needed refresher courses, business men who want to get a different kind of experience, housewives with grown-up families, and so on. In a generation or so, the whole picture of every science changes drastically: when a person is 50, the science he learned at 20 is no longer of the same shape nor does it deal with the same facts. In the humanities, although there are tremendous advances in fields like critical theory and linguistics and so on, the classics of literature remain what they were from the beginning. But while it is very desirable for a student of 14 to read Shakespeare's *Macbeth* and look up all the hard words, still *Macbeth* is not the same play to a person of 40 that it is to a person of 14. The person of 40 has perhaps a clearer notion in his own experience of just how lethal ambition can be.

So the development and progress of education lie in the direction of a kind of social planning of which education is a part but which depends on factors outside education as well. If we ask what is wrong with our present society, the left wing would immediately answer "imperialism" and the right wing would immediately answer "permissiveness." It seems to me that both of these answers are for the birds. However wrong or evil or foolish the American involvement in Vietnam or the Russian involvement in Czechoslovakia may be, these situations are not imperialism in any Leninist sense. There is something quite different going on. Similarly the word permissiveness might be extended to cover both very good things as well as very bad things.

I suspect, when people use these polemical and very largely meaningless words, they have in mind what is really the same thing, different aspects of the same fallacy: that the individual and society are in an antithetical relationship, that society is what diminishes the freedom of the individual. The approach to education which took the forms of the birch rod and the dunce cap also assumed an antithesis between the individual and society. It took the side of society and forced the individual student to conform to a social mould or role, but the fallacy at the bottom of it was exactly the same.

We are social beings first and our individuality is a delicate, complicated process of evolution out of society. Anybody can remain a merely social being. He may be simply part of a conforming mob. The individual is not born an individual. He is born a member of a society, and all his individuality has its roots in that society. We still tend to think of society as an aggregate of individuals, and of the individual as somehow prior to his society. That is one reason why one of the central problems of our time is the fragmenting of the social vision, and it is greatly increased by the influence of fragmenting experiences like those of the news media, television and radio — particularly television. These have enormously increased the amount of fragmented experience, which is forgotten or at best hazily remembered as soon as one has had it.

If we ask what is the easiest form of education, disregarding the question of what is the best form, the answer is obviously that education is easiest when society is at its most static — that is, if society does not change, the educational process is very simple or relatively simple. An obsessive or neurotic sense of continuity is maintained in the desire to keep some things stable. This anxiety of continuity is one of the oldest forms of experience, and has produced one of the oldest forms of our literature. In the Old Testament, for example, we have the Proverbs, which consist of a father handing on to his son maxims of conduct, the transmission of the cultural heritage. Of course the Proverbs in the Bible are based on Egyptian and Mesopotamian models centuries older than that. This same anxiety of continuity, of transmitting a heritage from one generation to another, is still going strong in Shakespeare's *Hamlet* when Polonius is haranguing Laertes and in the 18th century when Lord Chesterfield is writing letters to his son in the vain hope that his son would be something like him. Lord Chesterfield's maxims of conduct, according to Samuel Johnson, combined the morals of a whore with the manners of a dancing master, but as Chesterfield's son was an appalling lout anyway, it didn't really matter.

This kind of anxiety is what produces the notion in education which becomes recurrently fashionable, that the job of teachers is to teach students rather than subjects, disregarding the fact that you can only teach what is teachable and that only the subject is teachable. There is no such thing as a teachable student, and there never will be. It is that kind of anxiety which is the parody, the obsessive or the neurotic form of what seems to me to be the central need of our time, the sense of the wholeness of social vision, the sense of community out of which all individuality grows.

To understand how this sense of community operates, one has to distinguish very sharply two things that are often confused. One has to distinguish unity from uniformity. Unity means something which can comprise a great variety of opinions and views. Uniformity means everybody thinking alike or saying that they think alike.

It is at this point that the importance of reading comes in. Reading is above all a continuous and not a fragmented experience. The written document is the focus of a community because the written document is there to be returned to. It is the basis of all the repetition, of all the habit and the practice which underlies the genuine educational process. This is why the art of reading with its stationary book which keeps patiently saying the same things no matter how often one opens it, is still the basis of all education and can never be replaced by the fragmented and the temporary media, however large a part of our lives they may occupy.

The basis of education therefore is the habit of reading, and it might be said that if young people were taught not simply how to read but taught the habit of reading so that it became continuous, perhaps nothing else would be necessary in our education. One does run into such views occasionally. I studied in Oxford in the 1930s, and it was a strong belief in Oxford that English literature was a subject that did not need to be taught. You teach people to read and then you send them into the library. If they want to read English literature they can read it — they know how to read, don't they? This is an extreme view — in fact, I should regard it as a rather fatheaded view in 1971 — but it's useful because it is an extreme view. You may remember Mr. Bennett in Jane Austen's *Pride and Prejudice*. He had five daughters and a library. He made no effort to educate his daughters formally. He knew that the two sensible girls, Jane and Elizabeth, would make a sensible use of the library. The third, Mary, was pedantic: she would be studious and would read a great deal, but would not be able to absorb her social life into her reading. The two silly ones, Kitty and Lydia, would not read at all. So you have two out of five, which is a remarkably high average, and up to that point I suppose Mr. Bennett's view might work.

It is more important, however, to recognize that the habit of reading is not a simple matter, because elementary reading is for the most part a passive operation and it becomes essentially the reading of instructions. The elementary reader is trained above everything else to read things like traffic signs. The art of reading has to be continued throughout life in order to keep presenting to the student the fact that reading is an active and creative process and that it is also a constant act of judgment. This sense of reading as an act of judgment lessens the panic that so many of us feel when we are confronted with the immense quantity of reading that there is to get through, the feeling that there are so many square miles of print that one needs to read just to keep up.

The nightmare of information retrieval which our libraries present to us is a part of the same thing. I don't know what it is like in the sciences, but I do know what it is like in the humanities. Most of the information to be retrieved from whatever source is not information at all; it is either misinformation or else it is a repetition of what has been said elsewhere, and the trick is to get rid of it and not to absorb as much as possible of it.

The act of reading as a continuous act of judgment is the key to equality, and the key to freedom. Its purpose is the maintaining of the consistent consciousness which is the basis of human freedom and of human dignity.

Reading 71 Conference, York University. In *University of Toronto Graduate,* 3 (June 1971).

# Research and Graduate Education
## in the Humanities

The humanities used to be regarded by administrators with a good deal of favour as low-budget departments. It was not long ago that when a dean of humanities presented his needs to his president, he would be met with a glazed eye and a reference to Mark Hopkins and his log. Of course, there are some aspects of the humanities which are extremely expensive, one obvious example being archeology, on which some types of humanist scholarship are heavily dependent. But, for the most part, the expenses of supporting research in the humanities consist of a paradoxical development: first, building up the library, because the humanities usually get the lion's share of the library budget, and, secondly, providing travel grants to bring scholars to better libraries. The immense resources, technological and otherwise, of modern libraries, which can bring so many streams of modern learning to the scholar's doorstep, are, of course, useful only to the scholar when he knows what he is looking for; but if he is doing original research, he probably doesn't. He still has to be turned loose, in the British Museum or Library of Congress with a sense of serendipity which has been built up by his previous experience of the subject.

One of the things that is not always realized about the humanities is the relative novelty of serious critical work. If I may give an example from personal experience, the first major problem that I attempted as a critic was an exposition of the meaning of those long didactic poems of William Blake which he called prophecies. They were written by Blake between 1788 and 1822, and the first serious study of them, which was Foster Damon's, came out in 1924. Previous to Damon's study, there had been, I suppose, well over a hundred books on Blake and countless articles and essays, to say nothing of thousands of incidental references, but there was nothing in this material, so far as I know, which was worth anything to a student working in this field. It was no more of use to him than treatises on the geocentric Ptolemaic universe would be to a modern astronomer: consequently, no devices of "information retrieval" from pre-Damon material would be of any help.

The question arises, why is there this curious novelty about so much serious critical work in the humanities? One reason, I think, is the survival of the superstition that the students of the humanities are custodians of values, that it is all very well for scientists to study mere facts, but, after all, it is values which make man, give him a dignity above the other animals, and it is the humanists who know about them. I have always attacked this notion that the end of criticism is the developing of value judgments. It seems to me that the study of literature is, first of all, a categorical and descriptive study, a study of what is there. It has been only very gradually that the inhibition caused by the sense of the importance of value judgments has begun to wane. First of all, there was the profound humanist belief that the only languages and literatures worth studying were those of the Latin and Greek cultures. It was at that stage of the humanistic cultivation of values that the Bodleian Library at Oxford got rid of its Shakespeare Folio, which it later on had to buy back again at a very considerably advanced price.

In the next stage, the modern languages were admitted to the serious humanities, but the study of their literatures was largely confined to a select canon of approved writers. Some years ago I was visiting another university and a man who did most of the ordering for the English department came in to me. He had a chance of buying a large amount of literature of the Gothic Revival Period in the 1790's, that is, the horror stories of the Clara Reeve and Mrs. Radcliffe period, and he wanted to know what he should do about this. I said, "Grab it at once." But he hesitated because he felt that this material wasn't really good enough from a literary point of view to justify spending all that money. Of course, the study of the Gothic novel is very much "in" at present, and I imagine he now greatly regrets having passed up this opportunity.

As time goes on, more and more things, which in the terms of the conventional value judgments of a generation ago were regarded as unimportant, become more and more integral to the serious study of literature. After having digested the modern languages, the humanities are now trying to digest the practical arts, including film. At the same time popular literature, children's literature, popular magazines, hard and soft pornography, and other peripheral material pushes itself inexorably into the literary critic's purview. Consequently, the use of a criterion of values as a means for discouraging research is on its way out, but I suppose that not long ago, and perhaps even still in some quarters, a person who would say of a minor poet of the past that his voluminous works have long since been forgotten would feel that he was paying an indirect compliment to his own taste and judgment. What he is actually saying, of course, is, "I know that this man wrote a great deal, but I have been too lazy and incompetent to look into it, much less put a graduate student on the track of it." In short, there undoubtedly is such a thing as "junk," but for the purposes of buying for a library "junk" is not definable in the conventional terms of literary values.

I mentioned archeology as an example of a discipline related to the humanities, and certainly in archeology it is much more fun to turn up a priceless work of art from the past than to go sifting through pots and the rubble of brick and the excreta of long dead dogs. Nevertheless, an archeologist who is looking for buried treasure instead of studying the past belongs, not in the tradition of the scholars, but in the tradition of the grave-robbers. The humanist who is obsessed by values is in much the same position.

Of course, a hundred years ago, even fifty years ago, there was a certain existential reason for this emphasis on values. It was one thing to decide to commit a large part of your life to making a concordance to Shakespeare or to collating the manuscript variants in Chaucer, but would you want to do that for a swatch of medieval homilies or for the kind of Elizabethan dramatist who was prolific around 1580? But now that we have computers and various machines like the one invented by Professor Hinman of Kansas for collating manuscripts, that particular kind of choice is a less decisive one than it used to be. The more mechanical jobs of criticism can now be looked after in more efficient ways.

When Professor Douglas Bush produced his book on classical mythology in the Renaissance a generation ago, he tells us that he had started out by making an immense number of observations about the treatment of some Ovidian myths like the Pyramus and Thisbe story in minor Elizabethan poets. He regards this work as a waste of time and says that the only way in which he can atone for his youthful follies is to keep his information to himself. He says, for example, "Not even the exalted consciousness of knowing more about Pyramus and Thisbe than anyone else gives warrant for setting down here a detailed comparison of countless versions of the tale from notes compiled in my lusty youth." But I suspect that this information is not really too trivial to be passed on: I think perhaps it may indicate an area where some kind of mechanical or other adult audiovisual aid might be of some assistance. In any case, the humanist finds that what was regarded highly in its day is just as important as what is regarded highly now, and that the more of a scholar he becomes of a certain period, the more clearly he understands why certain works were valued highly in their day.

That brings us around, of course, in a full circle, to the question: what about works of criticism themselves like the ones I mentioned, the books which deal with the prophecies of Blake before 1924? What use are they? It seems to me that they are of very considerable value. One of the jobs I had to do was to write a history of Blake scholarship, and it was a fascinating exercise to see how long people had stared at what was straight in front of them and had refused to focus their eyes and minds on it. In other words, one can learn a great deal about the anxieties and obsessions of the time it takes a great writer so long to come into his proper heritage of recognition. So in a sense you can't miss in the humanities. If your book is any good, it's a contribution to scholarship; if it's no good, it's a document in the history of taste, and has its importance there.

In the nineteenth century, when the modern languages became a respectable subject of academic study, a philological tradition, emanating mainly from Germany, set up a kind of quasi-scientific procedure in dealing, not only with philology, but with other literary and critical problems. Around the turn of the twentieth century was the time when a number of learned journals, often with *philology* in their titles, *Modern Philology, Studies in Philology, Journal of English and Germanic Philology,* and so on, were founded. About a generation later, around the 1930's, there came a strong reaction against this, and, instead of the philological journals, we began to get a crop of new journals with *review* in their titles, like *Kenyon*

*Review, Hudson Review, Sewanee Review* and *Southern Review,* which were committed very largely to critical problems and to a more direct commentary on literature.

When I write an article in my own field I send out some offprints to friends, as a kind of personal correspondence, but am only occasionally asked for an offprint by another humanist. But I remember on one occasion making an address to a group of psychiatrists. The address I gave was printed in a psychiatric journal, and I got several hundred requests for offprints from all over the world. It was no surprise to me to learn that people working in such disciplines as psychiatry worked with offprints and abstracts and progress reports more than with books. But it had never struck me before how comparatively small a percentage of humanists' work is really based on research articles. I am speaking, of course, primarily of critical students of literature. The humanist's instinct seems to be to wait for the book: if he comes across a good article he assumes that it will take the form of a book later on. The question then arises: Why has there been a reaction against the learned journal article and the growth of a tendency on the part of the student of literature to return to the book as his main tool of research?

I think the reason is that anyone seriously concerned with literature is seriously concerned with problems of criticism, that criticism is an activity which forces one to think in large and configurated patterns, and that a full-length book is the only means of providing such patterns. It is obvious, for example, that any scholar in the humanities tackling a new field in the humanities is going to begin reading the essential books in that subject. His patterns therefore tend to be large complexes of patterns, and the question of delimiting the subject in order to write within the fairly limited scope of a research article has to come later. For example, it would have been entirely impossible for anyone interested in Blake's prophecies to have written an article on them of more than peripheral interest or to have done a Ph.D. thesis on them until enough of the essential books had appeared to set up the central complexes of the critical problems involved.

There is, of course, a superstition in our time that this complex, configurated, and, in a sense, mythical thinking is something that can only be brought to us from the new media. I happen to be on a board in Canada concerned with communications, and this board had a committee of policy report to it which recommended that the board should issue publications from time to time. The sentence with which it began this recommendation read: "Despite the disadvantages inherent in the linear representation of a world that is increasingly simultaneous, print still retains its medieval authority." This sentence, I suppose, is typical of the kind of nitwitted McLuhanism which is confusing the educational scene. McLuhan himself, of course, is another matter, but I think that even he fails to distinguish between the actual operation of reading a book, which is linear, turning over pages, and following the lines of type from the upper left-hand corner to the lower right, and the effect of a book on the mind as a unit, once read. As that, the book is, and in the foreseeable future will remain, the indispensable tool of the scholar in the humanities.

The reason, then, for the reaction against the philological journal is in part that this kind of scholarship was felt to be concerned with matters extrinsic to literature. If you wanted to delimit a subject in order to write an article or do a thesis on it, you had to choose not so much something within the central critical confines of literature as something in the historical or the biographical background of literature. The reaction of what was called the "new criticism" (which is called "new" because it cannot be traced much further back than Plato, who is full of it) insisted on the central critical problems, beginning with the explicatory reading of the text and going on from there.

When you raise the question of what is the meaning of a work of literature, there are really two answers. There is a whole range of meaning which lies outside the work that you are reading and outside literature — the meaning which is to be found in the historical or the biographical background of which the work of literature is fundamentally a document. This is the concern of historical critics and of certain essential critical interests like the history of ideas. Then, again, there are other questions of meaning which relate literature to the arts. I suppose one area would take in the subject known as "aesthetics" in the sense of the unified criticism of all the arts. But that subject has not been developed yet and not many philosophers who are interested in aesthetics are technically competent as critics in any of the arts.

There are, however, two types of literary context within literature itself. One is the context of language, which is the one that used to be dealt with by comparative philology and is now by linguistics. The other is the type of criticism which sees the work of literature in the context of literature, that is, which studies such matters as conventions and genres and the way in which one work of literature is linked with another. There is, of course, a great deal in this study which is historical, but it is not purely historical study. That leads one to the fact that literature is inside a different kind of framework from that of the sciences. It has always been a principle of the arts that the arts do not improve; they do not advance or progress as time goes on; poets don't get better and better. What they do is produce the classic or model, and the critic (although criticism I think does progress and does advance and improve in its understanding) is bound to a kind of spiral movement, returning over and over again to the central masterpieces of literature, finding more and more depth in them and more and more relationship with other literary works of relatively less importance.

The relations, from this point of view, of literature are with certain aspects of religion, political theory, anthropology, psychology, and, in general, with that whole area which I should call "mythology," and which, I should say, deals with the study of what the existentialist people have taken to calling "concern." Man lives in two worlds. There is a world around him, which he tries to understand and know more about, and which is the particular preserve, I suppose, of the physical sciences. There is also the civilization that he is trying to build and live in, and this, because it concerns him to know what kind of a world he is going to live in, is the peculiar province of these interrelated studies which I have been calling "mythology" and of which literature is a central part.

In the eighteenth and nineteenth centuries, the student going to university in Oxford or Cambridge was exposed to an intensive treatment in Classical culture and might then be sent off to be something like a colonial administrator in India. From the point of view of, say, a contemporary student activist, nothing could be less relevant to life or to his own future career. My colleague, Mr. Sontag, will be saying something about relevance in a moment. And yet, you know, the classical training of the eighteenth and nineteenth centuries was, in fact, a study of another kind of mythology, from which the student was sufficiently detached to look at objectively. He could study the religion of Classical times without being committed to the religion. He could study the political movements of Greece and Rome without feeling himself a partnership in them. And yet at the same time he realized how deeply concerned, not only the people of that time, but he himself was in such questions. There could have been worse trainings for work in India, or any other different civilization.

In general, two characteristics of the humanities, which I think are of particular relevance to our discussion here, emerge from what I have been saying. One is the immense difficulty of limiting a Ph.D. topic in the humanities, because of the large, complex, configurated pattern of interconnected problems which criticism poses. For a keen student in the humanities, it is almost impossible to prevent the Ph.D. thesis from becoming at least the ghost of his first book, and so blocking up and preventing anything else he is ever going to do. But this is, it seems to me, a kind of a built-in occupational hazard, and no easy answers are possible.

The other is that teaching has a kind of functional role in the humanities which I think is distinctive of the humanities. All teaching of the humanities follows the general outlines laid down by Plato. We begin with dialogue, which is one of the great magical terms of our time. But we notice that whenever there is "dialogue" in Plato, the discussion is usually either indecisive or else somebody is talking nonsense. And as somebody, generally Socrates, begins to get hold of something else, which is not dialogue, but dialectic, that is, a particular argument advancing in a particular direction, the dialogue begins to turn into monologue, and the others follow his leadership. And we end in a kind of Darwinian mutation, where those in the symposium who have been weaklings and flaked out earlier are now lying under the table in a state of insensibility, along with a few survivors who, with Socrates, are still engaged in the silent contemplation of the form of the good.

From *Journal of the Proceedings and addresses of the Twentieth Annual Conference of the Association of Graduate Studies in the Association of American Universities,* ed. W. Gordon Whaley. Austin: University of Texas Press, 1968.

# On Teaching Literature

In every subject that can be taught there are certain rudiments to be learned first, and whatever is learned afterward has to have some kind of connection with those rudiments. For example, if we are teaching music, we can begin with the octave, the twelve semitones of the octave that make up the chromatic scale, the relation of the major and minor modes to that scale, and the way in which such musical elements are presented in notation. Knowing these rudiments will not enable us to compose like Beethoven, but it is a start in putting ourselves in command of the same technical apparatus that Beethoven worked with all his life. Such teaching is progressive in a way that "music appreciation" by itself is not. For many reasons teachers have been for a long time confused about how to teach literature (*and* language, but that is another subject) systematically and progressively, and hence their students often grow up with, at best, only a vague memory of attempts to get them to "appreciate" "good literature." The present series of books is designed to help a teacher to present literature in the same kind of coherent and planned sequence that one might use to present music or mathematics. The principles on which these books are based are the subject of what follows.

In learning some subjects we are forced to depend a good deal on sheer memorization. Political geography is one such subject. There is no reason why Bolivia should be in South America instead of Africa: it just is, and we have to remember the fact. If we try to teach literature without any principles of its construction in our minds, we are going to force a great deal of memorization on our students: names and dates of writers, historical and cultural facts associated with literature, allusions and references and other aspects of content, and so on. One great advantage of teaching literature systematically is that it then turns out to be a structure, like mathematics or science, and the memory work involved becomes a good deal simpler when there is something to hook it on to.

The first principle of literary structure is that all literary works are so presented that they move in time, like music, and yet, because they are structures, they can also be studied all in one piece, like paintings. First of all, we must read, or listen to someone read, or listen to a play in the theatre. This is a participating act: we *follow* the structure as it unfolds in time. It is also a precritical act: we are not studying or judging or commenting at this stage, but suspending all mental operations until the end to get a sense of the total form. Study and criticism begin at the second stage, where we see the structure frozen into a simultaneous pattern. For this second stage we have to have a printed text; but study of the printed text does not replace the original listening experience. In practice we may read or study dramas that we have not seen in the theatre, but even so we should keep some kind of ideal performance of them in our minds. And even if we are just reading for relaxation, not concerned with an educational process and so not going on to the second stage of study and analysis, we can still be aware that our reading experiences are attaching themselves to one another, and forming a larger pattern.

The word *convention* expresses one very important kind of similarity that we find in our reading. A detective story is a simple example of a conventional form: we know before we start reading it that there is going to be a corpse, a number of suspects, police called in, an inquest, and the eventual discovery of the murderer just at the end. If we bought a detective story and didn't find this kind of material in it we'd feel cheated. Of course every individual work of literature has to be just enough different from all the others to make reading it a distinct experience. But the similarities within the type are equally important. A radio or television serial will use the same characters, the same incidents, the same turns of speech, and if these familiar features didn't turn up, their programme's ratings would go down fast and far. So there are aspects of literary experience that are very like games. Each game of chess or bridge may be different, but the conditions within which the game is played do not change. We notice too that it is in popular forms like the detective story where this rules-of-a-game feeling is strongest. The word *genre,* like the word *convention,* expresses a similar sense of classification or type in the things we read. If we are told in advance that what we are going to read is a comedy or tragedy or romance or novel, we expect certain features that we should not expect if the indication were different.

A work of literature, therefore, not only has a narrative movement and a unified structure: it also has a context within literature, and it will be more like certain works of literature than like others. The first step in teaching literature systematically, then, is to establish a context within literature for each work being studied, first for the teacher, and eventually for the student as well.

Detective stories and the like are commercial products of a specific society, designed to meet a specific social demand, so it is perhaps not so surprising to find similarities among them. But when we turn to the popular literature of "primitive" (i.e., technologically less-developed) societies, and study their folk tales and myths, we find the same kind of similarities turning up. Sometimes, where the similarities are very striking and the societies that tell these stories are very far apart, we may even find the likenesses uncanny, and feel impelled to invent historical theories about a diffusion of myths from Atlantis or the Garden of Eden or the collective unconscious or what not. But we don't need such theories. If we go into a museum, and look at cultural objects from societies all over the world, such as textiles or pottery or masks, we find that the same principles of design keep recurring. Certain blends and contrasts of colors, certain geometrical patterns, will resemble one another even where there is no question of direct influence. There is enough uniformity in the human mind, in the order of nature that that mind works with, and in the physical conditions of the medium itself, to account for all such similarities.

### The Function of Archetypes

In one of the books in this series there is a story, told among a tribe of Californian Indians, of a man who followed the shade of his wife to the land of the dead and was allowed to return with her on condition that he did not touch her before they were back home. Anyone familiar with Greek mythology would say, on reading this story: "That is the same story as the story of Orpheus and Eurydice." We notice that there is no question of the Greek story's having influenced the Californian one, or vice versa. Even if there were, the fact that the same story makes an appeal to two such very different cultures would still be significant. But in what sense is it the "same" story? The incidents are different; the journey to the land of the dead is different; there is no mention of the hero as a musician, as Orpheus was, and the taboo is of touching in this story and of looking back in the Greek one. When we say that it is the "same" story, we are speaking of the shape the story assumes when we look at it all at once as a piece of verbal design, after listening to it being told. As something told and listened to, the story is a narrative or plot (the Greek word for plot, *mythos,* is the source of our word *myth); as something to be studied and compared with other stories like it, it is a theme. As a plot, it moves in time, and our reading of it is also a movement in time. As a theme, it exists all at once in space, like a picture. The Californian Indian story and the Orpheus story are the "same" story because they have the same theme.

We notice that the Californian Indian story incorporates an episode of clashing rocks. That incident is not in the Greek story of Orpheus and Eurydice, but it appears in another Greek story, the voyage of the Argonauts (where Orpheus was also present). This kind of motif, which can appear in any story, is an "archetype," that is, a repeatable unit of imaginative experience that turns up constantly and unpredictably. Just how unpredictable such units can be we can see from this account of the seduction of a girl by a serpent:

> Cinderella dressed in yella
> Went upstairs to kiss her fella
> Made a mistake and kissed a snake
> And came downstairs with a bellyache.

The verses are nonsense, but amusing nonsense, and no nonsense is amusing if it is *entirely* pointless.

The story of Orpheus and Eurydice is in the centre of the western literary tradition, and so hundreds of poets have referred to it and many composers have written operas about it. Consequently it comes to us with the resonance of these echoes around it, as the Indian story does not. But the Indian story, if we listen to it sympathetically, is just as haunting and suggestive, just as touching and as close to our own sense of loneliness and bereavement, as the Greek one. Thus the *quality* of literature does not depend on the technological development of the culture that produced it. Literature does not improve when social conditions improve, or are assumed to improve.

It is true of all forms of human creativity that, while we may in some contexts speak of a development from primitive societies to high civilizations, there is no corresponding development of quality in the arts. Just as the textile or pottery designs of "primitive" peoples may often seem to us as sophisticated as our own, and sometimes much more tasteful, so "primitive" myths and folk tales can be on at least the same imaginative level as our own stories. If we call such stories crude or undeveloped, we are probably misinterpreting them, or thinking of them as early efforts at conceptual thought. They are not forms of conceptual thought at all: they usually come from societies where conceptual thought has no real function. They are forms of imaginative thought, and that can be as subtle and suggestive in the tales of the "eternal dream time" told by Australian aborigines as in our own culture. That is why literature, no less than painting and sculpture, has continually to turn to the primitive, to ballad and popular song and folk tale, to find the sources of its own vitality, and why this literature program makes so much of these sources. Behind these sources, and even more important for us than they are, are the mainsprings of western cultural tradition, the Old Testament and Greek mythology.

**The Primacy of Poetry**

One of the things we learn, if we study such a people as the Eskimos, for example, whose conditions of life have kept them technologically restricted and close to the subsistence level, is that the simpler the society, the more clearly poetry emerges as one of the primary needs of that society. In a civilization like ours, poetry, like physical exercise, gets smothered under a mass of other activities. We forget how simple and direct a form of expression poetry is: how it is linked to singing and dancing and marching. Like singing and dancing themselves, however, poetry has come to be regarded as a difficult skill attained by very few people. But the three-year-old who learns to hear and repeat nursery rhymes with the kind of rhythmical swing that belongs to them is learning something about the real impact of poetry that many of us have forgotten or never knew. The editors of these books have assumed that the nursery rhymes and fairy tales that children hear in their preschool years, if they are lucky, are the right beginning of a literary education, and they have tried to continue this instead of interrupting it, as school education too often does.

The superstition that poetry is difficult and specialized has produced many anthologies and textbooks based on the assumption that the study of poetry should be either circumvented altogether or approached with the greatest caution, and that prose should be the staple of literary education. A culture like ours, submerged under great masses of print that pass for prose, tends to assume that prose must be the natural way to speak and think. But, if prose is more "natural" than poetry, how does it happen that the simplest and most primitive societies have poetry, whereas prose is always a much later and more specialized development? And, more important for us just now, if prose is the natural way to speak, why do young people, introduced to prose in the early grades of school, treat it as a dead language, with no relation whatever to the way that they actually do speak? And why is it that even at the university, by which time the propaganda has done its work and students have finally become convinced that prose is the natural way to write and speak, they still cannot write it, and never speak it consistently?

The truth of the matter is, first, that the natural way to speak is not in prose, despite the pleasure of M. Jourdain in Molière at being told that he had been speaking prose all his life. The natural way to speak is in an associative and repetitive babble which is neither prose nor verse. If we want to see what it looks like in print, we should read Gertrude Stein, the one twentieth-century writer who has completely mastered its peculiar idiom. Verse and prose are different ways of regulating and controlling this babble, but prose is a far more difficult and sophisticated way of conventionalizing speech than verse is. It is therefore better and more logical teaching to begin with poetry, and keep it at the centre of all one's training in literature. And, if we once understand the primitive and simple nature of the rhythm of poetry as compared with prose, we may go on to understand something of the primitive and simple nature of its use of language and its methods of thought. The poet, like the child, is dependent on sense experience rather than abstraction, and his primary units of expression are images, not ideas or concepts. Poetry has a limited tolerance for abstractions of any kind, including the abstractions of critical commentary.

## Image: The Unit of Meaning

Again, the poet thinks, not in logical sequences, but in the most primitive and archaic of categories, similarity and identity: A is like B; A is B. These are the categories that appear in poetry as simile and metaphor. "Eternity is like unto a Ring," says John Bunyan; "Grandfather of the day is he," says Emily Dickinson of a mountain. The programme begins with riddles, describing things in terms of other things:

As round as an apple,
As deep as a cup,
And all the king's horses
Cannot pull it up.

Such poetry makes a direct appeal to the intellectual excitement of childhood: the child wants to "guess," and thereby he recapitulates the whole history of literature, where the riddle, along with the riddle game and the riddle duel, is among the most ancient of poetic forms. In fact "riddle" was originally what one "read." I suppose no poetry will ever be written more difficult and elusive than that of the nineteenth-century French poet Mallarmé, yet Mallarmé's prescription for writing poetry, to describe, not the thing, but the effect it produces, is still essentially a prescription for writing riddles. Such mental processes as those that are involved in riddles, proceeding through pun and identification, are very close to the mental processes of young children. A generation ago T.S. Eliot said that poets writing in so unpoetic a time as ours have a moral obligation to be difficult. But a proper literary education would preserve a child's own metaphorical processes, not distort them in the interests of a false notion of reality. If it did, the child would grow up to find the most apparently difficult poetry a simple, direct, natural, even inevitable form of expression.

Literature is produced by, and appeals to, the imagination. The imagination is a creative and constructive power: it is different from reason, though it is intelligent, and different from feeling, though it is sensitive. If we are responding to someone else's poem, we should respond to it at first with intelligence and feeling, as we do to anything else outside ourselves. But sooner or later we come up against the question of how our own powers of creation can be related to what the poet has made. For, however unlikely it is that we could make anything like *King Lear* or *Paradise Lost,* our response even to that level of creation still has in it some quality of recognition. Lear on the heath is not like anything we have actually experienced, either in waking life or in dreams. Nevertheless he reminds us that besides actual worlds and fantasy worlds, we do have an imaginative world of our own, a world of possibilities, so to speak, and that Lear is within range of something that we can imagine. We know very little about our own imaginative worlds: even a great genius may not know much about what his genius is producing. Hence we are, at least at first, totally inarticulate about what we can imagine, until something in literature, say a poem, comes along and expresses it. Then we realize that that poem corresponds to something in a world that we have lived in and lived with, but knew nothing about until the poem spoke for us.

This imaginative world that remains within us, hidden and mysterious, until literature begins to call it forth, is a world with a shape to it. We have just said that each work of literature has a context within literature: it lights up a specific corner or area of our imaginative experience, and the other works of literature that are most like it are in neighbouring areas. The editors of these books have taken the logical next step, and have tried to sketch out for the student the outlines of his own imaginative world. That sounds at first like a formidable undertaking, but the two main principles involved are very simple.

### The Two Rhythms of Literature

First, the easiest way to impose artistic shape on material is to give it a recurring pattern. For arts that move in time, like poetry and music, this means the repetition of an established rhythm. The poet uses words, and it is not too difficult to put words into regular rhythm. But words, unlike musical notes, have to mean something besides their own sound: they also describe and refer to the world around us, or, as critics back to Plato have said, they imitate nature. The first thing poetry does, in transforming "nature" into an imaginative world, is to seize on the element of regular repetition in it.

This is the element provided by the cyclical rhythm of nature: the four seasons of the year moving from spring to winter and back to spring again; the daily cycle of the sun moving from dawn to darkness

to a new dawn, the cycle of waters running into the sea and returning in the rain. Next comes the fact referred to above, that the poet
thinks in terms of likeness and identity. And what likeness and identity suggest is adding to the cycle of nature the rhythm of life, with
human life at its centre, moving from birth to death and back again
to new life. But this step gets our own emotions immediately involved
with the cycle. And as poetry continues to express not merely the
rhythm of what we see around us but what we feel as part of ourselves,
a second principle begins to operate, a principle which tends to
separate what we hate or fear from what we want or love. Out of
this cycle of death and renewal, and out of separation of our feelings
about the cycle, there gradually emerge four fundamental types of
imaginative experience in literature. The editors call this sequence
of four types, the first time they appear, the "circle of stories." Later
they are referred to by their more usual names: romance, tragedy,
irony, and comedy.

Romance is the name we give to the type of imaginative literature
that takes place in an idealized or stylized world inhabited by brave
men and beautiful women, where all villains are easy to recognize
as villainous. Such a world is likely to be considerably simplified in
its setting also: the discomforts, frustrations, and confusions of ordinary life are largely cleared away. Opposed to romance is the world
explored in irony and satire: this is much closer to the world we live
in, except that irony puts us in a position of some superiority to the
characters in the story, though not so much as to prevent us from
being involved with the story. It will generally be found, however,
that the shape of an ironic story often takes the form of a parody
of romance, as stories of adventurous voyages are parodied in *Gulliver's
Travels* and stories of knights rescuing maidens and the like are
parodied in *Don Quixote*.

Then there are stories we call comedies and tragedies, the stories
that turn up or turn down at the end. Tragedy usually focuses on
a hero, a central figure of more than ordinary size, who is caught
in a situation that propels him inevitably into disaster, whether death
or a loss of freedom of action. The direction of the tragic plot is thus
from the romantic to the ironic. Comedy moves in the opposite direction, from a condition where (to take a very common type of comedy)
a hero and heroine are threatened with separation or a loss of freedom
by some obsessed or ridiculous character, but manage to evade all

obstacles and proceed to a happy conclusion, often marriage. Thus comedy normally moves from the ironic to the romantic worlds. But a tragedy may have its centre of gravity, so to speak, in romance, like *Romeo and Juliet,* or in irony (ironic comedy is generally called satire), like *Vanity Fair,* or in romance, like *The Tempest.*

We may feel that this "circle of stories" considerably simplifies the facts of literary experience. Three points in this connection are important. First, the simplification may be valuable for teaching purposes, giving shape and coherence to an inexperienced student's reading. Second, no boundary lines exist, except in diagrams: no classifying or pigeonholing is involved; literary works are simply seen as being in different areas, where they can be both distinguished from and related to one another. Third, and most important, this is not a schematism to be imposed on students. The teacher should have it in mind, but as a principle to give form to his teaching, not as something for the student to memorize and present as a substitute for literary experience.

We come then at least to the beginning of an answer to the question of what we should teach. We should teach literature, but in such a way that the primary facts emerge first, and the primary experiences are properly emphasized, so that whatever the student goes on to next will be continuous with what he has already experienced. That implies teaching the structure of literature, and the content by means of the structure, so that the content can be seen to have some reason in the structure for existing. Very often literary materials in schoolbooks are arranged by content, by what they say about love or time or death or what not. When well done, such an approach may overlap with the present one: putting poems on spring together is to some extent arrangement by content too. But the approach of this programme also provides a containing form for the themes: love and death are not taken as real classifying principles, but as aspects of literary genres, such as comedy and tragedy. This avoids the danger of classifying literature by what it says, and so making literary works into documents illustrating various Noble Notions. It thus avoids the moralizing of literature, of treating it as a collection of allegories of something else. Moral and allegorical approaches to imaginative literature have been experimented with from classical times down through the Middle Ages and Renaissance to the "Syntopicon" of a few years ago, which attempted to present all the great ideas of man in reference form. But somehow or other this approach has never really worked, except when the moral principles mainly featured were also those that the power structure of society was determined to enforce. It has not worked because it does not follow the actual shape of literature, but distorts that shape in the interests of something else.

## Myth and the Imagination

Every society has a verbal culture, which includes ballads, folk songs, folk tales, work songs, legends, and the like. As it develops, a special group of stories, the stories we call myths, begins to crystallize in the center of this verbal culture. These stories are taken with particular seriousness by their society, because they express something deep in that society's beliefs or vision of its situation and destiny. Myths, unlike other types of stories, stick together to form a mythology, and this mythology begins to take on the outlines of the imaginative world just described. Creation myths and other myths that account for the origins of things appear at one end of it, and myths of a final dissolving or transforming of the world may appear at the other, though this is normally a later development. Literature as we know it, as a body of writing, always develops out of a mythical framework of this kind. The heaven or paradise or Mount Olympus of the mythology becomes the idealized world of romance and pastoral and idyl, and its hell or Tartarus or Hades becomes the abhorred or grotesque world of irony.

The mythological framework of western culture has been provided mainly by the Bible, with the mythology of Greece and Rome forming a counterpoint against it. During the last century or so we have been learning more and more about the similarity of these mythical patterns to those produced by other societies all over the world, which, of course, in itself gives the study of literature an important function in a world where we have to meet so many other peoples on their terms as well as ours. The present literature programme is full of mythical stories from a wide variety of sources, and their similarity to more familiar ones is clear enough. But, as we said above, the biblical and classical versions are the ones that western poets have known: they are the ones with literary echoes around them, and they have an obvious priority in western literary education.

Of course the fact that the Bible has been traditionally associated with belief, and that classical mythology has not, at least not since the rise of Christianity, makes for differences in emphasis. There has been a long-standing notion that poets are just playing with words, and novelists just telling stories for fun. Hence the writer comes to be thought of as a kind of licensed liar, and the words for literary structure, *fable, fiction,* and *myth,* acquire a secondary sense in which they simply mean something untrue. This provides quite a hurdle for the study of literature to get over. When I became a junior instructor in English many years ago, I began a course on the imagery and symbolism of the Bible, which I am still teaching. I thought, as I still think, that without some knowledge of the Bible one simply does not know what is going on in English literature. Also that while the Bible may be many things besides a work of literature, it must be that too, as no book can have had its influence on literature without itself having literary qualities. Naturally some of my students found it hard to understand why poets did not confine themselves to classical mythology, where they could do what they liked, instead of meddling with really serious issues. To demonstrate that poets took their work very seriously was not difficult, but there was another set of objections when I carried the campaign into the opposite camp, and began calling biblical stories myths, and biblical images metaphors. The questions usually took some such form as "Do you mean to say that it's all just a myth, only a myth, nothing but a myth?" Here one had to explain that, in the first place, a myth is a certain kind of story, and that calling a biblical story a myth is simply making a statement about its form or mode of presentation, not about the reality or unreality of its content. Secondly, that the Bible employs myth and metaphor because it expects the active and constructive response from its readers that only the imagination gives. The fact that Jesus taught in parables and stories obviously increases the seriousness and immediacy of what he had to say.

In the last few years students have started to ask very different questions. They are, after all, living in an age where it is all too easy to see that anything, religious or scientific, becomes dangerous to society as soon as it is uncritically accepted. Whenever we try to place any subject beyond criticism, what we are really placing beyond criticism is our present understanding of that subject. The motivation for religious persecution, for instance, is never "You must believe in God," but "You must believe what I mean by God." The next step is to understand that what is real or true about any human form of understanding, whether religion or philosophy or science or literature, is not its relation to objective fact, but its relation to our own power to use it. So it is reassuring to find that students now seem to realize that active imagination is worth any amount of passive faith.

## Models for Action

There is, however, a still more important principle involved here, so far as the teaching of literature is concerned. Every belief or doctrine which can be expressed as a general statement or proposition is also the moral of a possible story. Literature addresses itself to the imagination, and the imagination is not directly related to belief. It is concerned rather with models of possible belief, structures which may be "just stories" in their literary form, but may also take on the outlines of a much wider and more comprehensive social vision. What we believe is not what we think we believe but what our actions show that we believe. Our actions in their turn are chosen by a certain kind of social vision, and if we were sufficiently conscious of our social vision to describe it, we should find it taking on the outlines of a story and a body of imagery.

One of the stories in this programme is of a medieval baron who is a werewolf, and is forced to become a wolf for three days each week. His wife, who wants to marry someone else, worms his secret out of him (Samson-Delilah archetype), steals his clothes so that he cannot become human again, marries the other man, and takes over his property. The king goes out hunting, finds the wolf, and the wolf proves so affectionate that he spares his life and takes him back to the court. Eventually the whole story comes out: the baron is restored to his normal shape, and the lady and her second husband are baffled. Just a story, and a very simple and childlike story at that. Yet the structural device employed is an extremely common one in literature, which implies that it belongs to a fairly important group of structures. In Homer's *Odyssey*, for example, the hero remains absent from home while other suitors of his wife lay waste his goods; he returns secretly and in disguise, and eventually reveals his true shape and destroys the suitors. In Shakespeare's *Measure for Measure* the Duke of Vienna disappears, leaving a regent in charge, returns secretly, disguised as a friar, and finally reveals his true shape, to the great discomfiture of the regent, who has not been behaving well.

There are no greater writers than Shakespeare or Homer, but still, we may feel, these are "just stories," told to amuse. But then we may begin to think about, say, the teachings of Christianity, which form not only a body of doctrines but a story. The story tells how Christ leaves the world after his ascent to heaven, returns in secret to the human heart, often neglected or ignored and his authority usurped, yet to be finally revealed in a second coming at the end of time. The story of Chrisitianity, we see, is, from the literary point of view, a comedy: that is what the greatest of Christian poets, Dante, called it. Then there is Marxism, which turns on the theme of a usurping ascendant class getting the benefits of society while an oppressed class remairis hidden within it, some day to manifest itself in full force and to return to its rights. In short, hundreds of millions of people today are thinking about the world within the kind of framework represented by that werewolf story.

## Literature in the Free Society

The social importance of teaching literature, then, does not stop, as so many people think it does, when children have acquired the skills of reading and writing. Nobody denies the importance of these skills: all social participation depends on them. But in themselves they are passive skills: the knowledge of how to read leads in itself merely to reading such things as traffic signs, to learning how to do what one is told. If we go on with the study of literature, it turns out to be, not something to fill in our spare time with, but an organization of human experience. It presents the human situation, not as we ordinarily know it, as a dissolving flux, but in structured forms like romance, tragedy, irony, comedy. To reach this kind of transformed imaginative reality, its rhythms have to be more concentrated, its imagery bolder, and its conventions at once more stylized and more varied, than anything we can use for ordinary experience. Literature in this sense is cultural mythology, the social vision which is not in itself belief or action, but the imaginative reservoir out of which beliefs and actions come.

Every subject worth teaching is also a militant subject, fighting against the social perversion of itself. To teach science is implicitly to fight against mental confusion and superstition; to teach geography and history is implicitly to fight against provincialism. And as we continue to study literature, we begin to realize that every society also produces a social mythology, or what is often called an ideology, that it has techniques of ensuring that its citizens learn it thoroughly and early, and that literature has the social function of trying to clarify and provide imaginative standards for this ideology.

There are two aspects of social mythology. One is its genuine aspect, as the body of beliefs or feelings that are held deeply, if often very inarticulately, by a society. American social mythology, for instance, has a concern for self-reliance and independence, for tolerance (which is really intellectual independence), for the democratic process, for an inclusive community that does not make second-class citizens out of any group. This mythology, like other mythologies, is a construct of historically chosen beliefs and principles, and is incorporated in the Constitution. The fact that it is a mythology, once more, does not mean that it is untrue, but that its truth depends on the way it is used. A great American writer, such as Whitman or Thoreau, will almost always be found to have struck his roots deeply into it. But there is also a strong tendency to project this mythology, to treat it as a body of established social principles, to be imposed on everyone without criticism. This produces a mythology which aims at conditioning all citizens in habits of docility and obedience, or, as it is called, adjustment.

This projected adjustment mythology may be studied in all anthologies and textbooks which assumes that the main function of education is to produce docile citizens. For several generations it was widely assumed that the student should learn as much of this adjustment mythology as possible, and as little as possible of anything else. In fact the study of this mythology frequently replaced the study of actual literature. The mythology in the United States presents a nostalgic version of the American past, with certain mythical figures looming out of it, some named, like Franklin and Washington, and some general, like the pioneer, the hunter, and the cowboy. The present was a middle-class world of comfort and security, where the main outlet for adventure was in operating the technological machinery. The rest of the world, including the rest of the United States, hardly existed at all, or existed only among certain exotic peoples who were to be tolerated and sympathized with, but of course at a distance. So far as it addressed itself to literature, it tended to vulgarize the imaginative response to literature, so as to make the student a part of the captive audience of the mass media in their present facile commercialized form.

The result was all too often to train the student in stock response, not imagination, and the end of the process to get him in adult life to repeat the liturgy of the adjustment myth, in a series of cliché-notions that show traces of the Christian myth from which it was, at many removes, derived. We have all heard these clichés: things were much simpler in the old days; the world has unaccountably lost its innocence since I was a child; I just live to get out of this rat race for a while and go somewhere where I can get away from it all; there is a bracing atmosphere in progress and competition, and although the world is threatened with grave dangers from foreigners, yet if we dedicate ourselves anew to the tasks before us we may preserve the American way of life for generations yet unborn. One recognizes the dim outlines of pastoral myths, fall-from-Paradise myths, exodus-from-Egypt myths, and apocalyptic myths. Genuine American mythology, we said, stresses independence, tolerance, and personal freedom. But no adjustment myth can possibly believe in such things: if it did it would cease to become an adjustment myth. It has to present such beliefs as ways of getting along in a benevolently authoritarian social establishment. Thus the belief in independence and individuality gradually turns into an acceptance of the power of a pervasive but almost invisible corporate state. More important for our present purposes is the principle involved, that if we neglect or misunderstand the teaching of literature, we create a vacuum in education, and adjustment mythology rushes in to fill the empty space. We have no choice about teaching mythology; we have only the choice between teaching genuine and perverted kinds of it.

## The Imaginative vs. the Imaginary

One trouble with the stock-response version of literary teaching is that this kind of education is performed far more expertly by advertising, especially television commercials. Advertising, being a socially approved form of drug culture, envelops us in an imaginary world, and promises us magical powers within that world enabling us to transcend the world we actually live in. As we grow older, we learn not to take this very seriously, but we acquire the habit of responding to advertising in childhood, and if we simply outgrow it, many of the elements in that response will remain with us. It seems to me that the study of literature should be accompanied, as early as possible, by the study of the rhetorical devices of advertising, propaganda, official releases, news media, and everything else in a citizen's verbal experience that he is compelled to confront but is not (so far in our society) compelled to believe, or say he believes. The rhetorical devices of advertising are easily analysed, and such analysis uncovers a primitive level of verbal response that literature as such cannot reach. In totalitarian states advertising turns into propaganda, and the element of competition, which, along with the separation of economic and political establishments, makes advertising something of an ironic game, disappears. The fact that first rate literature also disappears in totalitarian states is part of the same process.

Literature, as ordinarily conceived, is so small and specialized a part of one's reading that we forget how much of our total verbal experience is untouched by it. For many a student in grade eight whose verbal experience is centered on television, *The Lady of the Lake* may be a pretty meaningless collection of words, something that those unaccountable adults, for whatever reasons of their own, think he should read. The way out of this is not to try to choose the kind of literature that can compete with the appeal of television — no such literature exists. But the teacher should understand that teaching literature means dealing with the total verbal experience of students. The points of contact between literary and subliterary experiences should be kept in mind; obviously the same forms of comedy and romance and irony that appear in literature also turn up in television drama or rock ballads. I am not saying that a teacher should be constantly pointing such resemblances out, only that they are occasionally useful. Far more important, however, is the fact that students are being steadily got at by a rival mythology determined to capture their imaginations for its own purposes, armed with far more skill, authority, and prestige than any teacher has. This is why I think students should be encouraged to become aware of the extent to which they are being conditioned by the mass media, as a central part of their literary training. Some of them have reacted with a general hatred and contempt for everything their society produces, but that, of course, is quite as dependent on conditioned reflex as anything it revolts against. Besides, it does not distinguish between genuine and false forms of social mythology. What is absurd about growing up absurd is adjustment mythology, not society itself.

If I am asked how we should teach, therefore, I should begin by saying that the sense of urgent necessity about learning to read and write should never drop out of the teaching of literature, at any stage. We cannot take part in a society as verbal as ours without knowing how to read and write: but, unless we also learn to read continuously, selectively, and critically, and to write articulately, we can never take any free or independent part in that society. As we gradually become more aware that what we do and believe is the product of a social vision, we can see that this social vision is a product of the imagination. As such, it has been developed by our imaginative experience. Some of this has been formed by literature, but by far the greater part of it has been formed on the subliterary level of mass media and the like. The social importance of literature, in this context, is that it helps us to become aware of the extent to which we are acting out a social mythology. Part of this awareness is in realizing that there is a good deal of it that we don't really believe or respect, but are merely following out of habit and laziness.

When Flaubert wrote *Bouvard and Pecuchet,* an account of two cliché-ridden French bourgeoisie, he also drew up a "Dictionary of Accepted Ideas" to indicate the limitations of their culture. The dictionary arrangement of course conceals the fact that the accepted ideas form a mythology. *Madame Bovary* is much clearer on this point: it shows how Emma Bovary's life was dominated by the shoddy construct that her imagination had built, mainly out of subliterary sources. The people who want to censor everything have got one thing right: they do see that what addresses our imaginations does influence our lives, for good or for evil. But, apart from being mistaken in their tactics, they are nearly always on the side of bad social mythology rather than of genuine literature, and consequently it is genuine literature that they usually want most of all to attack.

## II

Whenever we read anything, whatever it is, we find our attention going in two directions at once. One direction is centrifugal, where we are associating each word we read with our memory of what it conventionally means. We may hardly realize we are doing this, but if we are reading something in a language we barely know, so that we have to look up a word every so often, we soon become aware of how important this direction is. I call it centrifugal because it moves outside what we are reading into our memories, or, if we don't know the word, into dictionaries. At the same time there is a direction of attention going the other way, centripetally, where we are fitting the words in what we are reading together. When Sandburg writes

The fog comes
on little cat feet

we remember what a cat is and what feet are, but we also have to know why these words are brought into a poem about a fog. Meaning is derived from context. The context of the dictionary meaning of *cat* is different from the context in Sandburg's poem, but the meaning of *cat* in that poem is at the point of intersection, so to speak, of the two contexts.

Now, suppose we are reading something specifically for imaginative pleasure, as a poem or story or the like. That means that what we are reading has a special context outside it called, however vaguely, literature. What we are reading is *like* other "literary" things we have read. I gave an example of this a while ago, when we found elements in a Californian Indian story that reminded us of similar things in Greek stories. Whenever we find something in one piece of literature that reminds us irresistibly of something in another piece of literature, we have found what we have been calling an archetype. If a reader who knows very little English has to look up *cat* and *feet* in Sandburg's poem, he will have two useful words in expanding his mastery of the language in general. Similarly, whenever we pursue the likenesses in what we are reading, we are beginning to expand our mastery and knowledge of literature. That is, perhaps, the most distinctive feature of the present programme: that students should be encouraged to pursue the resemblances in what they read.

It may be thought that this practice will require a great deal of erudition. But it should be realized, first of all, that what the teacher of literature is concerned with is the total verbal experience of his students. That includes conversation with families and classmates, movies and television, comic books and advertising. For all important archetypes, a teacher can start wherever his students are, and any question of the "What does this remind you of?" type will soon produce all the examples he can handle for some time. In *Wish and Nightmare* there is a telling of the Jack-the-giant-killer story. If we try this out on a junior high school class (as teachers have done: this is not simply theory), somebody may be reminded of the David and

Goliath story in the Bible or the story of Odysseus and Polyphemus in Homer. But there will also be a flood of analogies from other sources that show how archetypes are not at all confined to what we normally think of as literature. Sergeant York, up against a German platoon. Truman winning an election over Dewey after all the polls and news commentators had decided that it was in the bag for Dewey. Clark Kent turning into Superman. Aspirin defeating Headache in a television commercial. The wise teacher will not reject these as not being literary. They are literary enough to address the imagination, and they are part of the student's total verbal experience. The next question could be: Why is the audience's sympathy usually with Jack rather than the giant? Again there will be no lack of answers. People like to see the little guy win. People like to see brains beat muscles. It's more unexpected and exciting to see the little fellow come on top. Nobody likes bullies. Such answers are not just reflections about life: they are answers that take us deep into the structure of comedy and romance.

We notice that several of the examples given above illustrate some aspects of the archetypes and not others. Some suggestions may be too far away to be very useful, because in literature there is an immense amount of general and vague resemblance. The teacher's experience and guidance come into play in emphasizing the examples that illustrate rather than digress. In the same book there is a story of "Ashpet," or Cinderella. Some students may suggest that Cinderella and Jack are parallel, that Cinderella is really a female Jack. But with a little more discussion it will become clear that the two stories are quite distinct in both structure and feeling, though, of course, they are related within the general area of comic romance. Discovering analogies is fun, but discovering differences provides direction. Accepting the student's verbal experience as it is is the first step in transforming the teacher-student relationship into a common participation in the subject.

Of all the perverted adjustment myths dealt with above, one of the most pervasive is the myth which rationalizes the subordinating of some group of people in society. In Victorian times, for example, women were made the focus of certain anxieties. Their sensibilities, which were assumed to be exceedingly delicate, formed an imaginary criterion for society's constant dread of an unregulated sexual instinct, and for the enforcing of social standards connected with that dread, such as those which were assumed in the censorship of books. We remember Podsnap in Dickens's *Our Mutual Friend,* and his appeal to the blushing cheeks of the young person. Podsnap was not alone: even Tennyson could be seriously praised for never having written a line that would distress a sensitive female. This was part of a social code of allegedly sheltering and protecting the delicate sex from the rougher facts of life, in the middle class at any rate. But on the excuse of protecting womanhood, women were deprived of equal participation in society, not allowed to vote, or even to own property after they were married. We may look also at the way that blacks used to be treated in a good deal of popular white literature, as comic-strip characters who were generally good-natured and lovable, but not very strong on intellect. The implication of such writing was that, blacks being naturally just happy children, they wouldn't worry too much about being excluded from full participation in society. It looks as though the instinct to patronize and the instinct to exploit are rather closely related. This is not hard to see in, for instance, the African and Asian colonies developed by western powers during the nineteenth century: it has taken a little longer to understand how disastrous the working of such complacent mythologies in our own society can be.

It is most important to realize that we have been applying a very similar mythology to young people for the last three or four generations at least, and that the results have been equally explosive. The motive has been not so much exploitation as the dramatizing of an aspect of the social mythology referred to above. We remember that that mythology contained a pastoral, or primal-Paradise, myth. When people become adults, old enough to vote and hold jobs, they become involved in a social rat race, full of cares and worries and responsibilities. When they look back to their childhood, they reconstruct it as a world which was happier because it had less responsibility. Children, then, should be protected from the adult world as long as possible: why make them old before their time? School is there to keep them off the streets not only physically but mentally: the young should be in a special preserved world, like the Garden of Eden before the Fall. Most innocent worlds, including the Garden of Eden, are presexual worlds, hence books for younger people, especially schoolbooks, have to be ruthlessly, even hysterically, censored to remove any trace of a specific reference to the way that human life keeps going. Nobody is fool enough actually to believe that a young person's life is sexless, but books for the young have for a long time been expurgated as though this were true, in order to preserve the myth for the reassurance of adults.

## Genuine Literature for Real People

"Adolescence," in short, is not really a process that young people must all go through. A great deal of it is really a deliberate creation of adult social anxieties. In order to maintain the adult dream of a happy clean world of fun-loving middle-class children, we have to assume that a person takes twenty-odd years to grow into a genuine human being. During this period, everything he is "not ready for" should be kept from him, which in practice tends to mean that all genuine education should be postponed as long as possible, as explained above. Whatever is socially undesirable, such as violence, is also to be kept from him, on the theory , if that is the word, that if he never reads about violence it cannot occur to him to become violent. Sex and violence, therefore, come to be associated with adult books, the books one reads outside of school or after one has finished school, which is a major reason why the popular taste in reading, and entertainment generally, whether adolescent or adult, is so prurient and sadistic. I think a little more emphasis on genuine literature in school might make this tendency less automatic.

It is, of course, quite as easy for young people as it has been for women and blacks to see through the trick. They realize that what all the coddling and permissiveness really means is exclusion from serious social issues, and from any real participation in society. What is important is not so much to keep them in school as to keep them off the labor market. An overproductive economy would like to turn all children, as it would like to turn all women, into full-time consumers. And no matter how much "citizenship" young people may study, or how much they may learn about democratic processes, the fundamentally anti-democratic attitude of protection which surrounds them from infancy nullifies all this, and throws them on the world expecting more protection. This issue, which has always been serious, has reached a crisis with the coming of television. In an age of electronic media it is no use going on with the pretence that young people in their teens can be kept in a world by themselves. As we have already seen during the past few years, people who have no social function quickly get bored, and boredom leads to smashing things.

Although the literature programme is addressed to a specific age level, and uses material appropriate to that level, it does not condescend to its readers. There is no feeling of "this is all you are ready for at present" hanging around it. This programme covers the same area that adult literature covers, including the tragic and the ironic, not a special preserve fenced off within it. There are also stories by and about black and Indian groups indicating that American society and middle-class white American society are not the same thing. What the young student is "not ready for" may be more complex, like the later novels of Henry James or the poetry of Wallace Stevens, but it is not different in kind. Whatever else he reads, at the same time or later, can be seen to be continuous with what is presented to him here. Anyone, at any time of life, may become demoralized by the sense that the world is very different from what he had been told it was. But no teacher wants to feel involved in a process of systematically lying to young people. And while no book can be ideal, even for a single reader, I think that the books in this programme are the ones that students themselves will respond to eagerly. Some people may object to exposing "our children" to so many serious, even tragic and ironic, themes, and some may believe that children should be taught, in effect, nothing except what they cannot help discovering for themselves, hence such material as these books present is fantastically difficult. The difficulty is for them, not the students, and consists of panic and mental block, not of anything actually in the books.

## The Authority of the Subject

The title of a book in the programme already available is *Wish and Nightmare*. The title is significant in itself of the change which has come over social assumptions in the last generation. We understand better now how much "nightmare" comes into life at every age. Nightmares enter the life of the youngest child, to such an extent that it is no good trying to remove them from his experience, for nightmare is not something presented to us from outside: it is something that our own minds construct. The sound of children at play is often regarded, by those bemused with the paradisal myth of childhood, as the sound of the purest and most innocent happiness, but anyone who listens carefully to it, and to the amount of hysteria and aggression in it, can see that the facts of life are otherwise. The way to deal with nightmare, educationally, is not to pretend that it is not or need not be there, or, as in some of the more brutal movies and thrillers, to force it on us on the pretext that "society is involved with it," but to present it in its real context, the context of irony, where it can be seen with detachment, as the vision we must have of the world that we don't want.

As for "wish" we have also discovered that that is a far more powerful element in life than we used to think. Wishing used to be thought of as a natural but helpless reaction against "reality," including in that term both the objective world of nature and certain social conditions that men have made themselves. But clearly anything that men have made can be unmade by other men, and in the last few years there has been a dramatic development of the sense that wishing can be a concrete and revolutionary force: that we don't have to live with the mistakes of the past if we don't want to. Again, this feeling need not take the form of a querulous pseudoradical demand for everything to be much better right away, or some vague hope that an inspired political leader will somehow put everything right, but should be studied in its proper context, the context of comedy, or the vision of how desire is not always frustrated by reality, but is sometimes strong enough to transform reality, and force things to turn out better than habit and inertia had expected.

If we ask whom we should teach, then, the beginning of the answer is that we teach mainly young people, but we teach them as people and not as a special kind of people. Still less do we teach them as half-developed people who must be kept away from what real people, that is, adults, talk about. This sounds obvious to the verge of being offensive, but the implications of the attitude go a little farther. The emphasis on teaching by personal relationships has much that is good in it, along with much that is merely addled, if well-meaning. While many things can bring teacher and students together personally, only one thing can ever *equalize* them, and that is the authority of the subject being taught. In relation to the subject being taught the teacher is also a student, and so the difference between teacher and students is at a minimum. The role of teacher vis-à-vis the students has its embarrassing aspects for both, and every genuine moment of insight in a classroom carries with it a sense of momentary relief from that embarrassment. When either teacher or students dominate a classroom, there are, of course, likely to be very few such moments. When they do occur, they are moments when the one real authority in the classroom is supreme over both, and everyone is united in the vision of its power.

## The Reality of Metaphor

The student of literature is continually being brought back to the passage in Shakespeare's *Midsummer Night's Dream* in which Duke Theseus classifies poets with lunatics and lovers as being "of imagination all compact." These three groups are, in the first place, the only people who can take metaphor seriously. The "lunatic" is normally obsessed by some kind of identification, usually of himself with something or someone else; lovers desire, in Sir Thomas Browne's phrase, "to be truly each other," the poets assert, or seem to be asserting, like Lady Lowzen in Wallace Steven's poem "Oak Leaves Are Hands," that what is is other things. We notice that this progression moves from the negative through the playful to the positive. The same thing is true of another characteristic of these three groups: that they seem to be unable to distinguish fiction from fact. The lunatic, that is, anyone so disturbed mentally or emotionally that he needs help in managing his own affairs, is the prisoner of his own fictions, which he insists on substituting for the world he is in. The fiction need not be his own creation: anyone who believed advertising literally, for example, would be for all practical purposes a lunatic. Whenever a social mythology is accepted as something beyond criticism, it becomes a fiction or construct taken as fact, and so creates a form of social neurosis. The neurosis may be mild, as it is when criticism and dissent are still tolerated, or acute, as it is when they are suppressed. Here again, the confusion between fiction and fact is negative: one is unable to recognize either or any distinction between them. We move into a more playful area with the lover: if he asserts that he loves the most wonderful girl in the world, we recognize that some illusions are not only more important than some realities, but may also be truer in the context of personal truth.

When the poet presents us with a work of fiction, and insists, again, that if not literal fact it is still truer than fact, he is giving us the positive side of the identifying of the two. He also raises a good many questions that are harder to answer than they look. The traditional, common-sense view is that literature is an imitation of life, or reality, or nature, of whatever we may think of as outside it, and owes what truth it has to its relation to whatever is not literature. The reversed thesis of Oscar Wilde's *Decay of Lying*, that life imitates literature, and is not real life unless it resembles a literary form, is more recent, but is something much more than just the clever paradox it seems to be. We notice, for example, that we are continually playing roles in society. We are reading by ourselves, let us say: a friend comes in to talk to us, and we instantly throw ourselves into the social role suggested by his presence. Or we decide to maintain a certain public attitude, say in politics, and find that everything we say, or even believe, is being carefully selected by ourselves to fit the role demanded by that attitude. Some psychologists call this role-playing aspect of ourselves a *persona* or mask. But, as the soliloquies of Hamlet remind us, we dramatize ourselves to ourselves, and the mask never really comes off. At present there is a great vogue for "unstructured" personal encounters in which it is believed that we can get past the persona to our "real" attitudes. But there are no real attitudes of this kind: there is never anything under a persona except another persona. It follows that we spend our entire lives playing roles, and are never in any situation which is not to some degree a structured and dramatic situation.

The feeling that there is a "real" self underneath the persona is a tribute to something important, however. It is part of sanity to be aware that we are playing roles, and a part of our larger freedom to understand what shape those roles have, and why we are adopting them. Looking over some of the books I have been reading recently, I find a book on existential philosophy that said, in effect," the human situation is tragic," a book on religion (by Kierkegaard) that said, in effect, "God is ironic," and a book on Marxism that said, in effect," the historical process is a romantic comedy." It is clear that the study of literature has a good deal of usefulness in clarifying such attitudes: none of the authors seemed to realize that his argument was also a literary fiction. Poets are often more versatile. Socrates devoted his life mainly to ironic roles, and Byron to romantic ones, yet Byron wrote satire and Socrates fought with great courage in battle: they were not prisoners of their roles.

The fallacy about the "real self" is of a different kind, and important for our conception of education. Most of us are brought up in a half-baked Rousseauism which makes the individual prior to society. On this theory, tne more we explore the hidden or suppressed parts of ourselves, the deeper we are getting into the individual, and the closer we come to the real core of him. But clearly we belong socially before we are individually: if we are born twentieth-century middle-class white Americans, for example, that context is given us long before birth. Below the social comes the generic, what we share with all other human beings. If I know the intimate details of another's sex life, I know only something that is generic about him; if I glimpse his suppressed resentments and aggressions, I see only the aspect of him that can become part of a mob. Individuality is the visible part of the iceberg, the last part of ourselves to be achieved. Our opinions on poetry, music, religion, politics; our relations with one another that deserve the names of friendship or love — these are the things that are individual about us. Individuality, which is the condition of freedom, is never achieved without some genuine form of education. There are of course many forms of that outside the schools, but still there is infinitely more reality, and infinitely more to be discovered about our real selves, in encounter groups with Shakespeare or Milton or Tolstoy than merely with one another.

## Relevance to What?

What I have been trying to explain is, to use a vulgarized word in what for me is something close to its proper sense, the "relevance" of teaching literature. Relevance implies a relation to something else, but the question of what relevance is relevant to is often not raised. It seems to me obvious that any subject taught and studied is a part of the whole of human life, and its relevance is to that wholeness. There is no such thing as inherent or built-in relevance; no subject is relevant in itself, because every field of knowledge is equally the centre of all knowledge. Relevance is a quality which teachers and students alike bring to a subject of study, and it consists in a vision of the human possibilities connected with that subject. Some subjects, such as car-driving, are obviously and immediately useful; for those that are not, such as the arts and sciences, the question of usefulness moves from an actual into a potential world. They are useful for living a genuinely human life, but of course one can neither prove that a genuinely human life is better than other kinds, or that a certain programme of study will necessarily enable one to live it. Teaching is not magic, and it would be a very impudent or self-deceived charlatan who would assert that if we only teach literature properly, certain social benefits are bound to follow. Still, a sense of the worth-whileness of what he is doing is what keeps a teacher going, and surely that sense should be made as specific as possible. If he teaches science, he is trying also to teach intellectual honesty, accuracy, the importance of relying on evidence rather than authority, and the courage to face results that may be negative or unwelcome. If he teaches history, he is trying also to teach the dimension of consciousness that only the sense of continuity with the past can give, the absence of which makes society as senile as loss of memory does the individual. If he is teaching literature, he is trying also to teach the ability to be aware of one's imaginative social vision, and so to escape the prison of unconscious social conditioning. Whatever he is teaching, he is teaching some aspect of the freedom of man.

I have put so much emphasis on the social function of literature because, in my experience, it is very little understood. In an age when silliness, or, more politely, absurdity, is sometimes thought to be an attribute of genuine vision, it is not surprising to hear some people say that all teaching of literature is an "establishment's" effort to impose a fool's paradise of imaginary values on the rest of society. One may see this to be nonsense and still not be able to formulate a social role for literature beyond the orbit of refined leisure-class amusement. But even if we do recognize its social role, we know that the real answer to any question about why we teach it does not lie in its relevance, or its social by-products. Some subjects, like car-driving again, are a means to an end; the arts and sciences are not. Studying them is a process which is its own end, and exists for its own sake. Its products are incidental, and the usefulness of those products does not represent the value of the process, which is something quite apart from them.

In literature there is much to admire, but the end of literary study is not admiration of something remote, but the recognition that it corresponds to something within ourselves. Admiration is thus succeeded by possession, as we make what we read part of our own vision, and understand something of its function in shaping that vision. So far, it is true that education has been for the sake of the student: one wants literature to be something he can appropriate, and its study a process of transferring its power of vision to him. It is often said that there is no disinterested learning process for its own sake; that every such process is conditioned by the society it is in. Hence all scholarship is in a sense political: if it claims to be disinterested, it is really only defending the status quo. This is another way of saying that all our beliefs and actions take shape around a social vision constructed by the imagination. The important thing is to realize that no social vision is ever definitive; there is always more outside it. The circle of stories (or ocean of story, as it is called in India) is there to keep us continually expanding and reshaping that vision. It exists for us; it exists for itself; perhaps we may even feel, for a few moments in our lives, that it really is ourselves on an infinite plane.

**Definitions**

*Ritual* is a special human action maintaining rapport with the natural cycle.
*Symbol* is a unit of poetic meaning.
*Myth* unites ritual and symbol, giving action to thought and meaning to action.
*Mythology* is a set of myths that take root in a particular society. The most fully developed mythologies form an imaginative encyclopedia providing answers to questions of the deepest concern to society.
The *narrative patterns* of literature represent the absorption of ritual action into literature.
The symbols of literature recurring in different works of literature are called *archetypes*.
Literature shows various degrees of *displacement* of myths in the direction of the plausible, the moral or the "real."
*Literature* is the total body of stories and symbols that provides hypotheses or models of human behaviour and experience. The central story of all literature is the loss and regaining of *identity*.

New York, Harcourt, Brace Jovanovich, 1972.

# Criticism as Education

It is a great pleasure to be here and to inaugurate this series of lectures in honour of a distinguished educator. I was in some doubt in my mind as to just what path to take: true, I rather rashly joined a committee on children's literature, but I have not yet been able to attend a meeting of it, so I feel that I have not been properly instructed in the subject. On the other hand, I did not begin to believe in my own critical theories until I began to see ways of applying them to elementary education. In a book published over twenty years ago, I wrote that literature is not a coherent subject at all unless its elementary principles could be explained to any intelligent nineteen-year-old. Since then, Buckminster Fuller has remarked that unless a first principle can be grasped by a six-year-old, it is not really a first principle, and perhaps his statement is more nearly right than mine. My estimate of the age at which a person can grasp the elementary principles of literature has been steadily going down over the last twenty years. So I am genuinely honored to be able to pay tribute to an educator who has always insisted on the central importance of childrens' literature.

The teaching of literature has certain problems peculiar to our particular state of society. There were many good reasons for separating church and state in American life, but of course one inevitable consequence was the creating of a kind of religious vacuum. In that vacuum education became a kind of denatured religion. That aspect of education increased in the proportion to which the church and home continued to abdicate more and more responsibility to the schools. So I have often been asked, quite seriously and by adults, that if the study of literature is supposed to make you a better person, why doesn't it?

My original answer to this question was "who supposes this?" But I found that it was understood to be my colleagues. They had, or were assumed to have, some hazy notion that scientists studied the mere mechanics of things, whereas they were the ones who had values and the elements that really made for fuller human life. So, very early in my contemplation of these problems, I came up against what I still think of as the magic potion fallacy. I had to make it clear to myself, as well as to anyone who would listen, that nothing good inheres in any subject of education as such. If somebody wants to be a better person, there is plenty of literature that will certainly help; but if there is no "want", the engine has no gas.

This fact, in turn, connected with my lurking distrust of value judgments as the distinguishing aspect of a literary education. It was clear to me that value judgments were really disguised moral judgments: consequently they were socially conditioned. Being socially conditioned, they had a limitation in them that did not extend to the central thing that literature is about. Bringing value judgments, either explicitly or implicitly, into the classroom strikes me as a dangerous procedure, and invokes a tricky analogy with the school cafeteria, in making a distinction between that awful tasting stuff that's so good for you and that junk food that you like. It seemed to me that students' likes and dislikes should be approached rather differently. If a student prefers the movie he saw on television to the play of Shakespeare he has to study, the emphasis should fall on the structural analogies between the two works, on the assumption that while the difference in value will eventually become clear to him, the perception of it cannot be hurried or forced. There is such a thing as value in literature, certainly, but a work of literature establishes its own value. What we really mean by such terms as "classic" and "masterpiece" are fundamentally works of literature that insist on their value, and refuse to go away.

I can understand why Matthew Arnold, a century ago, took so seriously the conception of literature as a denatured religion. He felt that culture would come to occupy the place in our lives that religion formerly did. When I was a graduate student, T.S. Eliot was the dominating force in criticism: he dismissed Arnold's confusion of culture and religion as nonsense, which I think it is, but he went on playing the old value game. It seemed to me that something more pragmatic and more connected with the learning process needed to be invoked. It has often been said, when I have attacked the undue reliance on value judgments, that after all I write a great deal more about Shakespeare than I do about, say, Thomas Churchyard or Barnabe Googe. Doesn't that imply a value judgment? Of course it does: that is where value judgments ought to be, in the area of tentative working assumptions, where they can be subjected to revision.

The revision is nearly always a revision upwards. If I accept society's traditional value judgment on Shakespeare and begin the study of Shakespeare, I find only that that value judgment is confirmed in practice. That helps encourage me to continue, but the study itself is not founded on the value judgment. On the other hand, it often happens that a poet who has been ridiculed or neglected for centuries, such as Skelton in the early sixteenth century, may turn out, to a fresh eye, to be an extremely interesting and original poet. And just as value judgments are not the beginning of the literary process, so they cannot be the end of it. The end of the study of literature is not an act of genuflection in front of a masterpiece, but the incorporation into the student's mind of the articulateness which literature represents. That is a devious and subtle process, I know, but none the less I feel quite sure about the validity of the general process involved. The final aim of studying works of literature is, in some way, the absorbing of their verbal power into oneself.

There are also a number of confusions in the theory of education which are hangovers from a class-structured society. Compulsory education assumed a leisure class on top and a working class underneath, and it sought to extend the benefits of what the leisure class had in the way of education to everyone else, to the whole of society. That was benevolent enough, but it eventually raised a second question, and a rather more difficult one to answer. If the study of literature is supposed to give you a better job or a better social status, why doesn't it?

Again, the answer is that the change from a closed class system to an open class system is not a simple or a one-way process. Some months ago, I found myself in Italy, in something of a dream state, in Urbino, the home town of Castiglione, and lecturing on Castiglione's *Courtier,* which I have always regarded as one of the supremely great textbooks on education as well as one of the most beautiful books in the world. It is a book written at roughly the same time and in much the same environment as Machiavelli's *Prince*. In Renaissance society the most important social facts were the prince and the courtier, so it was natural that two seminal works of the period should have these titles. Renaissance education took as a theoretical model the ideal education of the king, because the king was the most important person in society to get educated. This had produced a genre among educational treatises which had come down from Greek times with Xenophon's *Cyropedia,* the account of the training of Cyrus the Great, and it was still a very active form in the sixteenth century.

This cyropedia form splits in two with Machiavelli's treatment of the prince and Castiglione's of the courtier. There is a curious tension between the two books which is still central in our educational confusions today. Machiavelli's prince is a person for whom moral principles are something of an inhibition, in short, hangups. He has to remember that the people over whom he rules are animals as well as men, and have the animal qualities that he himself needs to rule them, the ferocity of the lion and the cunning of the fox. As the prince is constantly on view, his reputation, or what we should call his image, is much more important than the reality behind that image. It is good for the prince to be reputed virtuous, much more important than for him to be virtuous. It is essential for the prince to be reputed liberal, though he is probably more sensible if he saves his money.

Castiglione, on the other hand, stresses an educational programme for the courtier plunging into all the arts: painting, sculpture, music, and literature, but on an amateur level, in order to give glamour to the prince's court and to be an advisor to the prince. These two aims run into certain paradoxes. If the courtier is to be the advisor of the prince, he should be an older man with experience; but if he is to cut a dash as a musician or poet or cavalry officer, he has to be a young man. And if he teaches the prince moral principles, is he not reducing him simply to the rank of a justice of the peace? One can only answer these problems today by remembering that in our society every man contains his own prince and his own courtier. The education of the prince in Machiavelli is the pattern for the education of the will, the tradition of which culminates, perhaps, in Nietzsche. The importance of Dewey in the history of educational theory is mainly in the emphasis he laid on the education of the will, on the active or performing force in man, as distinct from the more contemplative virtues which have been more traditional in teaching.

Similarly, the education of the courtier represents the education of leisure class virtues, but the phrase "leisure class" makes very little sense now. One rather suspects that the phrase "working class" would not make much sense either, if it were not a holdover from an earlier phase of society. Work and leisure are different aspects of the same person (according to the Bible they are even different aspects of the activity of God, in a ratio of six to one). Traditionally, there has been a lurking analogy between the hierarchy in society and that in the human body, in which the brain, the directing force and the power behind vision, corresponded to the leisure class which was "on top" in society. But even this had been questioned for a long time. In Shakespeare's *Coriolanus* there is what amounts to a civil war in Rome between the patricians and the plebeians. One of the patricians attempts to rationalize their ascendancy in society by telling the fable of the belly and the members. The members of the body rebel against the belly which, they say, does nothing but sit there and absorb food; but they soon find that they cannot get along with the belly. The moral of the fable is that the leisure class is not really parasitic; it is a digestive force in society. But if it is digestive, then, unless my anatomy is very mistaken, it is not the brain of society. Neither in work nor in leisure, nor in any precedents in the classes with which they were formerly associated, can we find the controlling vision which is, as I think, the real driving force in education and the one to which literature is centrally connected.

The ideals of our society are, I think, still the same revolutionary ideals of liberty, equality and fraternity. Liberty and equality have become mass movements in our day, but the third one, fraternity, the sense of personal relationships, is one that has been largely ignored. Yet it seems to me that it is an ideal very deeply involved in all forms of humanistic education, where all knowledge is ultimately personal knowledge. Although one may plunge into impersonal scholarship for a while, one has finally to come out on the other side with some kind of personal absorption of what one has learned.

Over against the individual whose knowledge has become personalized is society itself. It is, I think, an essential educational principle that the morale of society is more important than its morality. It is, of course, much better if you can have both, but, if society believes in its values, it can function with some efficiency even if some of those values are wrong. Consequently, the clichés of forty years ago, about "starting education where the child is" and "the whole child goes to school", need reshaping in view of the individual's actual relation to society. You can't start education where the child is; the child isn't anywhere. The whole child doesn't go to school because he is not a whole child or he wouldn't be in school. The first step in education, in other words, is acquiring, or rather recreating, the sense of one's social context. We all belong to something long before we are anything. We were predestined to be mid-twentieth century middle-class North Americans before we escaped from the womb.

The elementary forms of education have much to do with rediscovering this fact, a fact which by itself leads to adjustment, to docility and to obedience. Learning to read on the elementary level is fundamentally an act of responding passively to a verbal stimulus. That is, the essential or primary reason for learning to read is to learn how to respond to traffic signals and the like. It is because the demands of society are prior to the needs of the individual that literacy is a social requirement. If we can read and write, the first use we make of this skill is to discover what society expects us to do . There has been a good deal of repetition of the phrase "back to basics" in Toronto during the last few months. I distrust all slogans that begin with the phrase "back to" because I suspect that they derive from some kind of pastoral myth, like the little red schoolhouse, where "back to" meant something fairly specific. Again, these "basics" are the things that society primarily demands from its citizens. That is why the study of literature can be shunted off to one side in favour of things like "language arts" or "language skills". The difficulty with such phrases is that there are many language skills, which are in quite different compartments, each with conventions so different from one another that they are not transferable. A poet or novelist cannot immediately start to write advertising copy or good journalism without some training in the specific conventions of advertising or journalism.

The educational process begins with continuity, or with what in the Middle Ages was called *habitus*. At that time a person who could read Latin was said to be a person who had the "habit" of Latin. There can be no education without the kind of creative continuity that goes with incessant practice. But this right and essential continuity gets mixed up with another kind which is far less legitimate. This is the continuity of instinctive conservatism, or what I call the anxiety of continuity in society, the desire to keep going with the same things as far as possible without change. It is, I think, largely because of the anxiety of continuity that education acquired, for so many centuries, that curiously penal quality which sometimes made it a positive hell on earth for young people. Education that depends on punishment and terror goes with the authority of seniors, the tried and tested way, the primitive notion of wisdom in which the wise man is the man who does what society has found to be the right thing, and in which the fool is the man with the new idea which always turns out to be an old fallacy.

One of the most popular stories in the later Biblical period is the story of Ahiqar (the spelling varies), an elderly man who was betrayed by his wicked young nephew but was subsequently brought back into favour by his king. He then took his revenge on his nephew by reciting to him several hundred proverbs, largely connected with the undesirability of ingratitude to one's elders. The nephew began to say he thought he had got the point, but Ahiqar kept on placidly reciting more proverbs until, so the text says, the nephew blew up and burst. This was an immensely popular tale echoed in the fables of Aesop, in the Bible and the Apocrypha, in the Koran. With a story like that you can't miss, from the point of view of conservative wisdom, because the senior man is the hero and we have a sense of the customary thing being upheld and re-established.

The anxiety of continuity is really an anxiety of hoping never to meet a situation in which there is a dialectical conflict. In modern society it is entirely impossible to do that, so we have to educate in a way that provides for the possibility of such conflict. Dialectical conflict implies, among other things, a group of individuals who have grown out of the social body, not to the point of breaking with it, but to the point of seeing it in proportion. We belong to something first; we are something afterwards, and the individual grows out of the group and not the other way round. But it is the group of individuals linked in the fraternity of social vision that constitutes the real brain of society. Society by itself can hardly distinguish the visionary who is above its standards from the criminal or lunatic who is below them. The social vision I am speaking of, the real directing force in society, is one which is aware of its own social conditioning but is not wholly imprisoned by it.

I have always been deeply impressed by a poem by Wallace Stevens called "Description Without Place". He points out that man does not live directly and nakedly in nature as the animals do. Man lives inside a kind of insulating envelope of his own construction which we call culture or civilization. It is the verbal aspect of this culture which concerns us here. This verbal aspect is what I think of as a mythology, a body of words which contains literature, or the products of verbal imagination, and provides the context for each work of literature within it. But there are many layers of this verbal mythology. Being a transparent envelope between us and nature, it may, in its earlier stages, make statements about nature, and so be a primitive form of science. So far as it does so, however, it is eventually displaced by real science, which is designed to study nature directly, as geology, astronomy and biology displaced the mythology of creation. But this does not affect its importance as a structure of human creation, made up of human hopes and anxieties and fears. This is what is encapsulated in our literature, and is what constitutes the distinctively human part of the world we live in.

In early stages of language we get a strong sense of the word as a power in itself, as something that may have a magic force uniting consciousness and nature. Warriors will begin battles with boasts because they may be words of power for them. For the same reason the gods of Greek mythology are extremely nervous about people who start boasting: they are afraid that they may get hold of the words of power which will threaten their authority. In the language of Homer, such words as time or motion or courage or thought or anything that sounds in the least abstract is strictly connected with parts of the body or with physical images. The word *kairos*, which came to mean a specific moment in time, originally meant the notch of an arrow. Such language is totally concrete: there are no true abstractions, and in this stage of language there is little sense of the separation of subject and object. This kind of language is succeeded by other approaches to language, such as the metaphysical constructs from Plato and Aristotle down to Kant and Hegel, and by the descriptive and defining language of our day. Yet the metaphorical structures thrown up by primitive societies are just as subtle and powerful as the constructs that succeeded them. I think it is particularly Lévi-Strauss in our own time who has insisted upon the importance of this, and its importance for childrens' literature, which to some extent recapitulates the primitive experience, can hardly be overestimated.

It is the function of literature, as I see it, to recreate the primitive conception of the word of power, the metaphor that unites the subject and the object. Such metaphor flies in the face of the contemporary use of language which implies a rigid separation of subject and object and calls for a descriptive accuracy in the use of words. There is nothing wrong with this use of language either, but other kinds must not be ignored. That means, among other things, that within our present attitude to language some words have lost their meaning. The words God or soul or spirit mean nothing in a world where words have to be specifically objective if they are to mean anything. Nietzsche's phrase "God is dead", which has received so much acclaim even in theological circles, is really a specialized linguistic observation extended to other areas. It means essentially that God is dead as the subject of a predicate. That is, if we ask "is there a God?" the answer, if it is in terms of the language we customarily use, can only be no, because any question beginning with the words "is there" is, so to speak, an ungodly question.

I spoke of various layers of our mythological envelope. The innermost layer is a phony mythology, made up of prejudice and gossip and the shallow and superficial reactions that inform so much casual conversation. This is the aspect of verbal mythology which is conveyed through advertising and propaganda. The distinction between reality and illusion is one of the most important activities that we use words for, and, as advertising and propaganda are designed deliberately to create an illusion, it follows that they form, in a sense, a kind of anti-language. Their effect on the modern world has been analyzed by, for example, Roland Barthes in *Mythologies* and by Marshall McLuhan in *The Mechanical Bride*.

Beyond this layer of phony mythology, prejudice and cliché comes the serious mythology, or genuine social vision; the vision that makes us believe in things like democracy and liberty to the point of being ready to fight and die for them. On this level I think we might relax our fever over the word "indoctrination", because I keep coming back to my principle that only a society that believes in its own values can really educate. I notice a tendency among people of my own generation to nag younger people on the grounds that they are much too indifferent and apathetic. They say: when I was young I was very radical, taking nothing for granted and questioning all established values — I think. Why can't you be the way I was? But what was radical and questionable thirty and forty years ago has changed its social role by this time, and this whole approach seems to me to be an arrogant misuse of seniority. It is little good questioning values if what you need at the moment are a few answers, however tentative and inadequate they may be. We are surrounded by various forms of verbal illusion, and the genuine magic that inheres in the metaphors of poetry and the words of power is sometimes replaced by the degenerate magic of vogue or cliché words.

I was recently attached to a government commission in Ottawa, and the chairman, who was a distinguished humanist, was reading a directive from higher up in the civil service. Being a humanist, he was unable to understand gobbledygook, and said helplessly: "what are we supposed to do with this?" I said: "it's very simple; we just establish our parameters and keep our interface clean." This is an example of the use of vogue words thought at one time to have some special clarity about them. But the clarity has gone dead, just as a cliché is often a fossilized epigram where the wit has gone dead. All ways of using words fall under the general educational law that they are powers to be acquired and developed by continuous practice. That is true of thinking, for example. One cannot think at random: how well one will think at any given moment will, like playing the piano, depend entirely upon how much of it one has already done. The resistance to continuity on the part of a good many muddled educational theorists has created another social vacuum, which is partly filled by things like meditation cults, where there is no argument about the necessity for regular practice and continuity. People will undergo a degree of discipline in studying yoga, zen, or transcendental meditation which undoubtedly surprises themselves. The only trouble with this from the educational point of view is that so much of it stops with tuning the instrument, rather than going on to take part in the social vision that I spoke of as the community of fraternity.

In the sciences there is a curious factor which we may call a factor of alienation. It was a wonderful achievement when mythological space, which put a fixed earth at the centre of the universe, was replaced by the scientific space brought in by Copernicus and, more effectively, Galileo. It was a wonderful achievement when the mythological time that started with a creation in 4000 B.C. was replaced by the scientific time brought in by Lyell and Darwin. Yet there is in science also the realization that man is essentially unrelated to the world of nature, except through his own mythological envelope. We live in a world that got along without us for billions of years, and could still get along without us, in fact still may. When this fact penetrates the public consciousness, a kind of alienation develops. If we go into paperback bookshops, we see rows of books on out-of-body experiences, reincarnation, telekinesis, survival of death, space ships arriving in the past, and the like, invariably described in the blurbs as utterly shattering to orthodox notions of science. Whatever the validity of any of these subjects in themselves, I think their attraction for the public has something to do with the sense of an intellectual holiday, of the mind breaking free of the laws of nature into a more uninhibited form of speculation. This is not hard to understand in a world so rigidly split as ours is into subject and object. The word "subject" means two things, an observer, and a person subordinated to a ruler or to society, as when we say that one is a British or American subject. It seems to me that cannot separate these two meanings. The modern mind "subjects" itself to the world: it crawls under it, like Atlas. Perhaps that is why we use that very curious word "understanding" to describe our attitude to nature.

In all this what is not objective soon becomes clear. The world of the observer observing the observed is too simple; the observer himself becomes a factor in the observation. The social sciences in fact are founded on the principle of observing the observer. So what is left that is subjective? It seems to me that man is subjective to the extent to which he participates in the community of the essential languages of mankind, starting with the verbal language of literature, but including mathematics and the languages of the other arts. Just as his relation to nature is under law and the conception of necessity, so his role in the participating community of observers is his heritage of freedom.

In the educational process we can reach no more elementary level than the level of coming to terms with the panic of time. A child of four is just as aware of the ticking of the clock as a man of eighty. The sense of relaxing the mind and the body, of making time for receptivity, seems to me to have a most important role to play in education from earliest childhood. That is why the most elementary forms of literary education, learning and chanting nursery rhymes, listening to stories, singing together, and the like, are so important as a way of relaxing this sense of panic. Joining a community, whether it is a singing community or a listening community, leads to realizing that literature is first of all something anchored in the body, something connected with dancing and singing, something which one's whole being must respond to. A literature cut off at the neck is not a literature at all. Reading whatever is worth reading cannot be hurried, because what we have to do is to take possession of it, absorb its power, and that will take time. We must not worry about the time, but let it soak in. If rushed or directed by too active a will, the process collapses.

I have been asked a good many times if it is true that if a man knows the 1611 Bible and Shakespeare, he is an educated man whatever else he may or may not know. I usually distrust the kind of assumptions that are behind such questions; nevertheless, it is perhaps worth remembering that these two great pinnacles of English literature are both primarily involved with speech. The reason why the 1611 Bible held the market against all comers for so many centuries was not the scholarly quality of translation, but the fact that its translators had an infallible ear for the spoken word. What is said on the title page of the King James Bible, "appointed to be read in churches", is the key to its supremacy. It is based on the spoken word, and the spoken word comes out of the human body. And what is true of the 1611 Bible is even more obviously true of Shakespeare's plays, which were intended to be acted and spoken on the stage. Literary education proceeds by intertwining a speaking style and writing style. No written style will be any good unless it is based on a good speaking style, which in turn means that a good speaking style must develop too. The usual schizophrenia in which we get "oral" composition on a level of sub-language not far removed from the orang-utang, and a written language of composition so dead that it sounds like something transcribed from Linear B, is not very close to that interplay of good speech and good writing which is the civilized use of words.

In the study of literature there is a historical factor, and in that factor there is a paradox. The plays of Shakespeare, let us say, meant something to his own time and his own audience; they also mean something, and something rather different, to us. We have to recognize both these facts and make some kind of bridge between them. If we ignore the fact that they are seventeenth-century productions addressed to a very different society from ours with very different assumptions, then we are simply kidnapping them into our own world of values. If we ignore their relevance to us and study them simply as seventeenth-century productions, they remain icons, or more accurately idols, set up to be admired but not to be incorporated into our own experience. The connecting of the two, the historical context and the contemporary context, is a process of what I can only think of as a process of continuing recreation.

There are many paradoxes raised in critical theory today, some of them very intricate. Where is the test, and what is a text? What is the reader doing when he reads, or the writer when he writes? How many masks intervene between the writer and the reader? One can easily get lost in these labyrinths, and I think one needs the conception of recreation to make sense of such problems. Everything that we read we recreate into our own orbits; that is, to some degree every reading is a translation. Even if we are reading a personal letter from a friend we are still translating it into our own forms of experience. Criticism, as I see it, is really the shaping of a central tradition of recreation. I say a central tradition because there are peripheral readers, critics who are crackpots or whose recreations we cannot accept. In the study of Shakespeare, Johnson, Coleridge and Bradley are as useful as ever, but Ignatius Donnelly, who decided that the Folio contained a scandalous court history which could be extracted by cryptograms, remains a crank.

I remember coming across a remark in the great Chinese Taoist philosopher Chuang Tse, who says "nine things out of ten that I say are metaphors; seven things out of ten are illustrations of valued writers". He goes on to say "a person who is not fitted to precede is not in the way of human life". It seems to me impossible to improve on that statement: each of us is engaged in the process of preceding posterity, however great the mess that we transmit to it. That is what I mean by recreation: in it there will inevitably be misunderstandings or perversions, but many of these may turn out to be creative too. This sense of recreation seems to me to be an improvement over that anxiety of continuity that I mentioned a while ago and identified with primitive wisdom. In our society, I said, education must include the possibility of breaks in continuity, of dialectic confrontations, even though a good deal of what has been said about "future shock" is expendable. That is why in, for example, the Bible, there is respect paid not only to wisdom, with its sense of the traditional thing to be done over again, but also for prophecy. Wisdom culminates in such figures as Jesus or Socrates, who confront their societies with a transcendent vision which triumphs over those societies even as they reject it.

Perhaps the oldest of educational ideas is that of the dramatic transformation of the mind, the sudden entry into a new plane of reality. We start with primitive shamans who seek moments of enlightenment and abnormal or supernormal powers. We have early philosophy developing with gurus and instructors who announce cryptic formulas but refuse to elaborate on them. A teacher who can get away without answering questions can be a great moral force, difficult as it may be for him to exist in modern society. The idea is that pondering the formula may bring insight. The same hope for the moment of transforming vision comes through such things as the dialogues of Plato, where a group of people gather, usually around Socrates, to see whether, if they follow a dialectic long and intensively enough, they may come to some vision of one of the Platonic forms, whether courage, justice or love. There are similar things in religion, such as the Quaker meeting, which quietly waits for the Spirit to transform it with a wisdom and knowledge not its own. The only thing that can be said about this conception of transforming inspiration is that it never descends on those who are totally unprepared for it. But, of course, neither can a system of education be based on it. I fully sympathize with students of the late sixties who wanted something exciting and existential to happen in every lecture they attended. But the first characteristic of this kind of enlightenment of spirit is that it is totally unpredictable, and may never happen at all.

Literary education seems to assume a kind of definitive response which in practice never occurs. A definitive response to a performance of *King Lear* would blow our minds, effect an unimaginable transformation in our whole sense of reality. But we are always dissatisfied with something in the performance, or some part of our emotional mechanism is not adjusted, or we may be simply too immature to understand what is happening. So we have to have Shakespearean criticism; we have to have repeated readings and performances of the plays; we have to look up the hard words and understand something of the editorial work that produced the text we read. After a while we may become aware that we are not simply making up for a failure in response, but gradually acquiring certain powers of our own, which keep moving us closer, even if we never actually get to, that final metamorphosis of experience. But, like Tantalus, we may always see what we may not reach, and what we see is that there is no real difference between criticism and creation, nor between education and vision; there is only our failure to abolish the difference.

The Leland B. Jacobs Lecture. New York: School of Library Service Columbia University, 1980.

# The Bridge of Language

As I understand it, my chief qualification for speaking to you tonight is my total ignorance of everything you know. That gives a certain detachment to one's perspective, but it does not provide many other clues. I think that, broadly speaking, the "two cultures" situation described by C.P. Snow some twenty years ago still holds in most respects. Lord Snow, you will remember, suggested that humanists and scientists did not see much of one another's point of view, and that humanists in particular tended to be intellectual Luddites or machine-breakers, probably members of a secret right-wing organization devoted to carbon power and the destruction of silicon chips. The literary critic F. R. Leavis, you will also remember, undertook to refute this case by asserting that in his opinion Lord Snow was a bad novelist. It seemed to me that what I hope might be a more civilized and pertinent statement of the humanist attitude, Ludditism and all, might be of interest to you. I call my talk "The Bridge of Language," because I understand that this is a pontifical conference, concerned with building bridges. I am not, however, a linguist but a literary critic, and that has led me into a different area of study concerned with the social use of words.

Lord Snow remarked that scientists "had the future in their bones". I take it that this is a reference to the fact that a progressive element is built into scientific method, so that any freshman today may know facts in physics or chemistry unknown to Newton or Lavoisier. As far as knowledge is concerned, this is equally true of the humanities: any freshman can also learn more about drama before Shakespeare or music before Mozart than Shakespeare or Mozart ever knew. But

the art themselves ( to quote the title of a famous essay on the subject) are not progressive. They have been assumed to be the ornaments
of a highly developed civilization, and of course they are that; but
they seem to have a curious affinity too with everything that is most
primitive and archaic in human society. Poetry thrives on superstition and fantasy; the formulas of popular fiction are the formulas
of the folk tales of pre-literary cultures; the structures and stock
characters of romance or comedy have persisted with astonishingly
little change in two thousand years. Science is generally assumed to
have something to do with the pursuit of truth, but the poet, as Aristotle pointed out, is not directly concerned with truth because he
says nothing in particular, and only particular statements can be true.
So while the mad scientist may be a stock figure of popular fiction,
it is perhaps significant that one of the great characters of literature
should be Don Quixote, a mad humanist trying to make the world
over in the pattern of his books.

This primitive quality of literature means among other things that
the humanist has the past in his bones: his focus of study is the classic,
the definitive masterpiece which may be many centuries old. Research
in the humanities, however new in itself, always has an aspect in which
it is more light on square one. In caricature, and to some extent occupationally as well, the humanist seems to resemble that heroic if
somewhat confused bird mentioned by Borges, who always flies
backward because he doesn't care about where he's going, only about
where he's been.

Because of the progressive element in science, questions of science
and technology are closely bound up with questions of the future of
society, and of how society is going to adjust to the discoveries and
techniques that have developed within it. We soon realize however
that not everything that is technically feasible is going to happen;
what will happen is only what society is capable of absorbing. That
in turn depends on society's present situation, more particularly that
of its power structures, and its inherited habits. Any such subject as
"futurology," in short, is based on the fact that we know nothing of
the future except by analogy with the past, hence the perspectives
on the past, including the perspectives of the historian and the
humanist, are inseparable from the future-directed concerns of
science. Further, we notice that we hear much less about future shock
and the like than we did a few years ago. One reason is that a widen-

ed horizon capable of taking in some speculation about the future is a by-product of economic expansion and political detente. Such conditions of clearing weather are not habitual to human life, however, and before long we are back in the recessions and political storm warnings that seem to be the normal lot of mankind.

A future-directed perspective is, in itself, very natural to the young, but it also is dependent on what for them is a well-functioning economy. Anyone who has taught students during the fifties and is still teaching is aware how their time-perspective lifts during expansive periods and how it shrinks again in times like ours. During the sixties the "activists" looking for revolutionary social change were mainly students of middle-class background, who seldom realized how much they had been conditioned by the assumptions of that background. These were largely the assumptions of American progressivism, the feeling that as their society had been moving ahead like an express train for two centuries, it was in the nature of the historical process for it to continue to do so, except that it ought to speed up. The students of the seventies, and probably of most of the eighties as well, have been forced into an involuntary caution like that of Cardinal Newman's hymn:

. . . I do not ask to see
The distant scene: one step enough for me.

In my own student days much the same thing happened: a native bourgeois progressivism was checked by the depression, and collided with Marxist vie vs about how a socialist economy would avoid such setbacks. We were assured, in a great deal of Marxist propaganda, that once man stopped wasting his energies in exploiting his fellow men the way would be open for the release of those energies in transforming nature. The assumption was that nature was still an unlimited field of exploitation, and the Marxist literature of fifty years ago resounded with hymns of praise to the tractors and hydro plants of the Soviet Union. But it is now painfully obvious that nature, at any rate as far as this planet extends, is finite too, and that the industrializing of human life is not an endless vista either.

It seems strange that the human race took so long to make a serious effort to develop its science and technology. The technology of the most advanced parts of the world in the early eighteenth century was closer to the neolithic age than it is to us. Even in the nineteenth century, with the Industrial Revolution fairly started, the speed and extent of the transformation of the world that a concentrated effort at technology would make was still beyond the most far-out imaginations. Edgar Allan Poe had about as far-out an imagination as the century produced, and used it partly to invent the modern forms of detective and science fiction. Yet in his story laid in the future, "Mellonta Tauta" (the things about to be), people are crossing the Atlantic in balloons at a hundred miles an hour, a thousand years after his own time, and even the balloon in which the story is supposed to be written falls into the Atlantic instead of landing.

The obvious answer is that for most of his history man has been preoccupied with a small-scale social coherence. Once the essential needs of life and survival are met for a sufficient number of people, the rest of human energy has to be reserved for intensifying the strength of a particular social unit. We can understand the past on this point well enough from the present, even though the social units are much bigger. Our governments feel that if they spent as much on science and technology as they do on armaments, they would create a political vacuum that other powers would be prompt to fill. At present there are certain kinds of scientific projects that only the United States or the Soviet Union can attempt, and it is obvious that some kind of global unity and cooperation is a necessary condition for the unfettered growth of science in the future. Science and technology thus follow the great centralizing movements of economics, which will eventually, we may hope, transform the world into a global unity. The contrast with cultural developments, in literature and the arts, is curious and striking.

The more a country's arts develop, the more they tend to decentralize, to break down into smaller units, or, more positively, to bring increasingly smaller areas into articulateness. We speak of American literature, but a great deal of what we learn about America through its literature we learn by adding up what Faulkner tells us about Mississippi, Robert Frost about New Hampshire, Hemingway about expatriates in Paris or Spain, John Steinbeck about southern California, Peter De Vries about New York. A similar decentralizing movement has been very marked in Canada in the last twenty years, and whatever "Canada" may mean politically, "Canadian literature" means very largely a group of regional developments. It is a mysterious law of literature that a very specific and local setting often goes along with universality of appeal: Faulkner confines himself to an unpronounceable county in Mississippi and gets the Nobel Prize for literature in Sweden. One hopes that this decentralizing movement will gradually loosen its grip on political activities, where it is mostly a nuisance, and confine itself to cultural ones, where it belongs. In some respects, clearly, the world should be a single unit; in other respects it should be a mass of small communities, where people can be aware of others as people.

One reason for the difference in social context is the kind of language literature uses, in contrast to the language of science or philosophy. In science or philosophy there is an underlying international language of subject-matter, so that abstracts of articles in foreign journals can be read even with a limited command of their languages. But literature enters into all the accidents and nuances of language, similarities in sound that make certain rhymes possible, associations in the meanings of words that one language may have and another may not, colloquial idioms that can be rendered into another tongue only by the most complete rephrasing of them. Science and philosophy remind us that language is a total human effort at communication; literature reminds us that language is also one of the most fragmented of human activities, so that it is a life's work to master completely more than one or two.

The word science, I assume, describes primarily a method, used wherever such a method is appropriate. A method involves the use of language, and so far as science uses the language of words in addition to the language of mathematics, it is committed to a certain kind of verbal style. Its language is descriptive, and, of necessity, highly technical, and except in popularized science, it avoids metaphors and similar figures of speech. It also avoids ambiguity, or using the same word in different senses. The language of poetry is a complete contrast: it is largely based on figurative and metaphorical language, and it thrives on manifold meanings and puns of all kinds. Poetry has a very limited tolerance for the abstract language of philosophy or the technical language of science, not because poets dislike these subjects — many poets are deeply interested in them — but because the language poetry uses has a limited power of assimilating their modes of language. The normal language of poetry is a language of colour and sound and movement, of immediate sense perception and concrete experience, of the existential rather than the contemplative or practical sides of human life, of the appearances of things rather than their underlying form.

In the eighteenth century, the work of Isaac Newton had a powerful impact on poets and humanists of all kinds. The sense of a regular and uniform natural law was like a new world to those tired of the anomalies and injustices of civil law, and his obviously sincere religious attitude was deeply reassuring too. So a great deal of poetry was written on the assumption that this new science could inspire a new kind of poetry, and we get such expressions of enthusiasm as this:

Let curious minds, who would the air inspect,
On its elastic energy reflect.

The eighteenth century was also the age of Jenner's discovery of vaccine, and another poem of the period begins: "Inoculation, Heavenly Maid, descend!". But this does not seem to be the kind of thing poetry can do. Obviously a more tactful and skilful poet would do a more convincing job, but it is the failures that point up the real problem.

What is involved is not a matter of vocabulary or subject-matter but of the inner structure of the discipline used. If we set a poem to music, we are putting two arts together, but each art communicates within its own conventions: we are not merging the structures of poetry and music. Similarly, poet and scientist may use, up to a point, the same language, or even treat the same themes, but the structure of poetry and the structure of science remain two things. The scientist quantifies his data; the poet, so to speak, *qualifies* his: he expresses its *whatness*, its impact on concrete experience, and at a certain point they start going in opposite directions. "I do not frame hypotheses," said Newton, meaning, I suppose, that he did not take anything seriously until he had verified it. But literature is a hypothesis from beginning to end, assuming anything and verifying nothing.

The same principle applies to science fiction, which is a form of romance, continuing the formulas of fantasy, Utopian vision, Utopian satire, philosophical fiction, adventure story and myth that have been part of the structure of literature from the beginning. What the hero of a science fiction story finds on a planet of Arcturus, however elaborate and plausible the hardware that got him there, is still essentially what heroes of earlier romances found in lost civilizations buried in Africa or Asia. The conventions of literature have to take over at some point, and what we see, in science fiction no less than in Homer or in Dante, is, in the title of a seventeenth-century satire set on the moon, *mundus alter et idem,* another world, but the same world.

There are different ways in which language can be used, three of them of particular importance. One is the descriptive way that we find in science and everywhere else where the aim is to convey information about an objective world. Then there is the language of transcendence that we find in large areas of philosophy and religion, an abstract, analogical language that expresses what by definition is really beyond verbal expression. And there is the language of immanence, the metaphorical language that poetry speaks, where anything can be identified with anything else, where natural objects can become images of human emotions. These are different languages, which accounts for the differences in structure I speak of; but they are mutually intelligible languages, so I should like to look at their relation again from a different point of view.

Even in the smallest social units, man does not live directly and nakedly in nature like the animals. Human societies live within a semi-transparent envelope that we call culture or civilization, and they see nature only through it. Societies vary a good deal in the extent to which their cultural assumptions distort their view of nature, but all views of nature are conditioned by them. There are no noble savages, in the sense of purely natural men for whom this cultural envelope had disappeared, nor any form of human life that does not restructure the world in front of it into some kind of human vision.

I am concerned here with the role of words in this situation. In most societies, at least, there seem to be traditional verbal structures that are particularly important for the members of that society, or some of its members, to become acquainted with. Laws, including rituals and customs, are at the centre of this material; myths and stories about the traditional gods and heroes, magical formulas, proverbs and the like, also enter into it. In some communities much of it is a secret knowledge, sometimes imparted to boys in initiation ceremonies. In its higher developments it comes closer to what in Judaism is meant by "Torah", the instruction of primary importance for the social identity of the student, which includes the law, but a good many other things as well. We may call this a structure of concern or social coherence, and it is usually a mixture of the religious and the political. Religious concerns, Christian, Moslem, Jewish or Hindu, invariably operate in some political context; political concerns, democratic, Marxist or fascist, always have a religious dimension to them as well.

This structure of concern is often called an ideology, but I think that that is a rather limited and inflexible term, one that does not allow for all its variety and its capacity for growth. I prefer to call it a mythology, in spite of all the misleading emotional reactions to that word. We tend to think of such words as myth, fable or fiction as meaning something not really true. This is partly because they are literary words, and literature is often thought of as a form of socially acceptable lying. Even more important, they are words for verbal structures, and there is a long-standing habit of mind that associates truth with a content that can be separated from structure. Thus we often say of a doubtful proposition that there may be some truth in it. We mean that if it were restated in a different structure it might become true, but we speak as though the truth could be extracted from the structure, like grains of gold from river mud. Both of these attitudes, in my view, are products of prejudice and sloppy thinking, so I shall keep the word mythology.

I speak of a religious or political concern rather than belief, because the conviction of its truth is less important than the sense of the social necessity of accepting it. In practice this means that everybody should say that they accept it, or at least refrain from saying that they do not. For some societies, perhaps, the only really essential doctrine that holds them together is the conviction of their superiority to all other societies. For others, heresy, revisionism or skepticism may become criminal or subversive attitudes.

The social crisis of a battle is a good example of the way in which questions of truth or falsehood are ignored in order to meet the crisis. In the battle of Agincourt there was an English army with a war cry addressed to St. George and a French army with a war cry addressed to St. Denis. Neither saint had a very solid existence; one developed out of a folk tale and the other mostly out of a pious fraud. Even if they had existed, the question of whether they were still available for invocation, or would automatically respond if they were, might still remain open, But if one were present at the battle, one would be well advised to ignore all such doubts and shout with the rest.

The creative arts grow up in most societies mainly as vehicles for carrying the central messages that society regards as primarily important. Hymns of praise to the recognized gods or epics and tragedies about traditional heroes appear early in literature; sculpture developed in Greece because a polytheistic religion needs statues to distinguish one god from another; in the Middle Ages painting and sculpture and stained glass were largely absorbed in producing icons for Christianity. But this introduces a complication into culture; the arts turn out to have structural principles of their own, so a tension arises between what the artist wants to say as an artist and what he is obliged to say as an artist commissioned by a church or government or other agent of social concern.

No art ever gets completely away from its social and historical conditioning; nevertheless it has two poles, the pole of concern, or what society wants from its arts, and the pole of style, or what the poet or painter or composer is discovering within his art. Concern is what makes the artist socially responsible and gives him a social function; style is what demonstrates the coherence, power and influence of the art itself, style being, as Wallace Stevens says, the quality that makes everything in Spain look Spanish.

The arts are older than the sciences, but the development of science follows the same pattern. A mythology is not, except incidentally, a proto-scientific structure: it is meant to draw a circumference around a society and face inward to its hopes and fears and imaginative needs and desires, not to face outward toward nature. But of course it is bound to make or assume statements about the natural order: these often conflict with what further observation of that order suggests, and so, because of their sacrosanct quality, they become obstacles to science when science develops. An obvious example is the doctrine of a divine creation in 4000 B.C. When such conflict occurs, a mythological view of some aspect of nature has to be replaced by a scientific one. But a conflict of science and mythology means only that the sciences, like the arts, have inner structures of their own, and are trying to follow the trends of those inner structures instead of conforming to the prevailing mythological formulations.

There is always tension between the inner growth of the arts and sciences and the anxieties of a controlling mythology. The philosopher Berdyaev complains that nobody wants a disinterested philosopher: it is felt that if he is going to philosophize he should earn his keep, that is, justify or rationalize what people want to see generally believed. In the arts, everywhere we look we see the struggle of imagination against the restrictions of mythology. Islamic countries condemn representational art; the Soviet Union condemns non-representational art; some Marxist regimes, notably the so-called cultural revolution in China, maintain that no art is socially conscious unless it devotes itself entirely to proclaiming the dominant social faith; in our own countries censors to the right of us and censors to the left of us volley and thunder. As for science, there can hardly be a member of this audience who has not had to answer, perhaps many times, the question "Why should we spend money on *that?*" from someone in control of funds. Such a question, when genuine, always indicates a clash between the inner development of science itself and the social concerns connected with what I have called mythology.

The Greek satirist Lucian, writing in the second century A.D., who was apprenticed to a sculptor before becoming a writer, has a dialogue in which Zeus calls a conference of gods, who come represented by their statues. Zeus tells Hermes, who is marshalling the procession, to arrange them in order of costliness of material, gold statues in the front row, silver ones behind, bronze and marble in the back benches. Hermes protests that some consideration should be given to quality of workmanship: on Zeus' arrangement all the Greek gods would have to go to the bleachers, because only barbarians can afford gold statues. Zeus says that quality of workmanship certainly ought to come first, but preference has to be given to gold. It is not hard to see why. Giving praise and prestige to expense fosters the industry of the care and feeding of gods: and if workmanship became too important, the question would arise of the extent to which gods are really human constructs. Workmanship represents the language of culture and civilization; expense represents the language of concern, which may lag behind imagination and intelligence, but usually controls the power.

The arts and sciences, then, for all their obvious differences, have a common origin in social concern. In proportion as they follow their own inner structures, they become specialized and pluralistic. This is simply a condition of civilized life: they have to do this, and the degree to which an art is allowed to follow its own line of development is of immense importance in determining the level of a society's culture, and, ultimately, the level of the life of its citizens. The same applies to science, and resistance to political or religious interference with the arts and sciences is the sign of a mature society. Such resistance organized on an international scale could become an essential instrument of human progress. As Thomas Pynchon points out in his brilliant novel *Gravity's Rainbow,* an exclusive devotion to a mythology shuttles between a belief that everything has been made for man's sake and a belief that man is a uniquely cursed and doomed species, both views being paranoid. At the same time it is only their common social concern, their interests as citizens of the human community of which they are equally members, that can bring artists and scientists together. They cannot be brought together by trying to learn more about one another's totally different disciplines, any more than we can bring about world peace by trying to learn all the world's languages. The reason is much the same: there are more like two hundred cultures than two. But the notion that we can do without a common sense of concern, that religion can be absorbed by literature or all mythology replaced by science, seems to me a very muddled one. Such a civilization would be at best only another Tower of Babel, an unfinishable structure worked on by people who no longer understand each other.

What does happen, in the course of time, is that as the arts and sciences develop, religio-political units become larger and fewer, the unity of the world becomes a visible possibility, and so the different mythologies of concern become broader and simpler in scope. This becomes very clear when a non-human danger or catastrophe unites them in the sense of a common need for co-existence. Camus' novel *The Plague (La Peste)* is a brilliantly concentrated study of the way in which, in the face of a raging epidemic, all human concerns vanish into the two basic ones: survival and deliverance. Deliverance or emancipation includes all the forms of the expansion of consciousness and energy that are at the heart of the major mythologies; salvation in Christianity, enlightenment in Buddhism, equality in Marxism, liberty in democracy. If the question of survival is less urgent, these decline into various donkey's carrots of reward and punishment, either coming immediately from social authority or associated with a future life of some kind, either for ourselves in another world or our posterity in this one. But in the limit-situation of crisis, all human mythologies reduce to a very elementary basis: that life is better than death, freedom better than bondage, health better than disease, happiness better than misery.

The twentieth century has seen a growth of a sense of common crisis in which the essential concerns of survival and emancipation have slowly moved into the foreground. It is unnecessary to rehearse the major elements in this sense of crisis — the atom bomb, the shrinking of natural resources, the feeling that central economic forces, such as the value of money, have gone out of control, the overcrowding of the earth by the one organism too irresponsible to play the game of natural selection fairly. Long before in literature, in Blake, Ruskin and Morris in the nineteenth century and Eliot, D.H. Lawrence, Ezra Pound and others in the early twentieth, there had been a strong attack on the ugliness that modern civilization was creating out of its surroundings. Writers looked at the blasted and blighted outskirts of cities, at once beautiful landscapes buried in tombs of concrete, and felt that even if Nature were the whore that she is said to be in some of our earlier mythologies, there was no excuse for treating her like that. This was what produced the "two cultures" situation that Lord Snow misrepresented so grossly. For even at its most wrongheaded this protest was not a merely aesthetic one, and it was not a "Luddite" attack on science or technology as such. It was a protest in the name of human concern for survival and freedom against what these writers felt to be a death-impulse in the human mind, an impulse that they saw as trying to get control of science and technology. More important, they saw the exploitation of nature to be essentially the same evil thing as the exploitation of other men that has produced all the slavery and tyranny of history.

Snow speaks of Orwell's *1984* as typical of the humanist's wish that the future did not exist. But it is reasonable enough to wish that *that* future would not exist. Man is quite capable of producing the hell on earth that that book records: to deny or refuse to face this is to be a far more reckless Luddite than the most reactionary of poets. We are very near to the chronological 1984 now, and if the particular fear that Orwell's book expresses is no longer our primary one, at least for ourselves, it is mainly because a new element has entered the picture: the sense that human survival depends on the well-being of the nature from which humanity has sprung. The days when a scientist could use his scientific detachment and the artist his freedom of expression as excuses for withdrawing from this concern are long past.

At the beginning of the twentieth century there was a strong sense that reality was divided into the subjective and the objective, and that science was concerned only with the latter. But even in the physical sciences it soon became clear that the observer himself was part of the scene to be observed, and of course the social sciences are entirely based on this principle. The corresponding development has taken place in the arts: such a movement as abstract expressionism in painting, for example, does not mean that the painter has gone on an ego-trip of "self expression": it means that he is studying the expressing process in himself as a part of his pictorial vision of the world.

In the twentieth century Einstein has had an impact on the popular consciousness rather similar to that of Newton in the eighteenth century. Like Newton, this impact was based on his obvious concern with the implications of his work in physics for human survival and emancipation. He made several cryptic, even mystical, utterances in this area, and Niels Bohr is said to have urged him, rather impatiently, to stop telling God what to do. On closer inspection, however, he seems to have been talking less about God than about the way in which nature, though with no language of its own, none the less makes humanly intelligible responses to the mind. The inference is that the structures of physical nature and the human mind are linked in a common destiny, discoveries in nature being also discoveries in human nature. I suspect that this is as central an intuition for us as the sense of the regularity of natural law was for the contemporaries of Newton. Further, it is an intuition that the metaphorical language of poetry, where natural objects and human emotions are so often identified with each other, can help to express.

If we split the world into subject and object, we tend to assume that the objective is real, the world of waking consciousness that we can agree we are seeing, and that the subjective world is one of dreams and resentments and wishes and desires and similar products of illusion. This was the view, fifty years ago, of Freudian psychology with all its hydraulic metaphors of blocks and drives and channels and cathects, and with its assumption that we retreat every night into a world of dream and futile wish-fulfilment, waking up again to face the real world. But this distinction between reality and illusion arises only when we stare at the world passively. For the 1980's, I think, we need different assumptions. First, practically all the reality we wake up facing is a human construct left over from yesterday. Second, some of that construct is rubbish, and needs to be cleared away. The importance difference is not between reality and illusion, but between what we can make real and what it is time to get rid of.

When we think of things this way, we can see that the arts and sciences, though they have different functions, have essentially the same kind of place in the human scene. If we think in terms of reality and illusion, we may concede that science deals with reality, but we don't know what kind of status to give the arts, because they are so concerned with subjective elements of desire and other products of the dream-world. But when we think of reality in terms of a world to be remade, we find that we need a model or imaginative vision of what we are trying to achieve. The world of dream and fantasy can be a source of models as well as illusions, and models are the first product of the chaos of hunch and intuition and guesswork and free association out of which the realities of art and science are made. This is the starting point of all creative work in any area, however different the products may be.

If we go to the theatre, the show we see on the stage is, we may say, an illusion. But we could search the wings and dressing rooms forever without finding any reality behind it. The reality-illusion distinction clearly does not work for plays: the illusion *is* the reality. If the play is, let us say, a comedy of Shakespeare, there are things inside it that look like real things, such as law-courts, and other things, like fairies and love potions and magic rings, that look impossible. What is important is where all this is going. At the end of the play a new society is created: four or five couples get married, and things which looked strong and threatening at first, like Shylock, get left behind. We look back over the play, and see that what we thought was just fantasy and wish-thinking was actually a force strong enough to impose itself on things that looked so well established at first, and transform them into a quite different shape and direction. The comedy is a miniature example of that drive toward deliverance that has fostered all the great myths of emancipation in the world, and is still capable of fostering the great emancipation myths of the future.

It is not for nothing that dramas are called plays: in fact Shakespeare's contemporary, Ben Jonson, came in for some ridicule when he published his dramas in 1616 under the title of *The Works of Ben Jonson*. In his endlessly suggestive book *Homo Ludens*, the Dutch scholar Huizinga distinguishes play and work on the basis, more or less, that work is energy expended for a further end in view, and that play is energy expended for its own sake, or as a manifestation of what the end in view is. A chess or tennis player may work hard to win a game or improve his skill, but chess and tennis are forms of play. An artist may work hard to perfect a work of art, but the work perfected is an expression of play, an energy complete in itself that shows what the work has been done for. Science and technology work hard to help achieve what would be, once achieved, a life of play, where nature is no longer conquered territory held down by man but lived in as his home, and where the mental work of solving problems has become *scientia* or *philosophia,* the love of knowing, the play at the heart of all genuine work.

The Book of Proverbs in the Bible describes wisdom as a female principle who was part of God's mind at the creation. The King James translation speaks of her as "rejoicing," but this is a very weak form of the tremendous Vulgate phrase *ludens in orbe terrarum,* playing throughout the earth. This world of play or spontaneous energy is the deliverance to which all religious and political ideals point, and some glimpse of it is accessible to any artist or scientist at any moment. The ordinary division of our lives into work and play makes work the endless pursuit of a donkey's carrot into the future, and play a relaxation from this that reminds us of the carefree days of our childhood. But the genuine human energy of the arts and sciences converges on a world where work and play have become the same thing. A gathering together of such people with such interests, including this one, would be in the deepest and most serious sense a play *ground,* a common meeting point where all forms of language are interchangeable, all statements of identity, whether metaphors or equations, balance out, and scientists and humanists shake the past and the future out of their bones and join together in a present life.

Keynote Address at American Academy for the Advancement of Science, January, 1981. *Science* 212 (April 1981).

# Culture and Society in Ontario, 1784-1984

Most of the cultural factors that exist in Canada as a whole also exist in Ontario in a reduced but identical form. Geographical displacement is the most obvious. The entire province is half as large again as Texas, but most of its people are huddled near the American border, in a territory no larger than Michigan. The hinterland in the north has been explored by painters, but in this paper I have time and space only for the literary aspect of Ontario culture, and northern Ontario does not seem as yet to have found a Rudy Wiebe to interpret it. The chief exception, so far as I know, is Wayland Drew's remarkable but rather neglected story *The Wabeno Feast,* and Drew has also written essays on what this vast territory ought to be contributing to our imaginations. It is a type of irony familiar in the modern world that in most respects it is easier to get from Toronto to Moscow or Tokyo than to get to Moosonee, at the other end of the province. It may be an irony more typical of Ontario that it seems to be easier to get into genuine social contact with Asians or Africans than with the indigenous peoples. The impact of native Indian consciousness on white settlers has been remarkably narcissistic: Pauline Johnson was very much a whitecomer's Indian, and when Grey Owl turned out to be an Englishman obsessed with noble-savage ideology he repeated a pattern set up in Ontario's earliest historical novel, *Wacousta*, where the allegedly Indian hero is actually a rejected suitor of the heroine's mother, back in Great Britain.

In the nineteenth century the central activity was the clearing of the land for farming. "Clearing" meant for the most part cutting down trees, the trees being regarded not as a potential resource but simply as obstacles. Catharine Parr Traill remarks in her *Backwoods of Canada:*

> Man appears to contend with the trees of the forest as though they were his most obnoxious enemies; for he spares neither the young sapling in its greenness nor the ancient trunk in its lofty pride; he wages war against the forest with fire and steel.

Anna Jameson makes the same observation, but carries it a step further:

> A Canadian settler *hates* a tree, regards it as his natural enemy, as something to be destroyed, eradicated, annihilated, by all and any means . . . [She goes on to say that there are two ways of killing a tree, by burning it and by draining the sap out of it.] Is not this like the two ways in which a woman's heart may be killed in this world of ours — by passion and by sorrow?

Leaving this terrifying remark to speak for itself for the moment, we note that clearing the forest means, among other things, a slaughter of the animals who are thereby made homeless. Here is Samuel Strickland, the male literary representative of that celebrated family:

> The deer are not now (1853) nearly so numerous as they formerly were . . . To give my readers some idea how plentiful these wild denizens of the forest were some years since, I need only mention that a trapper with whom I was acquainted, and four of his companions, passed my house on a small raft on which lay the carcasses of thirty-two deer — the trophies of a fortnight's chase near Stoney Lake. The greater number of these were fine bucks. I once had seventeen deer hanging up in my barn at one time — the produce of three days' sport, out of which I had the good fortune to kill seven . . . I do not know anything more pleasant than these excursions . . . This is one of the great charms of Canadian life, particularly to young sportsmen from the Mother Country, who require here neither license nor qualification to enable them to follow their game; but may rove in chase of deer or other game at will.

There are any number of ways in which such activities can be defended or rationalized; but to begin one's culture by severing so many links with nature and the earlier inhabitants poses the most formidable problems for its development. As Anna Jameson suggests, can one really destroy so many trees without stunting and truncating human lives as well? I have often had occasion to notice the curiously powerful resonance that the killing of animals has for Canadian writers: Irving Layton invests the death even of a mosquito with dignity. Among Ontario writers, we notice how the action in Margaret Atwood's *Surfacing* is directed toward reversing the current of the destroying and polluting of nature: the heroine, searching for what is both her father and the as yet unspoiled source of Canadian life, wants "the borders abolished . . . the forest to flow back into the place his mind cleared". Al Purdy's "The Death of Animals", a very intricate and subtle poem among many of his that deal with similar themes, shows us how the real horror in man's attitude to nature is not so much deliberate cruelty as total indifference, a feeling that man and nature have no life in common whatever:

When mouse died, a man coughed, stirred,
Went to the bathroom. No connection, of course.
When the lady slit her lover's throat with a nail file,
owl was already dead. Again, no connection.
Fox screamed, but the lady with lacquered nails
already owned a fur coat. No real connection.
Deer died later of a bullet wound, having trailed
a broken leg through miles of red snow . . .
What's the point of all this? None at all, really.

It is also Purdy who, in "Watching Trains", depicting some Indian boys staring at a railway train, shows us, without wasting a syllable on moralizing, an abyss between two ways of life too wide even for conflict: the boys might as well be on a different planet, as in some respects they are. And I doubt if any other book on the First World War calls our attention more distinctly to the sufferings of animals than Timothy Findley's *The Wars*, when describing a situation in which men have started to treat each other the way they have always treated wild animals. The slaughter of animals, so often ignored as a feature of war, is one of the major elements in the demoralizing of the hero, and toward the end of the book we have a description of a mare and a dog, mute and helpless victims in a nightmare, and remember that this episode is repeated verbatim from the opening page, as a central emblem of the story.

It is often said that if it hadn't been for Niagara Falls, Ontario would have been a most idyllic and pastoral community. Of course the sense of something idyllic and peaceful represents only a pause, a sort of plateau, in the "clearing" of nature. Technology, however, is a second twist in the destruction of so many of its features, and the cultural opposition to it is vocal and versatile. Lampman's poem "The City of the End of Things" is a familiar example, as is Grove's late Ontario novel, *The Master of the Mill,* where the theme is mechanophobia hitched to a sorcerer's apprentice myth, the mill compulsively continuing to grind flour after the world has been smothered with it. George Grant's *Technology and Empire* approaches a similar theme philosophically. Canada, as I have often had occasion to remark, missed out on eighteenth-century enlightenment, and has no counterparts to such cultural heroes as Jefferson and Franklin. But, as Grant insists, it did participate, very fully, in the Hegelian antithesis that the enlightenment turned into, the oligarchic exploiting of the country. It is probably Grant's influence that lies behind the sombre brooding opening poem of Dennis Lee's *Civil Elegies:*

Buildings oppress me, and the sky-concealing wires
bunch zigzag through the air. I know
the dead persist in
buildings, by-laws, porticos — the city I live in
is clogged with their presence, they
dawdle about in our lives and form a destiny, still
incomplete, still dead weight, still
demanding whether Canada will be.

Marshall McLuhan is often regarded as a prophet on the opposite side, but actually he thought of the coming of electronic media as bringing about a political reversal of development from technological imperialism back to a new form of tribalism, and was sustained by that belief as long as it was possible for him to hold it. No one has spoken more strongly of the dehumanizing effects of technology than he has:

When the perverse ingenuity of man has outered some part of his being in material technology, his entire sense ratio is altered. He is then compelled to behold this fragment from himself "closing itself as in steel" [the quotation is from Blake]. In beholding this new thing, man is compelled to become it.

The question that this paper faces me with is one that I have never seen dealt with in depth, and trying to cut through the jungle of jargon in contemporary critical theory will give one no help whatever. The question is this: when a new society begins to develop some cultural interests, that culture is bound to be, for some time, a provincial culture — I am not using this as a putdown term but as a characterizing one. After a culture has matured, it begins to show a decentralizing movement, as more and more commitments become articulate through the writers that grow up in them. For about 150 of the 200 years I am considering, Ontario had mainly a provincial culture, and a rather sparse one at that. For the last 25 years, at least, with the writers I have mentioned and others I have still to mention, it has had a regional culture, and a remarkably rich and varied one. Obviously there are affinities as well as contrasts between the provincial and the regional: what are they, and how does one get from one to the other? The central social process at work is the shift from a rural-based to an urban-based lifestyle, but the cultural changes accompanying this must involve more complex factors than that. I should say at once that I am not going to solve this quesition, merely to raise it, along with a few suggestions that I hope will be useful.

I arrived in Toronto to take up what turned out to be permanent residence there, in September of 1929. Toronto was then mainly a quiet Scotch-Irish town, its Yonge Street a curious mixture of an English midland and a middle-west American appearance, both of them deceptive. It was English midland in its array of second-hand bookshops and small grocery or butcher shops, with what appeared to be practically live rabbits hanging from the ceiling. The mean architecture, the grid plan, and the uniformity of the drug stores and branch movie houses were middle-western American features. It was a homogeneous city, with very little of the ethnical mix that Montreal and Winnipeg had: perhaps this is connected with the fact that the Jewish community in Toronto did not make the impressive contributions to Canadian literature that its counterparts in the other two cities did.

Toronto's spiritual life began on Saturday evening, where many downtown corners had a preaching evangelist, and continued through Sunday, a day of rest of a type I have never seen paralleled except in Israeli Sabbaths. One could then learn from a celebrated preacher that God was in his heaven and that the only events that bothered him were produced by the machinations of the Roman Catholic hierarchy. The Orange Order kept a firm grip on municipal government, demonstrating Communists, who began to appear in the depression, went to jail with broken heads, and, in imitation of the United States, the work ethic had expanded to the point of making any form of alcoholic drink illegal, drinking being bad for working-class morale. Outside Toronto there was a good deal of ridicule of "Hogtown's" somnolence and sexual prudery. It is still true that Ontario gives too much authority to censors, originally out of panic, though the real reason now is probably that censoring is a genuinely popular sport, with many votes to be got out of it. Even so, prudery in Ontario at its worst is mild enough compared to what one would find in Islamic or most Communist countries today.

What one noticed at once was the curious double-think about the loyalty to the British connection. There had been a good deal of resentment in the nineteenth century about some of the more spectacular ineptnesses of British colonial rule, and its obviously greater respect for American than for Canadian interests. One might have expected the aftermath of the First World War to have weaned Canada from much of its colonial fixation, the casualties being so hideously large in proportion to the population of the country. A holocaust is not less a holocaust for being a voluntary one. George Grant, speaking of Canada after 1918, says: "Those who returned did not have the vitality for public care, but retreated into the private world of money-making". Yet this was mainly imitative of American life in the twenties, where the Republicans, who thought of a president as an idol carried in the processions of big business, had a permanent majority. The imperialism which thought of Canada as one more exit from the globe-girdling highway of the British Empire was already in decline: its epitaph had been written, though few realized it at the time, in Sara Jeanette Duncan's *The Imperialist* (1904), where one of the main characters, an earnest but fairly articulate bore, keeps flogging what is clearly the very dead horse of "imperial federation."

So by 1929 the loyalty to the British connection in Ontario began to have a suspiciously vociferous quality to it: obviously it masked the fact that Canada was rapidly ceasing to be a British colony and was becoming an American one. A few years later, Frank Underhill said this openly, and the furore that resulted showed, first, that he had hit a social neurosis squarely in the bullseye, and, second, that is a genunine necessity for academic freedom, even though he left the university early to disappear into the civil-service vortex in Ottawa. I remember that the fiercest condemnation of Underhill I heard came from Charles G. D. Roberts, who had spent much of his productive career in the United States, but had received a new lease of imperial loyalty along with his knighthood.

And yet the ignoring of Canada by Americans effectively prevented much loyalty from going in that direction. American arrogance was all the more galling in that it was so largely unconscious. Apart from a few Fenians, who, like the murderers of the Donnellys, had brought their feuds from Ireland with them, there was little awareness in the United States that a different country bounded them on the north. In the year 1826 the citizens of Ancaster were insulted by a travelling American exhibition showing a diorama of the glorious American victory over the British at New Orleans ten years earlier. Doubtless, like their descendants today, the showmen had forgotten or never realized that the war that ended at New Orleans had begun with an invasion of Upper Canada.

It was much more important, of course, that in proportion as the United States began to exert its strength as a world power, the continentalism of the Liberals, as expressed in the later Underhill and elsewhere, began to look increasingly reactionary. Nineteenth-century Canadian critics of the American way of life had tended to attack from both the right and left, criticizing the absence of social standards in American democracy but also reflecting on the gross inequalities, including the retention of slavery in the South, in American oligarchy. In the depression the new CCF party, which hoped to become the Labour Party of Canada and force the Conservatives and Liberals to unite against them, represented a new kind of British-centered ideology. The British model faded along with the party, but an uneasy kind of Tory and radical mixture, expressed in very different ways by Donald Creighton, George Grant and Dave Godfrey, continues the fight to try to define just what kind of social contract Canada in general, and Ontario in particular, does have to hold it together. The fight has not been made any easier by the more childish aspects of French separatism, which tend to divide the continent into Quebec and the United States.

With so much agreement that Ontario probably does not exist, it is hardly surprising that earlier studies of its culture, such as E.K.

Brown's *On Canadian Poetry* (1943), should have expressed some wonder, not that it had a provincial culture, but that it had any at all. Tracing the criticism of Canadian literature back into the nineteenth century, it is extraordinary to find so unflaggingly persistent a desire to produce a literature, so constant a hope that a few contemporary seeds will burgeon into a bumper crop. The desire and the hope were genuinely heroic, and right in that our provincial heritage has become an essential cultural asset, not something to repudiate or get away from. The continuity between provincial and regional literature is primary: if we understand something of that, most of the differences will fall into line. An English friend once remarked to me that a Canadian's conversational opening gambit seemed to be invariably "Where you from?" Two of our most memorable novels, Margaret Atwood's *Surfacing* and Margaret Laurence's *The Diviners,* trace the development of their heroines backward to its source, in an effort to answer the same question to the satisfaction of the heroine herself. Both novels are Ontario-based, even though one heads east to Quebec and the other west to Manitoba. Often such a journey to the source includes the cultural sources. Margaret Atwood's *Journals of Susanna Moodie* indicate how creative an act it can be to absorb and exploit one's own cultural tradition, and Susanna's sister Catharine Parr Traill plays a significant role at the end of *The Diviners.*

These two novels employ, in reverse, the commonest formula of Canadian fiction, the *Bildungsroman.* The theme of "How I Grew Up in Zilch Corners" is inevitable for the young writer who as yet knows nothing except his own impressions, and of course the great bulk of all writing, in every age, consists of filling up prescribed and fashionable conventions. You will note that I fell into the idiom myself a moment ago. Even so, the theme seems to have an unusual intensity for Ontario writers: the best and most skilful of them, including Robertson Davies and Alice Munro, continue to employ a great deal of what is essentially the Stephen Leacock Mariposa theme, however different in tone. Most such books take us from the first to the second birth of the central character. Childhood and adolescence are passed in a small town or village, then a final initiation, often a sexual one, marks the entry into a more complex social contract.

In Ontario literature the large proportion of women writers comes out of a tradition established at the very beginning of settlement. It was not that nineteenth-century women had any more leisure than their husbands, or that the physical effort involved in the work they did was less intense. But they did have a more creative notion of what to do with the leisure they had: we may compare Samuel Strickland's three-day orgy of deer-killing with his sister Catharine's delighted discoveries of new plants and birds in her environment. The Strickland sisters worked mainly in a genre which had an actual market, of sorts: diaries, journals, reminiscences aimed, not at readers in Ontario, but at prospective immigrants "back home". We owe many of our clearest insight into the social and cultural development of the country to such work. Very occasionally we see some awareness of its function: thus Anne Langton, writing in 1840:

> . . .The bride looked much better than on . . . her first appearance. Her dress was of another shade, richer than the former. I think it would have stood erect by itself . . . If the follies and extravagances of the world are to be introduced upon Sturgeon Lake, we might as well, I think, move on to Galt Lake. I am afraid women deteriorate in this country more than the other sex. As long as the lady is necessarily the most active member of her household she keeps her ground from her utility; but when the state of semi-civilization arrives, and the delicacies of her table, and the elegancies of her person become her chief concern and pride, then she must fall, and must be contented to be looked upon as belonging merely to the decorative department of the establishment and valued accordingly.

The woman who loses her commanding position in a household to become part of the furniture is familiar enough today: in the literature we are considering, the dead end of the process is reached by the heroine of Margaret Atwood's *The Edible Woman,* the victim of a cellophane-wrapped consumerism. It is more common, however, for Canadian fiction writers to feature the woman who is determined to hold on to that commanding position even after her real function is past. Male-dominated societies are constantly turning into matriarchies and vice versa, and some reflection of this is perhaps what has produced the literary convention described, again, by Margaret Atwood in *Survival:*

> If you trusted Canadian fiction you would have to believe that

most of the women in the country with any real presence at all
are over fifty, and a tough, sterile, suppressed and granite-jawed
lot they are. They live their lives with intensity, but through gritted
teeth.

One of the earliest of such women, though not one she mentions,
is the mother of the heroine of Raymond Knister's novel, *White Narcissus* (1929), a book I shall come to again in a moment. This is a
story of how a young man's love for a young woman is frustrated by
the latter's parents, who are emotional vampires sucking all the life
out of her. They are feuding with each other for some reason, communicate only through her, and the mother retreats into an epic sulk
and raises white narcissi. The funereal color, the sickly-sweet smell,
and the mythical overtones of "narcissus" provide the central image
of the novel. A rather forced ending breaks up this pattern of frustration, but the type itself marches across Canada from sea to sea. I
have occasionally wondered if some psychological transfer from a
political dependence on a "mother country" has affected Canadian
feeling about female establishments. Scott Symon's *Place d'Armes,*
for example, has castrating mother symbols all over it, and ends in
an apocalyptic prophecy of the fall of the "mommy bank", the Bank
of Montreal. The setting is Montreal, but the psychological focus is
clearly Ontario.

In writing a *Bildungsroman* about one's early surroundings,
especially if one is not thinking of the people one writes about as forming any large part of one's readership, it is often difficult to avoid
a patronizing tone that isolates the characters from the rest of the
world. That is, the author knows that his milieu is provincial, and
his knowledge is apt to work against him into identifying with it. Hence
a certain self-conscious archness in earlier Canadian fiction, in Ralph
Connor, even in Leacock's *Sunshine Sketches.* Leacock, however, is
aware of this tone and feels defensive about it, and so adds a sen-
timental epilogue to the book, describing a returning railway journey
to Mariposa after a life misspent in the big city:

> Don't bother to look at the reflection of your face in the window-
> pane shadowed by the night outside. Nobody could tell you now
> after all these years. Your face has changed in these long years
> of money-getting in the city. Perhaps if you had come back now
> and again, just at odd times, it wouldn't have been so.

It is easy to locate, and still easier to caricature, the limitations of a provincial culture. There is, for example, its resentment of realism, its feeling that it should not be studied before it has had time to put on its best clothes. There are the querulous complaints against academic critics, who know how it should be done but can't do it, through which one can always hear the voice of the provincial appeal "Please go away until we get better". And there are all the fallacies engendered by the wrong kind of literary study, such as the notion that poetry is an elegant varying of meaning instead of a higher concentration of it. Thus Wilson MacDonald in *The Song of the Ski:*

I land erect and the tired winds drawl
A lazy rune on a broken harp

where the skier may have landed erect but his metaphors are a basket case. I am more interested, however, in the genuine difficulties encountered by dedicated and isolated writers. May I turn again to *White Narcissus:*

> He smiled bitterly. "It is always of her you speak," he added, with a surprising acrimony, for this thwarted feeling was being transferred to annoyance in behalf of the representative of his own sex in this generation-long quarrel. "Doesn't your father feel? Do you think he doesn't know the bitter of loneliness and misprision as well as your mother?"
> "Father, of course. I know that, and it is why things are as they are. Possibly if I could take sides, there could be some outcome, even to strife. But I see, I understand too well, so that there is no hope. I see the sadness of both, and how oblivion awaits it all . . . across a mist of pathos like dreaming."

This is provincial style: the heightening of tone, so that the conversational idiom is smothered in rhetorical rhythms, and the conscientious tracing of motive, indicate a writer who thinks of the highest standards of his craft as being already established outside his community (Henry James is the chief ghost haunting this passage, I should think), and as having to be met by very deliberate efforts.

It was a similar concern about meeting external standards that produced the dream of "The Great Canadian Novel," by which was apparently meant a Victorian type of character-crowded panorama, on the model of *Bleak House* or *Middlemarch*, or, if one ventured to hope so high, *War and Peace*. But such forms now exist, so far as they do, chiefly in historical romance, which is an international commercial product for the most part, though Antonine Maillet's *Pélagie-la-Charrette* indicates that something much more could be made of it. In any case, as we saw, prose in Ontario began with the documentary realism of journals and memoirs, and when fiction developed, that was the tradition it recaptured. Documents, when not government reports, tend to have short units, and the fact may account for the curious ascendancy in Canadian fiction of the novel which consists of a sequence of inter-related short stories. This form is the favourite of Alice Munro, and reaches a dazzling technical virtuosity in *Lives of Girls and Women*.

As a way of approaching cultural through social phenomena, let me give one example of how a provincial situation is affected, first, by the rural-urban population shift, and then expands into a more complex social issue. I remarked earlier that it was impossible to get legally any kind of alcoholic drink in Toronto in 1929. I forget whether the first tentative post-prohibition beers were available then or not, but I should not consider them an exception if they were. Many Protestant churches, at least, seemed to attach more importance to abstaining from liquor than they did to all the clauses in the Apostles' Creed together. Whenever we have a token anxiety symbol of this kind, we should look for unacknowledged change in the social process. The process here, as mentioned, was the rapid shift to an urban-based ethos. The churches adhered almost obsessively to the rural one, and in rural communities there was some justification for assuming that one either did not drink or took to drink. Where the industry was strongly seasonal, as with Newfoundland fishing, this was proportionately more true. However, according to Catharine Parr Traill:

> Intemperance is too prevailing a vice among all ranks of people in this country; but I blush to say it belongs most decidedly to those that consider themselves among the better class of emigrants.

The word "emigrants" goes a long way to annotate the remark: the "better class" in Ontario at that time had not come to Canada so much as left Britian or the United States, and like other refugees they felt a lack of social context, especially in moments of leisure. Ontario is a place to stand, we are told: the cultural complications begin with sitting down.

So "temperance," meaning total abstinence, may have been so vigorously supported by the more evangelical churches partly as a native protest against manners imported by the self-styled gentry. If so, this would explain why the political affinities of temperance movements were liberal to the verge of radical. A very easy generalization from denouncing "the liquor interests" and their control of politicians and the press would soon bring one to radicalism, or at any rate a kind of radical populism. The alliance between the evangelical and the populist was noted as early as Tiger Dunlop:

> It is long since the French reproached the English with having twenty religions, and only one sauce. In Canada, we have two hundred religions, and no sauce at all . . . The mode by which religion and politics are joined is, I believe, peculiar to the American continent, viz., by newspapers inculcating the tenets of a sect, and at the same time the politics of the leaders of it; and this unholy alliance have the Methodists set up to blend treason with the Gospel.

I became aware of the blending of "treason" and the gospel from some of my contemporaries who came from missionary families, and had spent much of their childhood in China or Japan. The Student Christian Movement, a very influential organization among students at that time, drifted rapidly leftward, partly under their influence. The tragic career of my classmate Herbert Norman is perhaps too well known to need more than a reference. So it should not be surprising that if, on a Sunday afternoon in 1931, there were 18,000 people at Denton Massey's York Bible Class in Maple Leaf Gardens, the children or grandchildren of those people should be listening to left-wing speakers imported from third-world countries in the same place in the late sixties.

If we add to this issue a dozen others, we can begin to understand how it was that Toronto was able, in half-a-dozen years after 1945, to transform itself from the "Hogtown" of the thirties into a cosmopolitan city with a minimum of ethnical tension. The immigration of those years was not of course confined to Toronto, though it was most dramatic there, and it was not the cause of the contemporary transformation of Ontario literature from the provincial to the regional, though it accompanied it and had many connections with it. The process itself by which a provincial writer isolated in a part of the world becomes a regional writer who from a sense of being in the world strikes his roots in his social environment remains a mysterious one. James Reaney has a poignant poem called "The Upper Canadian":

I shall always sit here in this hovel
Weeping perhaps over an old Victorian novel
And hear the dingy interwinding tunes

Of country rain and wind
And lame fires of damp wood.
Especially shall I hear that starved cricket
My mind, that thinks a railway ticket
Could save it from its enclosed, cramped quality.
That mind where thoughts float round
As geese do round a pond
And never get out.

Alvin Lee, in his book on Reaney, identifying the narrator of this poem with Reaney himself, remarks that his way of handling the problem "was not to export himself elsewhere but rather to learn an order of words or literary language comprehensive enough to swallow up the place and society which had brought him into being".

Lee is certainly right in pointing to language as the key to the process: it is a new sense of language that makes a writer realize that he must establish his own standards and not try to meet those of someone or somewhere else. There are many other factors: sometimes a railway ticket does help, as a ticket to Toronto helped E.J. Pratt to become a Newfoundland poet. Sometimes one can see a definite influence. One of the first Ontario writers to whom this metamorphosis occurred was Morley Callaghan, and the impact of Maritain on Ontario Catholic culture was operative there. But critics, when they identify such an influence, are apt to exaggerate it, because the actual process eludes them as much as it does the writer himself.

The point is that the transformation did occur, however it occurred. If the Nobel Prize Committee were to ask for Canadian nominees, anyone reasonably conversant with the field could name eight or ten people in English Canada alone, without feeling in the least apologetic about any of them, and a good proportion of them would be Ontario writers. At the beginning Ontario struggled along in what Douglas LePan calls "A Country Without a Mythology", having both obliterated the Indian mythology and discarded its own. A mythology is a framework of thematic imagery within which a literature operates, hence a country without one is a country with a provincial literature and a largely undeveloped imaginative potential. A mythology emerges when the mental landscapes of a group of writers begin to fuse with their physical environment. In another article I have tried to show this process at work among some contemporary Canadian poets. If I had another hour of your time and another month of my own (which I do not), I might attempt a similar study of Ontario fiction, showing how the *Bildungsroman* form, and others closely related to it, so often works through to some intuition or private epiphany that is an aspect of an emerging coherent mythology. LePan's own novel *The Deserter* affords an impressive example, as does each of the three Deptford novels of Robertson Davies, especially *Fifth Business*. Fable and fantasy forms, such as Marian Engel's *Bear*, Timothy Findley's new novel *Not Wanted on the Voyage*, or in a still different way Graeme Gibson's *Perpetual Motion*, have an important role to play here. Predictably, perhaps, the unifying theme of the fantasies is nearly always a renewed relation between humanity and nature. And there is also, of course, the ironic version of the *Bildungsroman*. To win through to a genuine mythical vision means casting off any number of false ones, and the failure of some characters to do this is quite as significant as the success of others. An example would be the heroine of Margaret Atwood's *Lady Oracle*, who exchanges a physical obesity for equally overstuffed myths, because, as she says, "the truth was not convincing".

When an imaginative coherence of this kind emerges within a literature, it becomes genuinely communicable, and provokes an immediate response in other parts of the world. It is not geographical curiosity about Canada, and certainly not its political importance, that has caused universities in Germany and Italy, in China and Japan, in Holland and Scandinavia, to set up centres of Canadian studies. Perhaps, as has been suggested, Canada has passed up or abandoned a genuinely political identity. But as long as it retains its imaginative one, it will do infinitely more for the benefit of the world.

---

Address at McMaster University in the Ontario Historical Series, 7 September 1984.

# The Authority of Learning

This year, 1984, seems to be the only year that has had a book written about it before it appeared, and discussions of Orwell's *1984* have become one of the most hackneyed themes in current journalism even before we are out of the January of that year. Nevertheless, I insist on beginning with one more reference to it, and for two reasons. In the first place, most of the discussions of the book I have read have failed to grasp its central thesis. Second, that thesis coincides with my own conviction as a student and teacher of English, which I have been trying to pound into the student and public consciousness for nearly half a century.

I remember well the impact that Orwell's book made when it appeared in 1949. The Communists turned on their scream machine, and in those days a lot of people in the democracies listened to it. For there was still a very large group of leftist sympathizers who, in regard to the Stalin régime in Russia, were in exactly the situation that the book itself calls "doublethink". The deliberately engineered famines in the Ukraine, the purges and massacres, the concentration camps in Siberia (a) didn't exist (b) maybe did exist, but nobody but a mean old Fascist would mention them. So the book was decried a good deal as reactionary propaganda. I reviewed it over the CBC in 1949, and I remember the comment of my producer, who himself was clearly in the state of doublethink I mentioned: "why didn't you just talk about the prose style"?

What I then said about the book was what I would say now: it is a twentieth-century *Inferno*, a vision of hell where there is no hope and no end. The liberal bromide that tyrannies will disappear when certain ends, however selfish, have been achieved, is carefully taken away from the reader. "I understand the how but not the why," the hero says, and is told that there isn't any why. The tortures and spying are not means to an end; they are the ends; the object of power is power; the reason for torture is torture.

In the ensuing years Orwell's prophecy began to look very accurate indeed. True, Stalin died, as the Big Brother of *1984* cannot die; but much of his structure of tyranny survived him. China set up a very similar structure during the so-called gang-of-four régime, and the fact that it has a more reasonable, or at any rate more pragmatic, régime now is the luck of a power struggle, not any uprising from the people: this is another mirage that Orwell's book sets aside. In the United States, the spying and frame-up trials of the McCarthy era went on and on and on. Everything Orwell said would happen has happened, but in bits and pieces, not, so far, in the consolidated global form that makes the book a real *Inferno*. Why not?

The central thesis of the book is that there is only one way to create a hell on earth that we and our children can never escape from, and that is to smash language. As long as we have the words to formulate ideas with, those ideas will still be potential, and potentially dangerous. What Orwell's state brings in is a pseudo-logical simplification of language called Newspeak, in which, for example, instead of saying that something is very bad you say that it is "double plus ungood". This kind of talk is rationalized as making language more logical; what it actually does is to make it mechanical, like a squirrel's chatter. Orwell devotes an appendix to his book in which he impresses on his reader the fact that the debasing of language is the only means to a permanent tyranny. We can no longer change a world like *1984* when the words that express the possibility of change have been removed from speech.

The appendix ends by quoting the opening paragraph of the preamble to the American Constitution, and then seeing how it could be translated into Newspeak. A Newspeak translator, Orwell tells us, could only stare at the paragraph and write down the word"crimethink". Even that indicates that his society is still in a state of transition. "Ultimately it was hoped," Orwell says, "to make articulate speech issue from the larynx without involving the higher brain centres at all." If we know we are in hell we are no longer wholly there: it is our consciousness that tells us where we are, and consciousness is a function of language, not the other way round.

Orwell's central case, then, is that the inner citadel of human freedom is language, and that language is not simply a content or subject-matter, such as we have in mind when we say that a speaker "has something to say". The way in which something is said is the reality of that something, and anyone who says "just give the ideas; never mind the words" is taking a step in the direction of the subconscious quacking and barking of Newspeak. We know that this is Orwell's view from his other writings, notably a wonderfully incisive and pungent essay on "Politics and the English Language". So while *1984* is a satire, the position from which it satirizes is the traditional humanist position. Again, *1984* belongs to a specific literary genre, the mock or parody-Utopia. The genre includes, among many others, Swift's *Gulliver's Travels,* which in its last book describes a society in which the horses have taken over because they can talk, while the counterparts of human beings, whom Swift calls Yahoos, cannot talk, and have consequently turned into the most noxious and vicious of animals.

So everything that comes after food and shelter and makes life worth living, Orwell says, is bound up with language. The rest of us simply take the humanities for granted, assuming that they are pleasant but secondary ornaments of civilization. In some ways it is better that this should be thought: it could be an advantage to have the real importance of language overlooked. Yet it is clear that the twentieth century is an age in which we cannot afford to take anything for granted. We have been accustomed to take air and water for granted, but we have managed to pollute both. Another thing we take for granted is compulsory education, which seems to be a benevolent and well-meaning thing for a society to provide. So it is, up to a point. But society supports compulsory education because it must have docile and obedient citizens. We learn to read primarily to read what society says we must read: traffic signs, advertising, labels on merchandise. We learn to count to make change and figure out our income tax. The thought of a citizenry unable to do these things fills us with such panic that we periodically hear complaints that the schools are not enabling children to grow up in a real world, so we get such slogans as a "back to basics" movement. The "basics," however, are not bodies of knowledge: they are skills, and the cultivating of a skill takes lifelong practice and repetition.

The simple ability to read, write and count is essentially a passive acquirement, a means of social adjustment. All genuine teaching starts with this passive literacy and then tries to transform it into an activity, reading with discrimination and writing with articulateness. Without this background, one may be able to read and write and still be functionally illiterate. It is discouraging for a student to find that he has reached university and is still totally unable to say what he thinks.

But by this time an odd kind of schizophrenia has begun to afflict public opinion. However "basic" it may be to read and write, as we go on doing it public opinion begins to push these abilities toward the periphery of society. The humanists find themselves fighting a rear-guard action, faced with supercilious questions that take the general tone: assuming that your area of interest is expendable, what are the serious things in society you can attach to it to defend its continued support?

One would assume that the simplest answer would be: people need political and social leaders who can define policies, articulate problems, and express the aims and ideals of their society for those who cannot express them for themselves, though they may feel them very deeply. But the evidence is overwhelming that voters in a democracy want, and expect, bumble and burble from their leaders, and seem to be disturbed, if not upset, by the impact of articulate speech. Without exhaustive examination, I should guess that if we read Hansard we might have to go all the way back to Arthur Meighen to find a political leader who habitually used the language with skill and precision, and the correlation of his ability to speak with his success at the polls seems to me significant, like the similar correlation for Adlai Stevenson in the United States later. There is a story, which I understand to be true, of a late colleague of mine, a professor of English who was private secretary to Prime Minister Mackenzie King during the war. In working on King's speeches, he inserted various quotations from Canadian poets, English and French, touched up clichés with a few metaphors, rounded out stock formulas with more concrete and lively language. These were regularly and routinely struck out. Eventually the Prime Minister said: "Professor, the public memory for a picturesque phrase is very retentive".

All this is a kind of negative indication of the real significance of what the humanities bring to society. The basis of my approach as a teacher has always been that we participate in society by means of our imagination or the quality of our social vision. Our visions of what our society is, what it could be, and what it should be, are all structures of metaphor, because the metaphor is the unit of all imagination. Logical thinking in this field seldom does more than rationalize these metaphorical visions. Occasionally we realize that a metaphor is no longer useful, and doesn't fit any more. One such metaphor is that of political and economic structures, including that of government, as machines. We speak of people "running" a business or a department so habitually that we forget we are using a metaphor showing that we think of such things as mechanisms. So anything that symbolizes to us the efficient running of a machine in public life creates a feeling of reassurance in us. When we hear a political candidate talking in a continuous series of uniform burps suggesting a breakfast coffee percolator, our conscious minds may be bored, but our metaphorical imagination feels that, so far, all's well with the world. There would be no harm in this except that I think we are beginning to feel an uneasy sense that social structures are not really machines at all.

It is obvious that social change would be reflected in changes of language: what interests me much more is the reverse possibility: that the teaching of language, and the structures of literature in which language is contained, may foster and encourage certain social changes. Not long ago I was asked to speak to a group of alumni in a neighbouring city, and a reporter on a paper in that city phoned my secretary and asked if this was to be a "hot" item. My secretary explained that Professor Frye was what his late colleague Marshall McLuhan would call a cool medium of low definition, and that he could well skip the occasion, which he did with obvious relief. The incident was trivial, but it started me thinking about the curiously topsy-turvy world of "news"as reported today.

What would the historians of the future, say of the year 2284, assuming the human race lasts that long, make of the history of Canada in the 1980s? In that remote future such historians would be puzzled by the exclusion of most news about universities in them. For they would also know that nothing of any historical importance whatever was taking place in Canada during the 1980s except what was happening in the universities, and in certain specific fields out-side that were directly reflected in and by the universities. These fields would vary widely: there would be environmental control, related to the biological area of the university spectrum; computer technology related to engineering and physics, literature and the performing arts, related to the humanities, and so on. If Canadian universities are underfunded so badly that they can no longer function effectively, Canada would disappear overnight from modern history and become again what it was at first, a blank area of natural resources to be exploited by more advanced countries. This is not empty rhetoric: it is a verifiable fact, though I should not care to become known as the person who verified it. What is connected with the universities is what is really happening: the political and economic charades also going on are what are called pseudo-events, created for and blown up by the news media to give us the illusion of living in history. The human lives behind these charades, of people losing their jobs or finding that they can no longer live on their pensions, certainly do not consist of pseudo-events. But they are not hot news items either.

I am leading up to, or circling around, the question: what kind of social authority does language, and the study of literature which is at the centre of language, really have in the social order? Every society, if it is to hold together at all, has to develop a body of concerns, assumptions in various areas, political, economic, religious, cultural, that are generally agreed on, or sufficiently agreed on for members of that society to communicate with one another. As society gets more complicated, various bodies of knowledge appear within it: these bodies of knowledge develop their own authority, and that authority may conflict with the concerns of society. We can see this most easily in the sciences. Galileo upheld a heliocentric solar system when the anxieties of a panic-stricken church were screaming to keep the geocentric one. That meant a conflict of loyalties in Galileo's mind, one to his science and the other to society as a whole.

It is not hard to see this authority within science. It is much harder to see that literature and the arts also have their own authority, that a writer may have to persist in his loyalty to the demands of what he writes even when threatened with censorship or personal persecution. Marxism, for example, when it comes to power in society, simply denies, as a point of dogma, that literature has any authority of its own at all. Literature in a socialist country, it says, should reflect and follow the demands of socialist concern, otherwise it will turn into the neurotic, introverted, decadent, etc., kind of literature produced in bourgeois countries. Christianity said much the same kind of thing in the past, and the Islamic religion repeats it in the present. The United States has no actual dogmas on the subject, but there have been startling outbreaks of hysteria, from Anthony Comstock in the eighteen-nineties to his descendants in our day.

There are no easy answers to this problem. For one thing, social concern certainly does have its own case. Nuclear bombs, the energy crisis, the pollution of the environment and the choking off of the supply of air, all indicate that scientists have a social responsibility for what they do. In literature, too, I think there is such a thing as a moral majority to be respected, even though I don't believe that the people who call themselves that represent it. Once when I was very young I found myself on a train with nothing to read, and in desperation bought a thriller from a news agent. It told me, in effect, that practically all the Chinese in North American cities were engaged in drug-running and in kidnapping young white women. It would be against the law to distribute such stuff in Ontario today, and I thoroughly approve of the law.

None the less, censorship is practically always wrong, because it invariably fastens on the most serious writers as its chief object of attack, whereas the serious writer is the ally of social concern, not its enemy. I can remember a time when even university professors (not at my college, I should add) would tell their students that D.H. Lawrence and James Joyce were degenerates wallowing in muck. This is not concern for society, but only anxiety directed at token or phony symbols of concern, four-letter words and the like, and its basis is a resentment of the authority that comes from the fresh and expanded vision of the serious writer. The failure to grasp this results in some very grotesque situations: people in Canada snatching Canadian books out of high-school libraries that are read and studied with the greatest enthusiasm in a dozen countries elsewhere.

In society there is a level of anxiety which is instinctively exclusive, suspicious of outsiders, and distrustful of any new developments from within. By itself, this level becomes a lynching mob, where any clearly defined individual, simply by being that, becomes a marked-out victim. Above this is the level of genuine concern, most clearly represented by the arts and sciences. I say most clearly, because they still attract us after many centuries, no matter how foul the anxieties of the society out of which they emerged may have been. We return again and again, with the same shuddering delight, to the opening of *Macbeth:* "Thunder and lightning. Enter three witches", even though we know that these witches were contemporary with the most hideous and pointless tormenting of harmless old women. Perhaps the witches were put into *Macbeth* to amuse King James, who was an ardent and gullible supporter of witch-hunting, but the authority of the play is unaffected by that.

I think Canada is in a unique position from which to study the role of language and the humanities in culture. Its political and economic structures may be in something of a shambles, but its culture, and I speak here more particularly of its literary culture, is flourishing and exhilarating. As we study this situation, we begin to see that two different social rhythms are involved. Political and economic movements tend to expand and centralize; cultural ones tend to decentralize, to bring to articulateness smaller and smaller communities. One has to keep the contrast steadily in mind: if we hitch a political development on to a cultural one, as in separatism, we get a kind of neo-fascism; if we hitch a cultural development to a political one, we get a pompous bureaucratic pseudo-culture.

Some time ago an American official, an appointment of the Reagan administration, remarked to me that he didn't approve of intellectuals in government. Somewhat to my surprise, I found myself agreeing with him, if somewhat tentatively. The social role of creative people, and of most of the group known vaguely as "intellectuals," is at this time probably to create possible models of human behaviour and action. Orwell created the terrible model of *1984* and remarked: "all a writer can do today is to warn". I think writers can do many things besides warn, however important warning may be. Every social change brings opportunities as well as dangers, and there are still a lot of people of good will around eager to respond to a more positive challenge than simply "avoid that". But models are one thing, and social machinery is another, and the nervous itch of many intellectuals to help turn the wheel of history, and show that they are of some practical use after all, has produced mainly illusions. This perversion of culture has been studied in a now famous book, Julien Benda's *Le trahison des clercs,* the treason of the intellectuals. Such people are frequently very vocal in the first stage of a revolutionary situation, and its first victims in the second stage.

It has often happened in the sciences that a new discovery, even a new invention, seems to be of no immediate practical use. But fifty years later it may turn out to be exactly what that science is then looking for. Similarly, it has been noted many times that what poets have seen in any given period becomes what the whole world is doing fifty or a hundred years later. Among those who have seriously studied our possible futures, we find, apart from those who prophesy tyranny or total destruction, a large number who see our present expanding of political and economic technologies as having reached its peak, and they tell us of a possible world which has become decentralized into smaller units, of the kind defined by a maturing literature. In short, the metaphor of society as a vast interlocking machine may succeed to a metaphor of society as a group of social organisms. At present, it seems that our culture, especially our verbal culture, is all that Canada has to contribute to the world that the world appreciates for its own sake. I have often been puzzled by the intensity of the interest shown in Canadian writing in European and Asian countries whose social conditions are very unlike ours. But perhaps before long we shall see the reason for that interest. If the world really does outgrow its vast jungle cities, its strangling international cartels, and the deadlocked hostility of its superpowers, it may break up into smaller units where the individual can find once more an identity and a function.

In such a world Canada might gain a quite new significance. In many ways Switzerland is the model for a peaceful and cooperating Europe, and Canada, ringed around with the world's great powers, is a kind of global Switzerland. Politically, it is constantly falling apart and being patched together by *ad hoc* compromises; economically, it has been trampled over by exploiters from three continents. But somewhere in its literature, its universities, its scholarship staggering and limping under budget cuts, there may be buried the model vision of a new world, where nightmare visions of tyranny and destruction have vanished as even the worst dreams do.

Empire Club, 19 January 1984. *The Empire Club of Canada, Addresses 1983-84*. Toronto: Empire Club Foundation, 1984.

# Language as the Home of Human Life

I assume that in this programme my role is to try to speak for the part of the academic spectrum usually called the humanities, which has the study of languages and literature at its centre. The title of my paper adapts a phrase from the philosopher Heidegger who remarks that language is the dwelling-house of being. We may notice two things about this phrase. First, "dwelling house" is a metaphor, and implies that even philosophers can't get along without the metaphorical picture-writing that's the backbone of poetry. Second, "being" for Heidegger is the profoundest subject that man can think about, because, Heidegger says, the first question of philosophy, and the hardest to answer because it's also the simplest, is: why is there something rather than nothing?

As this is a question we can't answer but can only talk about, we're really starting with the fact that man, unlike anything else in nature, is a talking being. He is often called a tool-using being, but language is by far his most useful tool. Many things are natural to man that are not natural outside human life, such as wearing clothes, and that means among other things that there are no noble savages, that is, human beings who can live directly in nature as animals can. All human societies without exception are enclosed in an envelope of culture, of certain social, religious, legal and other practices, and most of this cultural envelope consists of words. Completely natural societies, if they could exist, would probably communicate by telepathy or some kind of body language or gesture.

In societies as complex as ours anyone who cannot read or write is far more handicapped than the blind or the paraplegic. Consequently society supports elementary education, on the ground that reading and writing are necessities on much the same level as food and shelter. Society does not show much concern for education beyond the point where the student has acquired certain essential units of knowledge, like the alphabet or the multiplication table, and has developed out of them an essentially passive education. All genuine teaching begins at that point, and tries to transform this passive education into an activity, of a kind appropriate to citizens of a free society. The transforming process takes place through the encouraging of a factor in the student's mind that is, in the broadest sense, critical.

The cultural envelope I spoke of is something that I, for many reasons of my own, call a mythology. A mythology has two aspects. One aspect contains all our really deep and committed convictions and loyalties: our beliefs in freedom, human dignity, the values represented by our religious or social visions: that is, all our mental models of what our society should be. But such mythologies are also exploited by advertising and propaganda interests of all kinds and that is why we are compelled not just to read, but to read actively, that is, critically, trying to separate what speaks to our real beliefs from the sales pitch that asks us to support the ascendancy or prosperity of some particular class or group. If a political leader says "this is anti-democratic," when he means "this will affect the interests of my party," we have to learn to distinguish the two aspects of what he says, even if we ourselves belong to his party and accept his general position. So teaching the humanities is a militant activity: it has constantly to fight for the freedom that the critical faculty represents against passivity and uncritical acceptance.

Most of us realize, whether we consciously realize it or not, that the words confronting us in advertising, propaganda, and most news and casual conversation have to be taken in an ironic context. That is, they do not say precisely what they mean, and we have to recognize the difference between real meaning and presented meaning. We have just got through the year 1984, during which we heard a good deal about George Orwell's book of that title, and we remember that Orwell's main point was that the only way to establish tyranny permanently in society is to destroy the integrity of language. So his state promotes such slogans as "Freedom is Slavery". We may find this a bit crude even as satire, but nevertheless the satire reflects the century that has discovered the effectiveness of the big lie, and of the controlling of information in a way that cuts off access to the real meaning of what is said to us.

We are constantly making judgments about the irony of advertising and propaganda, and many of them have to do with fairly harmless situations. A restaurant promises "an evening of leisurely dining," and we have to estimate how much of that really means "we're doing our best, but we're understaffed and the service is slow". Or a college tells prospective freshmen that their teaching staff directly engages students in the existential problems that will confront them in society, and we have to decide how much of that means "our staff doesn't amount to much as scholars, but some of them are quite decent people to talk to". Or we may even find ourselves reading the opposite meaning into what is said: if we pass a theatre advertising "adult entertainment", we know that "adult" in such contexts generally means "infantile". So my special interest, which is literary criticism, is not really specialized at all in its elementary stages. The examples I've just given are critical judgments, and if we didn't make them every day of our lives we couldn't manage our own affairs.

But of course there are more important social aspects of language than that. It is very common for both social establishments and for the conspiracy groups that oppose them to develop secret or in-group languages, where words have special meanings not shared by outsiders. For centuries criminal groups have used special languages, and the drug cults of a generation ago also had their own jargon. By jargon I mean a language specialized for dubious social reasons, not the use of technical terms in a technical subject.

At the other end of society, we may recall the use of Latin as a mode of maintaining the ascendancy of both church and state for so many centuries, in Great Britain down to the end of the nineteenth. During that time, even the dumbest member of the upper classes, if male, would be sent to a public school to get some Horace and Cicero whacked into him. I say male, because Latin was also used as a sexual symbol. In Scott's *Guy Mannering* the heroine has a tutor who teaches her modern languages, and then innocently proposes to go on to Latin and Greek. At this point she balks, because she is a proper young lady conceived by a very sexist writer, and she, like Scott, feels that the Classical languages are not ladylike. In *Tom Jones* there is a very funny scene of a dinner party where the local parson keeps quoting tags of Latin, then oozes over the heroine and says "That is a Latin quotation, young lady, and it means," etc. If you have been following this critically, you will realize that I am not reflecting on the teaching of the Latin language, which is an admirable practice, but on the misuse of it for irrelevant social purposes. In imperialist days pidgin English grew up in the Orient, and it has often been suggested that one motive, perhaps wholly unconscious and perhaps not, in developing pidgin English was to make non-English speakers sound foolish and ignorant.

Again, social prejudice, as we find it in racism and elsewhere, is often embedded in a use of language peculiar to itself. We speak of people as black and white, for example, and this can get involved with other metaphorical uses of the words black and white that have nothing to do with the social groups called by those names except in prejudiced minds. Thus Huckleberry Finn, brought up on the clichés of white supremacy and not old enough yet to see through them, can say approvingly of Jim: "I knowed he was white inside". And yet the distance, in ordinary human decency and dignity, separating the "black" Jim from most of the technically "white" characters in the story has been quite as obvious to him all along as it is to us. Not long ago a neighbour's child, a boy of eleven, came in to see me with a questionnaire. The first question on it was "What kind of a picture comes into your mind when you think of the word teen-ager?" I said none whatever: in my opinion it was not only silly but morally wrong to make up stereotypes about so large and miscellaneous a group of people. He said that if that was my attitude there was no point in going on with the questionnaire. I think I understood what his teacher was after, but the tactics in my view were mistaken.

George Orwell remarks, in commenting on the deliberate destruction of language in his horrible 1984 society, that the ultimate aim was to make speaking a purely mechanical gabble, like a squirrel's chatter, involving no conscious thought at all. We can see such tendencies very clearly at work in all mob language, whether used by criminal gangs or by bureaucracies. One subdivision of bureaucratic jargon is academese, with which I have some reluctant familiarity. The other day I picked up a volume of essays concerned with critical theory, and read the following opening sentence of an essay on literature and phenomenology: "To question at our present intellectual juncture the relationship of phenomenology to literature implies beyond a reelaboration of an extension of familiar concepts the re-examination of a relationship which is essentially problematical". I did not read the second sentence, because it took me so long to decode the first one. What I think it means is: this is a tough subject, and maybe it's tough because it doesn't really exist. At least, that's what "essentially problematical" sounds like to me. But he couldn't say that openly and still go on for another twenty pages, so he retreated behind this barricade of polysllables. What is important here is that it is actually easier to write this way than to write in lucid prose, although the difficulty in deciphering it may convey an illusion of something profound.

This is still a fairly harmless issue, and only a few misguided people like myself are likely to suffer from brain sprain over it. Other aspects of the social use of language are more crucial. During the discussions I referred to over Orwell's *1984* last year, some journalists asserted smugly that the issues Orwell raised had been by-passed and were out of date. They forgot to notice how important it was that the press is still sufficiently free to observe the difference between what such a thing as the nuclear arms race means in plain English and what it is said to mean in press releases. It is quite simply true that the survival of the human race depends on the way that it responds to language over the next few years.

Language comes to us with a long history behind it, and has to keep adapting itself to changing conditions. Its power of adaptation is very considerable: there are, for example, few if any abstract words in the language that were not at one time concrete and metaphorical, but they are abstract now, for better or worse, and their use is not affected by their origin. We don't have cockfights any more, but we still say "crestfallen" and "showing the white feather"; we don't shoot with flintlock muskets any more, but we still speak of "hanging fire" or "a flash in the pan". We should notice that using these phrases does not give us the slightest nostalgia for bringing back cockfights or flintlocks, even if we know their derivation. If I speak of a member of the Society of Friends as a Quaker, I am using a term that was originally hostile, but has become so sanctioned by usage that it no longer conveys any sense of hostility. In fact, thanks to the advertising of the Quaker Oats Company, so far as any popular stereotype is concerned, it is one of stolidity rather than neurosis. In the seventeenth century there were Puritans who refused to pronounce the word

"Christmas" because the last syllable was "mass", and there are people today who refuse to pronounce the word "chairman" for very similar reasons. However, people kept on saying "Christmas," and Christmas did not turn Roman Catholic in consequence: it merely turned pagan. I see no reason why such words as "chairman," "spokesman," "mankind" and the like could not fossilize in the same way. We sometimes forget how much the language has already changed in this respect. When I was growing up, in the early years of this century, men and women spoke appreciably different languages: different in vocabulary, in rhythm, in intonation. The flattening out of these differences is a sign, I think, that society has gone a long way in normalizing the relation of the sexes.

It should be clear by now that there is nothing "natural" about language, except that for a conscious being, the natural and the artificial are the same thing. There is no freedom in human life that does not come from long and disciplined practice, and free speech is no exception. If we associate freedom with doing as we like or, in a most illiterate phrase, "doing what comes naturally", our freedom is simply a matter of obeying compulsions developed in childhood that keep pushing us around because we don't know that they're there. Playing games may be a natural activity, but playing them well means a lot of work. Every so often public opinion comes to realize that elementary education is not doing a good many of the things it ought to be doing in a free society, and so a demand arises with some slogan attached like "back to the basics". But the "basics" are not bodies of knowledge: they are skills. The important thing is not merely the ability to read and write but the habit of reading and writing critically, and that takes years of practice. If you listen to the speech of people in public office, you'll be impressed by how easy it is to become fluent, and how hard it is to become articulate. You can become fluent by simply repeating formulas that are supplied for you, where the speech is semi-automatic. But articulateness means developing your own rhythm of speech and speaking in your own voice, and that takes independence and not a little courage. So the skill involved is not purely technical: it's partly moral as well.

It must be admitted that there is a certain aggressiveness in framing fully articulate sentences. Like the songs of birds, they set up a territorial claim and create a space and a silence around them. You look at the speaker, perhaps with attention, perhaps only with resentment, but you look at him anyway, in a way that separates him from others. Anyone who has much to do with young people soon becomes aware of their obstinate silences: it often happens that the more obviously troubled they are the more silent they became. They are apt to feel that silence is their only defence: to speak, they feel, would let in the enemy, and they can't yet distinguish the enemies outside them from those inside them. But behind the insecurity, which is normal enough, there is also a kind of shame about speaking out. If, like the hippies of a generation ago, you confine yourself to formulas of the "like wow, man" type, you know that you can be invisible in a crowd. As soon as you are actually speaking language you become naked and exposed. That is what I mean by the courage of articulateness.

## II

All human societies have some sort of verbal culture, and in ancient or primitive societies the bulk of this culture takes the form of stories. Usually two kinds of stories develop: perhaps we could call them, oversimplifying things a bit, folktales and myths. The most striking quality of folktales is that they are nomadic: they wander over the world through all the barriers of language. Some of them are quite long and elaborate stories, and some are mere anecdotes, but they all have a well marked story line and a specific theme that tells you what sort of story it is. In fact their motifs are so clearly outlined that they can be counted and indexed by scholars. They also keep interchanging their themes, so that a new story may emerge from older materials. All this is of course completely anonymous: a folktale may start in India and wind up in Ireland or Japan, and scholars may, up to a point, be able to trace the path of its migrations. But nobody knows who started it off in India, and nobody gets any royalties. It's a long time before anyone starts thinking of a story as a story-teller's property.

But there are other stories that seem to have a different and much more serious social function, and these are what I call myths. These are the stories that tell a specific society what that society most needs to know about its recognized gods, its legendary history, and the origin of its class structure and customs and rituals. Myths may have the same structure as folktales, but their place in society is different. They don't wander over the world: they do travel within limits, but they also send down their roots into a specific culture and transmit a heritage of shared allusion to posterity. In the course of time they become a mythology in the sense in which I used that word at the beginning. That is, they form the core of the beliefs and values a society holds. That is what the stories of the Old Testament did for Hebrew culture and the Homeric poems for the Greeks. There is, of course, a vulgar sense of the word "myth" in which it simply means something not true. But this is derived from the notion that it is possible to convey definitive truth in words, and everything is wrong with that assumption.

However changed the conditions, one can still trace the same contrast even in complex civilizations like ours. Most of our verbal culture, in books and magazines and newspapers, in movies and radio and television and comic books, is geared to the expanding rhythms of marketing. It flows out from the big distributing centres, New York or London or Hollywood, into smaller and more remote communities. To keep things simple I shall speak mainly of books, and, for the most part, of books of fiction.

This is the rhythm of what is usually called mass culture, or popular culture. Such phrases don't imply any value judgment, because mass culture exists on every level of merit, from the best to the worst. But economically it is the direct descendant of the migrating folktales I mentioned, and like them it is highly conventionalized. The great bulk of it falls into certain obvious categories: there are detective stories, science fiction, romances, westerns, fantasies and so on: any good bookstore will provide the labels. In many of these categories there is much first-rate writing, and no book can remain on a best-seller list for long unless it is written with a good deal of professional expertise. But we nearly always know the kind of thing it is: if we pick up a book on the detective rack, we know the type of story that is going to be inside, and similarly with romances and historical tales. Knowing that we are going to read something highly conventionalized doesn't seem to put us off; on the contrary, we'd feel cheated if we didn't find the conventions observed. Books where the conventions are very clear remind us a good deal of games: each game of chess or tennis will be different, but there is a controlling set of rules that remains the same for every type of game. In the book trade this means that there will always be a constant pressure to turn out the predictable and highly professional product, whatever its category.

I should explain that all art is conventionalized, and convention works in two opposite directions. For a genuinely original writer convention sets one free to say what one wants to say. For a beginning writer, or a writer with some expertise but nothing much to say with it, convention provides a ready-made framework. But originality does not break with convention: it rediscovers it at a deeper level. Whether a given book is a good book or not will depend first of all on whether we like or accept its convention. Perhaps a very tentative standard of values might be established on the question: how much has to be sacrificed to keep the convention intact? To take an extreme example, hard-core pornography is writing that takes no interest in story, characterization, or social comment, but passes over all this in favour of an incessant prodding of reflexes. Those who respond to the reflex form the public for this convention: those who do not merely find such books a bore.

Canada has been, for most of its history, a provincial market for the big distributing centres. The pinnacle of success for a Canadian writer fifty years ago was a New York or London publisher, and this usually meant pulling his settings out of Canada. Stephen Leacock, for example, had to locate a good many of his stories in the United States even when they were as Canadian as Oka cheese. Gradually, however, there grew a demand for more unusual and out-of-the-way settings for novels, and in Canada this led to a certain amount of what we might call tourist literature, some of which might even be written by Canadians. We have Jack London and James Oliver Curwood writing about the Northwest, Robert W. Service celebrating the Yukon gold rush, and a mixed lot of historical novels about Quebec. In Quebec also we have work as different as the verse of W.H. Drummond and Louis Hémon's *Maria Chapdelaine*. What I call tourist literature corresponds to what in the history of painting is called the picturesque. Literature of this sort, like picturesque painting, looks at its settings with a kind of conservative idealism: it doesn't want to get close enough for actual realism, only close enough to distinguish its chosen setting from others.

Eventually we begin to be aware of a growing movement in the opposite direction from this, not the writing of a tourist looking in but of a native looking out, studying the immediate surrounding, ready to face the difficulties and the hositility involved in treating them realistically, and trying to communicate something through the imagination that we can't learn in any other way. This kind of writing may be, once again, on any level of merit, but good or bad it seems to follow the rhythm of myth rather than folktale: it strikes its roots into a specific community and tells us about that community. It's not a mythology in the sense of transmitting a distinctive set of social beliefs and values, but most of it does have a special kind of seriousness, even of urgency: it tells us the kind of thing we need to know if we're to understand the country it comes from.

This is how Canadian literature has grown up: not a literature that calls itself or tries to be Canadian, or tries to express some imaginary essence of the country from one sea to the other, but one that lives in restricted regions, in southern Ontario, on the prairies, on the Pacific coast. The best and most professional of its writers will sooner or later merge with the mass product of literature on its top level: this is what, for example, Margaret Atwood, Robertson Davies, Mordecai Richler and several others have done. Other books may remain for longer within a Canadian or even a regional orbit: that's nothing against them, just a characteristic of the kind of work they are. What is most important is the total enterprise. You don't find a twenty-thousand-foot mountain on a flat plain: you find it in a mountain range, where it's surrounded with a lot of others like it. Shakespeare was Shakespeare partly because he was one of about a hundred contemporaries, including nearly twenty dramatists, who have made a permanent impression on English literature. Nearly all of them lived and worked in a city far smaller than Edmonton. We begin to understand what the poet William Carlos Williams means when he says: "the classic is the local fully realized, words marked by a place."

It would of course be just as true of science that it's the whole enterprise that matters, not the individuals working within it. And yet every year Nobel prizes are awarded in the sciences, and these prizes carry a great deal of prestige. It's not too difficult for a sufficiently well-informed committee to discover where the front lines of research are in the sciences. The Nobel prizes in literature, though they get the same publicity, don't have anything like the same prestige. In the nature of things they can't have: it's not the diversity of languages that's the trouble, so much as the diversity of cultural situations behind the languages. There are too many variables, and the value-system changes every time you look at it. The first Nobel Prize for literature was awarded in 1901, a year when Tolstoy and Ibsen were still alive.

It went to a French poet of the Parnassian school named Sully-Prudhomme, and today even professors of French might have to do a double take to remember who he was. On the other hand he belonged to French literature, and the world's sensibility owes an immense debt to French literature.

Similarly, in Canada it's not the "greatness" of this or that writer that's important, but the sense of a total body of imagination emerging from the country with its own distinctive impact and integrity. This quality in a literature gets immediate recognition: that's why institutes of Canadian studies are now being set up in universities all over the world. So what begins as a kind of counter-culture, a handful of poets and novelists writing in a much overlooked provincial area, ends as an export product. Canada hasn't reached this stage as completely as, say, Ireland, where there have been dozens of world-famous writers who never thought of writing for the Dublin market even when they wrote about Dublin. And, of course, I very much hope it never does: it would be a miserable anticlimax to have a Canadian literature that Canadians weren't much interested in. That's where centres of education, like the University of Athabasca, get into the act.

## III

I've been speaking of books, but the same economic situation holds true for the other verbal arts. The movies at the beginnning of the century, radio in the twenties, television in the fifties, all seemed to have to go through a kind of archaic phase of rather crude beginnings. The gradual maturing of movies and radio had been assisted by the growth of television, which has pushed them out of the central place of entertainment and forced them to appeal to a more limited market. In Canada the growth of nationally subsidized media has also helped the maturing process, just as what used to be the Canada Council has played a major role in the growth of Canadian literature. As we all know, there was a golden age of radio and to some extent of documentary movies during the forties of this century in Canada. Golden ages seldom last: sooner or later the pressures of the mass market will bring about at least a partial return to the predictable professional output, or what I think of as the Agatha Christie syndrome. This has happened in all the media, but more particularly in the book business. More particularly, because in the United States the book business is no longer primarily in the hands of those who are really concerned with books, but in those of large corporations who have bought a publishing house or two as a hobby or even an investment. A publishing house I am connected with myself in New York is now attached to a zoo in Florida: what effect this will have on its interest in books I have yet to discover.

In all societies there is a built-in tendency to anti-intellectualism. Sometimes this is maintained by a state-enforced dogma, as it is in the vulgar Marxism of the Soviet Union or the still more vulgar version of the Moslem religion enforced in Iran. Sometimes, as in North America, it is simply part of the human resistance to maturity, and to the responsibilities that maturity brings, the instinct to stay safe and protected by the crowd, to shrink from anything that would expand and realize one's potential. It is this element in society that makes all education, wherever carried on, what I just called a militant enterprise, a constant warfare. The really dangerous battlefront is not the one against ignorance, because ignorance is to some degree curable. It is the battlefront against prejudice and malice, the attitude of people who cannot stand the thought of a fully realized humanity, of human life without the hysteria and panic that controls every moment of their own lives. Words like "elitism" become for such people bogey words used to describe those who try to take their education seriously. At the heart of such social nihilism, this drive to mob rule and lynch law that every society has in some measure, is the resistance to authority.

By authority I do not mean what is traditionally meant by it, the external power of church or state or big business or political party over the individual. That type of authority is one that a serious concern with democracy would reduce to a minimum. If we think of the people who have been presidents of the United States for the last quarter-century, we can hardly avoid the conclusion that it doesn't matter so much who is President of the United States, and that the real authority in society is something different and somewhere else. By authority I mean, for example, the kind of authority the sciences have when they appeal to evidence, logic, repeatable experiment, and accurate measurement. This is the kind of authority that, when we accept it, increases instead of limiting our own dignity and freedom. Further, a scientist's views on his science may collide with the anxieties of society, as Galileo's did. That means that he owes a loyalty to his science as well as to society, and whenever possible he should stick to the authority of his science in any collision with society. But a scientist may have social and political views not directly connected with his science, as Einstein did. Einstein held such views, not as a scientist, but as a man who had got where he was by exerting a considerable independence of judgment. And to exert independence of judgment, in any area of life, is a political act. It is very seldom really dangerous to society, but the hysterical will always think it is, and the political expression of hysteria, the police state, puts as many of its "dissidents" as it can in jail. That is why we have to have tenure clauses in university contracts.

Most people can be got to understand the authority of science, but the authority of poets and novelists is something we seldom think about. But they are more the targets of hysteria than almost any other group, and that is an impressive negative tribute to the importance of their work, little as they want it. Scientists have come to understand that academic freedom for other scientists goes far beyond the bounds of their science, and have started agitations for the release of scientists all over the world who are victims of tyranny and terrorism. Recently organizations of writers, such as PEN, have started parallel agitations for the release of persecuted writers. Such activity would not mean much, apart from ordinary humane feelings, without an underlying assumption that writers embody one of the genuine forms of social authority. It is a very difficult authority to characterize, because it is a form of prophetic authority. It has no techniques of verification like science, and it is often present in writers who may be obviously and perversely wrong about any number of things. This gives the university a delicate but very crucial role to play. However important Canadian literature may be or become in a university, it is not any university's primary duty to foster a national literature. Its primary duty is to build up a public receptive to it, a public that will not be panicked by plain speaking, not put off by crankiness, not bewildered by unexpected ways of thinking and feeling. Again, the importance of doing this goes far beyond the boundaries of literature. A society's tolerance for its own culture is the most accurate indicator we have of the level of its civilization. It is also the next step on from the critical approach to language I mentioned at the beginning.

When a university begins operations, or enters on a new phase of operations, as this one is doing, the situation I've been outlining faces it at once. The educational market functions like all other aspects of the market: it's centered in populous and wealthy areas like those of Harvard or Chicago or Berkeley, and it ripples out from there until it reaches the youngest, most remote, and most vulnerable seats of learning. The easy way to look at this situation is the cop-out way, to think of a new university as one where students go because they can't afford to go somewhere more central, and where the staff remains only because the employment situation is too bad to let *them* move somewhere more central. Such an attitude would kill any university, and would have killed Harvard or Chicago or Berkeley if it had got there early enough.

There are no peripheries in scholarship and learning: every university is fighting on the same front line, whatever its morale. A line of defence against Soviet missiles will be out of date long before it is built, but education's line of defence is never out of date, and it runs as directly through this community as it does through every community in Canada. The conception of culture as an expendable luxury, to be taken up only after we've done all the really important things like polluting the environment, is particularly strong in Canada, because two centuries ago Canada accepted the ethic of mercantilism that the Americans revolted against, and devoted itself to providing raw materials for centres outside the country. If Canadian education is persistently underfunded, Canada will disappear from history and go back to being again what it was at first, a blank area of natural resources to be exploited by countries that are more advanced and better organized than we are because they've spent more on their education.

The routines of teaching, lab work, essay marking and the like are quiet and undramatic. Breathing air and drinking water are quiet too: it is only when we run short of them that things get dramatic. The expansion of university work in Canada increases the supply of cultural air and water, and so represents an act of faith. Faith gives us, according to the New Testament, the substance of hope and the proof of the unseen. In that sense every act of teaching and learning is also an act of faith, with every step visible but the final goal unlimited. Those of us who have devoted our lives to the same process do not know, any more than you know, where the path to greater knowledge and enlightenment will take you. What we can say, with a confidence born of long experience, is that to such things there is no wrong path.

Athabasca University, 14 June, 1985

# "The Emphasis is on the Individual, the Handful of Shepherds, the Pairs of Lovers . . ."

I am preoccupied at the moment with a very large and complicated book on the Bible and the way in which the Bible set up the mythological framework within which Western culture operated for many centuries.

*And continues to operate?*

I think it does. There is hardly anything else with which to work. There is in secular literature — more particularly what I call romance — a curious kind of shadow effect. I have been looking at romance as consisting of a number of themes or narrative units, which make up the same kind of legend of the universe that religion also has, and which has certain recurring themes and images.

Every society has a body of stories that it regards as more important than others, and particularly important in explaining that society's customs and rituals and social structure. These stories become myths, as I call them, and they form the kernel of the kind of thing that the Bible is in Western culture. I'm trying to show that the traditional way of reading the Bible as a book with a beginning, middle, and end is the right way. Despite all the appearance of a hodgepodge that it presents when you open it, the Bible is actually a pretty well unified book. What unifies it is not doctrine and not history, but a certain narrative outline that runs from Creation to Apocalypse. There are also a number of other stories that have been recounted for entertainment. These become what I call fables , and they are the ancestor of romance.

*Fable being of a somewhat smaller order of magnitude than myth?*

It's a matter of social function. Myth and fable are the same structurally; they can tell the same kind of story. However, in social function and in authority, myth is higher in social acceptance, as a rule. Thus, myth is what defines culture; it takes root in a specific culture. It's the Bible that makes Hebrew culture; it's Homer that makes Greek culture; and so on. Then, as a culture develops, the folk tales and the fables that have been circulating around the world nomadically also begin to take root and contribute to the heritage of allusion, so that you get Dante and Milton writing in the Biblical area and Shakespeare and Chaucer in the romance area.

The theme of the Edenic paradise, the fall of man, and so forth, is central in American literature just because it is central in *all* Western literature. I can certainly see that many stories about the American West, for example, are a development of the pastoral convention, and I don't have any difficulty with the theses of books like R. W. B. Lewis's *The American Adam* or Leo Marx's *The Machine in the Garden*. These all make quite good sense really. But I think it might be found that there are other aspects of mythology that are also important in American literature. There is a great deal in Melville's books, for instance, that has much more to do with the tower of Babel and that kind of thing.

*Since we recognize a decline in our sense of community, Babel may be more to the point now than Eden.*

I don't know. In technology you get a continually increasing speed, and an increase in speed means an increase in introversion and a breaking down of personal relationships. But one of the things that attracts me about romance is its pastoral, Arcadian atmosphere. You find yourself in a world greatly reduced in numbers, where the emphasis is on the individual, the handful of shepherds, the pairs of lovers, and so on. Something of Adam and Eve wandering in the Garden of Eden comes back when you begin to think of that pastoral kind of human ideal.

*The extraordinary reception you've been having here — does this suggest to you any comparisons or contrasts with Canada?*

I think there is a certain difference in temperament, which is more the result of social conditioning than of anything inborn. Canadian students are not conditioned from infancy to be members of a great imperial power. They belong to a small, observant country on the sidelines of history. I find that responses are more personal and more direct in the United States as a rule.

I have been very fortunate in the particular generation I came to teach. If I had come here in 1968 or 1969, my reception would have been very different, I imagine.

There is now much more of a sense of the genuineness of history and of tradition. A country, like an individual, is senile if it has no memory. While there is a great deal of self-contempt of a kind that rather distresses me about the attitude of this country, say, to the Bicentennial, there is nevertheless a basis of pretty solid and serious feeling on the part of the students I meet. Still, there is something about American attitudes toward the eighteenth century that has always puzzled me. The Bicentennial is seen not as a celebration of 1975 — it is a celebration of 1775. The United States achieved its identity in the Age of Enlightenment and seems to have been revolving ever since around the kind of mentality that produced Jefferson and Franklin. I don't say that that is a bad thing. It merely strikes me as curious, coming as I do from a country that has no eighteenth century.

*In that same century Dr. Johnson was referring rather confidently to literary allusion in general as the parole of learned men, a* lingua franca. *Very few people speak this language any longer.*

It is certainly a declining market, I believe as a result of the ignorance and incompetence of professional educators. I would use an even stronger word than imcompetence — what has been called *le trahison des clercs*, a betrayal.

One reason I have so little difficulty with students is that they know they have been cheated. They are very serious people, and they rise to a challenge. There is also a strong self-preservative instinct in the human mind that makes them pick up the things they have been cheated of. If teachers are too dumb, too incompetent, to give their students some kind of coherent historical organization in their teaching, the students will pick it up themselves.

The cheating begins when a teacher avoids his essential job. There is a certain body of what you might call initiatory education — that is, a certain objective body of information, knowledge, and facts that you need in order to participate in a society as complex as this. To refuse to give that to students is to cheat them. Education is a long, repetitive thing. I went through all the hysteria of the late Sixties, when there was a great vogue for teach-ins and importing people at immense expense from other countries to come talk to students. Great enthusiasm was generated. What I said at the time was that these things were entertaining, and they were even quite useful, but they were not educational. Education is in the repetitive process — it is something that has to go on and on and on. Things *should* break into the continuum from time to time, but the continuum is the education.

Students want to make up for the time that they know they have lost. This is a recent development, but it is a very much saner and better proportioned development than that utterly indiscriminate rejection of traditional authority, which I think had something schizoid about it, in the Age of Hysteria.

*An age that has ended?*

I suppose it ended around 1971, perhaps around the time of the closing down of the Vietnam war, although I don't think that that was really the central thing about it. It ended with the collapse of prosperity, with the cutting down of the military commitment. A lot of it had to do with the physical impact of the television screen. The *containing* of television is something that is a feature of our lives now — keeping it under control, keeping it as a subordinate element of our cultural life. Television has driven many people back to the book, and that is a symptom of the fact that the human race is still motivated by self-preservation. I think university students will be driven back to the Bible and classical mythology for exactly the same reason, for self-preservation.

It is interesting to me that so many of the balladeers and folk singers of our time are extremely uninhibited in their Biblical, even in their classical, allusions, I'm not surprised at that — I think it is a necessary feature of all popular poetry. I'm interested for example in the fact that one of the best-known of the Canadian folk singers, Leonard Cohen, started out in the 1950s with a book called *Let Us Compare Mythologies*. The mythologies were the Jewish, the Christian, and the Hellenic.

*To come back to education, for a moment — you've expressed strong doubts about the notion of "teaching" literature to begin with.*

Literature has to be rather indirectly presented. The framework within which the teacher and the student operate is the framework of criticism, and that is what I have said consistently: What is taught and learned is the criticism of literature and not literature itself. I have always been rather distrustful of the importance attached to value judgments on the part of the New Critics and others. Values can be assumed, they can be argued about, but they cannot be demonstrated.

*Value judgments also encourage the arbitrary game of ranking writers.*

Well, that is the literary stock exchange. It's an utterly vulgar and futile form of activity. The primary criterion of value is a certain sense of genuineness. The conscientious reviewer of a book of poems, for example, will try to react to the genuineness of what he is reading. The questions of greatness — whether "A" is better than "B" and whether "B" is better than "C", and so forth — should be avoided as far as possible. I find myself browsing through anthologies, for example, and every so often I strike what seems to be a consistently interesting and intelligent mind. Then I want to look him up and read him in greater breadth and detail than the anthology gives me. It is a purely random operation. I could name a few names at random easily enough, but I would forget a lot of others. When I was about sixteen or seventeen I was excited by a great many different poets—Wallace Stevens, for one. Some of them did not stay with me. Others did. There are no reasons I can give as a critic why some of them turned out to be more permanent.

A great deal of contemporary literature that I read is Canadian literature, simply because that's where my roots are. I suppose there are about thirty or forty poets in Canada whom I find interesting to read. the output of good, genuine poetry in Canada is really astonishing. There is a reflective quality in the Canadian consciousness that is a good breeding ground for poetic expression. The very intensity of the American temperament sometimes works against this — its expression is so intensely political.

*What, would you say, turned you toward literary criticism as a vocation?*

Like other subjects, literature has a theory and a practice. I seem to have been drawn temperamentally and in other ways to the theory and have never seriously attempted writing poetry or fiction. I didn't feel that meant that I was noncreative. "Creativeness" ought not to be applied to genres but to the people working in them.

I had a rather intensively religious upbringing and thought of becoming a clergyman — which in fact I did do. But when I went to college I realized that my vocation was for university teaching. As an undergraduate I discovered Blake, which of course was exactly the right discovery for me at that point. He had all the religious — almost evangelical — pre-suppositions with which I had been brought up, but he turned them inside out in a way that made complete sense to me. What really interested me about him was his demonstration that the old man in the sky was actually Satan rather than God and that, consequently, anything that had to do with tyranny and repression in human life was Satanic and that there was no religion worth a second glance that hadn't to do with the emancipation of man.

I date everything, I think, from my discovery of Blake as an undergraduate and graduate student. Everything of Blake that I could understand convinced me that his mysterious poems would be worth working at. Thus I had to try to get inside his mind as well as I could, and that meant that my critical interest had to be central and primary.

When I came to write about Blake, I stressed the importance of the fact that he belonged in the eighteenth century. The historical took on a peripheral quality to me and receded to the circumference. It was relevant all right, but I had to get at the actual structure of Blake's mind at first. It's the way I would recommend to most students of literature — to try to grow up inside the mind of a great poet and to hang the history onto that, rather than start with the history, which has a way of cutting down the great figures of poetry into a kind of circus parade.

*You've described autobiography as a form of prose fiction. I wonder what you make of the present state of inflamed interest in the study of autobiography.*

I suppose it goes along with the kind of thing that made encounter groups so popular — the feeling that the more layers of the onion you peel off, the closer you get to the center. I think it is a fallacy myself. A person's real self is perhaps more clearly evoked by what other people think of him than by his own analysis of himself. The "real me" may be a layer of personae, the relationships with other people.

*The "real me" may be the work, then, and not the person at all.*

Yes, I think that is true. Somebody was in my office the other day urging me to write my autobiography. What I couldn't explain to him is that everything I write *I* consider autobiography, although nobody else would.

© Harvard Magazine, Justin Kaplan